Be careful when you read this book—your life could be forever changed. If you are not a bird-watcher now, you most assuredly will be after reading Brushed by Feathers.

Frances Wood has written an engaging account about the birds of the western U.S., with particular reference to their seasonal ebb and flow, eloquently pointing out what special haunts and habits are utilized for surviving the different seasons.

You will gain a special appreciation for every day of the year, as each day in the life of a bird represents major do-or-die events. Suddenly you'll find a pair of binoculars strapped around your neck observing nature's real-life drama.

—BOB RIGHTER,
author of Colorado Birds: A Reference to
Their Distribution and Habitat

Brushed by Feathers
A Year of Birdwatching in the West

FRANCES WOOD

FULCRUM PUBLISHING
GOLDEN, COLORADO

Library of Congress Cataloging-in-Publication Data

Wood, Frances L.
  Brushed by feathers : a year of birdwatching in the West / Frances L. Wood.
      p. cm.
  Includes index.
  ISBN 1-55591-480-2 (pbk. : alk. paper)
  1. Bird watching—Northwest, Pacific—Anecdotes. 2. Birds—Northwest, Pacific. 3. Wood, Frances L. I. Title.
   QL683.P162W66 2004
   598'.07'23478—dc22

                                        2004012367

ISBN 1-55591-480-2

Printed in the United States of America
0 9 8 7 6 5 4 3 2 1

Editorial: Katie Raymond, Faith Marcovecchio
Design: Ann W. Douden
Cover illustration: Frances Wood

Fulcrum Publishing
16100 Table Mountain Parkway, Suite 300
Golden, Colorado 80403
(800) 992-2908 • (303) 277-1623
www.fulcrum-books.com

CONTENTS

Contents

ACKNOWLEDGMENTS

Many people helped with the creation and editing of this book and I'm grateful for every contribution. I'm especially indebted to members of my birding community Brenda Senturia, Thero North, and Steve and Martha Ellis for their review of the entire manuscript. Also, I thank Libby Mills, Wezil Walraven, Jack Bettesworth, Jack Nisbet, Gary Ferguson, and Duncan Evered, who reviewed selected chapters.

Others have given help and encouragement in many, many ways. They include Colleen Bollen, Paul Freeman, Julie Jindal, Indu Sundaresan, and Phil Winberry; all are members of my writers' critique group. Also, I acknowledge ongoing support from Carla Hellekson, Susan Morrisson, Barbara Morse-Quinn, Nancy Satterberg Desonier, Paula Snyder, Louise Wilkinson, Sue Yates, and Susan Zwinger.

I am especially grateful for the love and encouragement from my sons, Munro and Alexander Galloway, and from my husband and favorite bird-watching partner, Bill Graves.

INTRODUCTION

Friends call me a bird magnet and tell me that I have good bird karma. The truth, I must admit, is more down to earth, more predictable, and much less cosmic. Simply put, I notice birds.

I watch for migrating birds to return in the spring. I pick out birds flying over Seattle's Safeco Field when all other eyes are watching the Mariners baseball team. The other day, when eating dinner on a friend's deck, I spied a great horned owl peering down on our seafood linguine. No one else, not even our host, had noticed it. They weren't looking.

Some mornings I walk along the county road where I live, listening for white-crowned sparrows issuing their plaintive, husky song in the grassy fields, and for winter wrens offering their cascading melody from the cool understory of the alder and hemlock wetland. Other mornings I scramble down the bluff behind my house to walk the beach. Bald eagles lord over me from Douglas fir snags and killdeer call out to divert me from nests hidden in the beach grass and rocky shore. On these walks I carry my binoculars and leave my Walkman behind; my goal is to enjoy nature rather than log a certain number of miles. I move quietly, which encourages the birds to stay in place rather than dive into the thick underbrush or scatter for the farthest treetops.

Last spring on a sunny Saturday morning (I remember the day well because sunny spring weekends are rare here in the rainy Pacific Northwest), I announced to Bill, my husband, "The violet-green swallows will return today." He replied with a distracted, "Huh."

At 2:30 that afternoon Bill glanced up, stopped mowing the

lawn, and charged into the kitchen. "How'd you do that?" he asked, implying that I possessed a magic wand that brought the birds back. My secret: I looked at the calendar that morning and realized it was March 21, the day the swallows always return to our meadow. This isn't metaphysics; definitely not rocket science. I just checked my journal for entries noted in previous years.

Birds visit my garden. But that's because I feed them, provide water for drinking and bathing, and leave tangles of blackberries for nesting. Also, Bill and I keep our garden pesticide-free, which leaves a smorgasbord of yummy grubs and insects. I'm allergic to cats and Bill is uncomfortable around dogs, so we don't keep domestic pets. Birds, as well as deer, bunnies by the hundreds, even the occasional coyote, weasel, or river otter find a safe haven in our three and one-half acres on Whidbey Island in northern Puget Sound. After house-sitting for a week, one friend described our garden as the setting for an animated Disney movie (was it *Snow White*?), with the baby deer, bunnies, and birds all singing and dancing together.

We do have one pet, sort of. A semiwild rock pigeon—known as a common city pigeon—dropped out of the sky one day, landed on our bird feeder, and adopted us. After a couple of days we dubbed it "Rocky." Later, I learned Rocky had escaped from a pigeon fancier a couple of miles away. I informed the owner, but he never made any effort to reclaim the pigeon. Rocky, who has been with us three years, sleeps on the light fixture out on the back deck, bathes in our three-tiered faux-Mexican fountain, eats at the platform bird feeder, and generally lives the good life.

This book, however, is about wild birds, the kind I first encountered while studying ornithology in college and have continued to learn about and admire during a thirty-year period since. I've lived in southern and northern California, Oregon, and Washington, and searched out birds in Idaho, Montana, Wyoming, Colorado, Arizona, British Columbia, and Alaska. This book focuses on the common birds of these western regions, the same birds that come to feeders, live in the back corners of gardens, in the park down the street, and in the protected wildlife areas miles away from cities. As the seasons progress, many of these birds migrate along the Pacific Coast flyway, while

California quail

Brushed by Feathers

others move from coastal lowlands up into the Cascade and Sierra Nevada Mountains or into inland valleys. Yet some, called residents, live their entire lives within one square mile. All of these endlessly fascinating birds are visible to anyone willing to pay them some attention, including residents of these western states, potential travelers to the area, and any naturalist interested in learning more about avian fauna.

Wild birds flutter, swim, fly, feed, call, hop, swoop, and sing all around us, but these activities often go unnoticed. This book will help you tune in, whet your desire to notice birds, and expand your understanding and appreciation of what you see. A world that has been an endless source of wonder and thrill to many other bird-watchers and to me awaits your discovery.

My love of birds brings to mind a beach hike last July with my son Alex. Every year on my birthday I hike out the Dungeness Spit on the northern coast of Washington's Olympic Peninsula. It is a healthy walk for one day, five miles out and five miles back. Alex, twenty-eight, was visiting from Manhattan where he lives. My beloved offspring is an assistant professor of media at New York University, but he doesn't know beans about birds. Whenever he visits, I drag him out into nature and try to remedy this obvious flaw in his liberal arts education. As Alex and I were hiking out the long Dungeness Spit, which gradually arches along a backbone of drift logs, I heard the brassy, rattlelike call of a black oystercatcher, a fairly unusual bird of the north Pacific Coast. We scrambled up through the beach logs and I saw a family of these chicken-sized, black-bodied shorebirds with long, sturdy fire engine–red bills. I was thrilled; Alex was blasé. I handed him my binoculars to give him a close-up look. He looked for a full five seconds, gave back the binoculars, and said, "Mom, I need more of a reward than that."

As we hiked the next two miles, I quietly pondered his remark. Why does birdwatching give me and countless others such joy? Why does it stimulate us and leave us feeling alive? When I see a bird species for the first time, my pulse quickens, my cares disappear, and I feel that I've received a very special gift. Obviously, not everyone feels this way, including my own flesh and blood. Yet, more and more, people are "getting it." Birdwatching is the fastest growing hobby in the United States, second in popularity only to gardening. We bird-watchers are now nearly 70 million strong.

For some, "getting it" means enjoying the birds that visit a feeder outside a kitchen window. For others, it's membership in a local Audubon Society and joining birdwatching field trips. And, for an increasing number, including me, it's traveling the world seeking out exotic species, keeping lists of all the birds seen, and becoming involved in movements to preserve habitats that sustain wildlife.

The main reason I go on walks looking for and observing birds is that it gets me out into nature. The sights, sounds, and smells of nature refresh me and help me relax. The exercise helps keep my body in shape and my mind alert. Watching birds is simple. The hobby is also intriguing and challenging since there are more species of birds than one person can see in a lifetime. Since birdwatching is usually nonmotorized, gentle on the environment, and free, it can be enjoyed by everyone.

Month-by-month this book introduces common birds in the western regions described above, starting with resident birds and adding migratory birds as they move through the region. Step-by-step we will examine bird behavior and learn the tricks of identification. But, more than that, we'll tap into the joy and fascination of watching birds. I invite you to have an identification field guide for the birds of your area and a pair of binoculars ready. Whether a novice, an experienced birder, or simply an armchair wanderer, your window into the natural world will open a bit wider.

CHAPTER ONE

January

I'm blessed. I live where I can watch the sun come up. In January it rises far to the south behind bare-branched red alder trees. The first rays peek out over Mount Index in the Cascade Mountains, send a golden-apricot shimmer across the waters of Puget Sound, define the long, low shape of Hat Island, filter through the trees, then meet me on my east-facing deck. Wrapped in a heavy robe with both hands hugging a mug of hot tea, I glance at my watch. The time is 7:58 A.M.

My house is perched on the edge of a steep bluff above a deserted rocky beach, which, as the tide recedes, exposes soft, sandy mudflats. Beyond the beach, the waters of Saratoga Passage merge with Possession Sound, forming a protective arm of Puget Sound. I'm near the southern tail of the narrow, glacial-tilled island, which snakes north for forty-one miles until its head nearly touches Canada. My family vacationed on this island for four generations, giving rise to my lifelong dream to move here permanently. That happened in 1999, when my husband Bill and I shucked off congested, noisy Seattle for island living, forty miles and one ferry ride to the north. I can't imagine living anywhere else.

Chestnut-backed chickadee

5

For several minutes I linger with my tea and enjoy the view on this first day of the new year. The vista of the bay is framed to the south by an ancient maple tree skirted with a dozen scrawny, misshapen alders. Many decades ago, when the old mother maple was a young sapling, the main trunk died, forcing three lower branches to thicken and share creation of a wide goblet shape. Now the broad trunk, softened by moss and licorice fern, welcomes raccoons and owls to its branches. A couple of years ago, a pair of wood ducks spent several hours discussing the cavities of the majestic maple as a potential nesting sight, but then deferred to a tree near my neighbor's pond across the county road.

The view is framed to the north by five tall, lean Douglas fir trees, standing sentry at the bluff's edge. Woodpeckers feed on the bare trunks and eagles alight on the top branches. Chickadees, kinglets, and siskins chatter among the deep-green needles while gleaning insects and grubs. Between those wide frames—the maple and alders to the south and the firs to the north—the expansive, ever changing panorama displays gulls and kingfishers. As the seasons change, shorebirds, seabirds, and thousands of ducks pass by, adding intriguing detail to the picture.

The weak January sun turns Whitehorse into a pink snow cone and etches the jagged top of Three Fingers against the soft-turquoise sky. I listen for early bird activity. A gull tries a lifeless call and then quits. Last night's high winter tide dislodged drift logs that floated out on the flat, gray water. One log holds two black bumps. Reaching for my binoculars, I identify the double-crested cormorants. A moist stillness closes in as a low fog bank snuffs out the sun and obscures the islands. I scurry back inside, shivering.

Pouring a second cup of tea, my attention is drawn to a side window where our birdseed feeders hang. Chickadees, both the black-capped and chestnut-backed varieties, snatch sunflower seeds and dash off. A single red-breasted nuthatch slips in during the infrequent quiet moments. A shy spotted towhee lifts from the ground onto the platform feeder, then shifts its long tail before dropping back to the ground. Among the shrubs below the feeder dark-eyed juncos, masked with dark hoods, flash their outer white tail feathers and dart away at my movement. Then a rollicking group of pine siskins descends on a hanging feeder.

Several hours later, fighting the urge to stay inside the warm house, I slip my binoculars into my jacket pocket and walk down our driveway toward the county road. The early January day has warmed a bit and the clouds seem thinner. As I reach the road, a lilting sound emerges from a nearby tangle of blackberries and I pause quietly. Hidden from sight, but full of promise, a song sparrow is dusting off its song, trying it on for another year. Soon the sweet notes burst out to enliven the dull day. I smile, relax my shoulders, and silently sing along with the familiar tune.

January begins a new cycle; not just a new calendar year, but a new year in the natural world. Days lengthen as the sun widens its arc through the southern sky, green sprouts emerge from early bulbs, and buds swell. Owls, a family of birds that nests early in the season, hoot messages of renewed pair bonding. A bald eagle soars along our bluff; a large branch dangling from its talons suggests its intent to add to its nest a mile to the north. The avian world prepares for a new season.

Barred owl

7

Pine siskins enjoying the feeder

A relatively quiet month for bird activity, January is a perfect time to learn about, or refocus on, birds. Dawn arrives at a respectable hour, so even the laziest bird-watcher needn't miss the first activity of the day. Bare branches of deciduous trees allow birds to remain in view so that they can be examined and identified. And since the migrating birds are far away to the south at this time of year, there is a manageable number of species to concentrate on.

This book is designed to introduce the birds in a logical, seasonal pattern. It begins with resident birds, the species that stay in one area year-round. These birds form the backbone of one's birding knowledge, and maintain a recognizable presence throughout the year as less-familiar migrating birds arrive and depart. The unfamiliar migrants will add a delightful confusion to the cast of locals, but we'll watch for and learn their identity as they arrive. As we move along, you'll learn what the birds look like and learn about their habits and habitats.

Since I'm often asked *why* I watch birds, "Why Watch Birds?" plays with that question. "Feeding Winter Birds" focuses on birds that visit bird feeders, and "Owl-Watching" discusses our resident owls. In the mild regions of the western states, owls begin nesting in February—so hooting and courting often punctuate January nights and predawn mornings. So, grab your binoculars and find an umbrella. Let's go January birding.

❑ California Quail *(Callipepla californica)*

❑ Barn Owl *(Tyto alba)*

❑ Short-eared Owl *(Asio flammeus)*

❑ Great Horned Owl *(Bubo virginianus)*

❑ Snowy Owl *(Nyctea scandiaca)*

❑ Barred Owl *(Strix varia)*

❑ Great Gray Owl *(Strix nebulosa)*

❑ Burrowing Owl *(Athene cunicularia)*

❑ Black-capped Chickadee *(Poecile atricapillus)*

❑ Mountain Chickadee *(Poecile gambeli)*

❑ Chestnut-backed Chickadee *(Poecile rufescens)*

❑ Red-breasted Nuthatch *(Sitta canadensis)*

❑ White-breasted Nuthatch *(Sitta carolinensis)*

❑ Pygmy Nuthatch *(Sitta pygmaea)*

❑ Spotted Towhee *(Pipilo maculates)*

❑ Song Sparrow *(Melospiza melodia)*

❑ Dark-eyed Junco *(Junco hyemalis)*

❑ Purple Finch *(Carpodacus purpureus*

❑ Cassin's Finch *(Carpodacus cassinii)*

❑ House Finch *(Carpodacus mexicanus)*

❑ American Goldfinch *(Carduelis tristis)*

Black-capped chickadee

WHY WATCH BIRDS

*There is no other door to knowledge than the
door nature opens; and there is no truth except
the truths we discover in nature.*

—Luther Burbank

What do writer Luther Burbank and 70 million Americans share? What is the Zen of birdwatching that brings peace and awe? Why do people around the world spend hours peering through binoculars for a glimpse or two of a flighty, feathered creature?

In many ways, birdwatching represents futility: The bird always has the advantage. A bird's ability to fly often allows us but a quick glimpse of tail feathers as it dives into a deep blackberry bramble or soars to the top of a faraway tree. If you think golf is frustrating, be grateful that the object of your attention—the ball—doesn't fly off the tee just as you begin your swing.

So why watch birds? Why not admire pretty flowers or red sports cars? Before answering these questions, I must tell you about Phoebe Snetsinger of Saint Louis. I never met Phoebe (yes, that really is her name!) but I've read her story. Phoebe had done some birding before she was diagnosed with terminal cancer. Three different oncologists gave her three months of good health and only a year to live. Phoebe began thinking about how she wanted to spend those precious months. She decided that as long as she felt up to it, she would do some serious birding, so she booked a birding trip to Alaska. While there, she added many new sightings to her life list (the total number of different bird species a bird-watcher has seen). She continued to feel good enough to bird so she decided to take another trip, this time to Australia. Off she went, adding new birds to her list by the hundreds.

Fifteen years later Phoebe was still actively birding. It seems that she got so busy chasing birds she didn't give her cancer time to develop. In 1997 Phoebe celebrated seeing her 8,000th bird species, the first person ever to cross that threshold. As with Neil Armstrong stepping onto the moon, it hadn't been done before. Could it be that birding, similar to laughter, is an antidote for serious illness? I wouldn't firmly make that claim, but I do know that nothing else gives me quite the peace of mind that I find when I am outdoors paying close attention to the natural world. In 2001 Phoebe died, not from cancer but in an automobile accident, while birding in Madagascar. By that time, she had seen 8,400 different species of birds.

One of the best answers to the question "Why watch birds?" comes from British writer Laurens van der Post.[1] When asked what creature he found most impressive of the many he had encountered in Africa, his answer was always some kind of bird. He was fascinated with the ability of birds to fly and to sing. "[There is] nothing so beautiful as the sight of a bird utterly abandoned to its song, every bit of its being surrendered to the music, the tip of the tiniest feather trembling like a tuning fork with sound."

But the main reason for his fondness for birds was their beauty. In most animals, color serves as camouflage. With birds, color is much more than that. "They had summer and winter dresses, special silks for making love, coats and skirts for travel, and more practical clothes that did not show the dirt and wear and tear of domestic use," commented van der Post.

In further support of his admiration of birds, van der Post noted the gracefully simple shape and color of birds' eggs, the diversity and elegance of the homes birds build, and the courage birds display when their homes or families are threatened. Finally, he suggested that birds have an eerie ability to sense in advance the coming of a major disturbance such as an earthquake, a storm, or the invasion of a foreign army.

Many birders are attracted to the hobby for less poetic and more competitive reasons. Like Phoebe Snetsinger, most serious birders keep a record of the birds they have seen. A prominent subgroup of birders, called "listers," takes this to a somewhat obsessive and competitive extreme. Not only do they keep life lists, they have backyard lists, state lists, North American lists, even lists of the birds seen while walking the dog. Phoebe Snetsinger was the Babe Ruth of listers.

[1] The following quotes are from *The Heart of the Hunter: Customs and Myths of the African Bushman* by Lauren van der Post.

Another subgroup, called "twitchers," watches for reports of rare sightings and sometimes goes to great lengths to see a single bird. A twitcher's goal is accumulating impressive numbers of birds, and they may expend large sums of time and money in doing so. The Internet is a godsend to twitchers, with its up-to-the-minute reports of bird locations. When a friend living near Seattle reported a black-throated blue warbler —a tiny bird typically found only in the northeastern United States—at her home feeder, hundreds of twitchers descended upon her doorstep, eager to add the warbler to their state or life lists.

Listing and twitching intrigue many bird-watchers, and I have no doubt some birders enjoy these challenges. However, most birders simply enjoy birds, without the competition and goals. They take great pleasure noticing the first canvasback duck's return in the fall, or hearing the song of the olive-sided flycatcher at the same bend in the road each morning. They enjoy responding when the rufous hummingbird buzzes the window asking for the hummingbird feeder to be refilled.

This and much more comprises the wonder of birds. They are the jewels of our planet, following the ebb and flow of our seasons. They can fly higher than the Rockies or swim with the fishes. One species, the arctic tern, flies more than 30,000 miles in one migration season. Another, the belted kingfisher, burrows up to fifteen feet deep into sandy cliffs to hollow out a nesting area. There are more than 9,700 different species of birds, each with a unique plumage and many with a personalized song, all ready to bring awe and delight into our lives.

When Phoebe Snetsinger was asked when she would be content to stop birding, her emphatic reply was, "Never!" To her, even after 8,400 species, birding was endlessly fascinating.

FEEDING WINTER BIRDS

We did not weave the web of life;

we are merely a strand in it.

—Attributed to Chief Noah Sealth

I turn off my computer at four in the afternoon, pull on a fleece-lined Gore-Tex jacket, step outside, and huddle under the eaves. A January rain, deliberate, soaking, and unending, hangs in the air like wood smoke circling a smoldering campfire. The temperature registers barely forty degrees and winter darkness has already stolen the day's light, turning the bare alder trees that rim the lawn into dark pewter giants.

My desire to go outside for a bird walk quickly erodes on days like this, when the Puget Sound region seems to sit in a big, gray puddle. I retreat back inside, make a cup of tea, and settle onto the family room couch. Thank goodness for bird feeders. They bring winter birds close to my window so I can enjoy my favorite pastime from the comfort of my warm, dry house.

Common birds that visit bird feeders are often the first birds novices learn to identify. The birds come close enough for viewing and return often, affording second and third chances to examine them. Most feeder birds are year-round residents, so there is plenty of opportunity to learn and practice their names.

Watching birds at a feeder trains the eye to distinguish size, shape, and plumage color, as well as the mannerisms of different species. A bird's behavior, or gestalt—how it perches, moves, and flies—is called a bird's "jizz." As with people, some birds meander, some dart, some are high-strung, and some are mellow. You can observe all this as birds flutter around the feeder. But first, let's learn about bird feeders.

Feeding birds used to be simple: sprinkle some birdseed in a bowl and set it on the porch railing. Now, like so much else in our lives, bird feeders have gone high tech. There are all sorts: some feeders are designed to attract specific birds, some have moveable parts, and some have suction cups that attach to your office window.

Specialty stores exist just to equip one for feeding wild birds.

Brushed by Feathers

These stores stock enough merchandise to send the novice bird-watcher humbly backing out the door, unable to cope with demanding questions from the clerk such as: "Tube or platform?", "Hulled or whole?", "Droll Yankee or Duncraft?" Before you head for the store, let me simplify the process for you.

Let's start with what birds eat in nature. The more we learn about what different bird species eat naturally and how they forage for food, the better we can simulate the habitat with bird feeders. For example, two common birds, the jaunty short-tailed, red-breasted nuthatch and the spunky chestnut-backed chickadee, feed on cone seeds in conifer trees, so they readily adapt to hanging feeders. Other species, including the spotted towhee and song sparrow, feed mainly on the ground and prefer low platform feeders.

To attract the greatest variety of birds—without getting so involved that you have to give up watching your favorite sports teams this winter—I recommend three types of feeders. The first, the platform feeder, has a flat space to sprinkle a seed mixture for the birds that feed on or near the ground. To keep things simple for now, just use the old-fashioned, shallow-bowl-on-the-porch idea. An old plate, the saucer normally used under a flowerpot, or a flat baking dish will work. The platform feeder needs to be heavy enough to stay put in wind and shallow enough so the birds can keep a watch out for predators as they feed. Any mixture of millet seed, sunflower seeds, bread crumbs, or even cut-up pieces of fruit can be offered. Later on, if you get caught up in feeding birds, you can replace the shallow bowl with a fancier platform feeder. My husband, Bill, made the one we use; it has a roof to keep the rain off and the bottom is fine mesh, which allows any moisture that does get in to drain away. It sits on a pole, which is fitted with a home-made baffle to discourage the resourceful squirrels in our neighborhood.

The second feeder, the most popular one at my house, is a hanging plastic tube filled with whole black sunflower seeds. Black sunflower seeds are sold either with the hull or without the hull. Selecting hulled seeds will decrease the pile of rodent-attracting refuse under your feeder. There are several types of tube feeders; most are made of clear plastic. It isn't necessary for the birds to see into the feeder, but the clear tube tells us when the seed level is low. Be sure to choose a good, solid feeder with metal reinforcement around the feeding holes.

The third feeder is a hanging wire cage to hold suet, or beef fat.

Certain birds, including the diminutive downy woodpecker and chestnut-backed chickadee, can't resist that fat! I keep the first two feeders, the platform and the hanging tube, full of seed all year. However, the suet tends to melt and drip in the summer, so I only fill that feeder during the cooler months. (In the spring I set out a couple hummingbird feeders, but we'll get to that later on, in March.)

Now you are ready to face the sales clerk with confidence. Wear a frumpy safari-styled hat, assume that faraway look birders use, and say, "I'd like a hanging tubular feeder, the Droll Yankee Model A-6 (six holes) with saucer, and five pounds of whole black sunflower seeds." The clerk won't dare question you about extra accessories. Then ask for "A wire cage to hold the suet and a couple suet cakes." The suet cakes are a commercial mixture of fat, seed, and fruit shaped into a four-inch by four-inch block. The flavors remind me of Baskin and Robbins ice cream. (I'm not sure what the birds prefer, but I'm partial to the peanut-sunflower mixture.) Finally, you'll need a bag of mixed seed with mostly millet and some sunflower seeds for your platform feeder, the shallow bowl on the porch. Later, if you find that the mixed seeds attract only crows and blackbirds, you can substitute straight sunflower seeds to encourage a greater variety of visitors.

If your bird feeding needs are unique—perhaps your "garden" is a ten-foot-wide balcony or you live on the twentieth floor with no outdoor access—go ahead and explain this to the clerk. Her eyes will light up with the challenge, and you may go home with a feeder that attaches to a window or with a long metal hanger—shaped like Little Bo Peep's staff—for your hanging feeder. There are lots of ways to feed birds; my system is just one solution.

After you get home, examine your house and garden for the best place for your feeders. Position the feeders where they are easily seen from inside your home. The hanging tubular and suet feeders do well under an eave or on the low branch of a tree. My tubular feeder and platform feeder are outside our family room window, but I put a suet feeder outside my home office window, since I spend so many daylight hours at my computer. The platform feeder can be from two to four feet off the ground. Birds like a tree or bush nearby where they can wait their turn at the feeder or quickly return to if they sense a predator.

Watch to see which bird finds your feeders first. I'll bet it will be a black-capped chickadee at the hanging tube feeder. If you live on the coniferous Northwest Coast, once this adventuresome explorer shows the way, the chestnut-backed chickadee will probably follow. At higher elevations, the mountain chickadee is likely to join the chickadee parade to your feeder.

Before long a new species will sneak in undetected. This stealthy ball of fluff will dart to the hanging feeder, grab just one seed, and escape back to cover without a pause. (That's its jizz.) A short-tailed loner with a black-and-white face pattern, the red-breasted nuthatch is all of four and one-half inches long. Later in the spring it produces a monotone call like a toy tin horn. This bird and one cousin, the white-breasted nuthatch, which favors higher, drier pine forests, cling to the trunks of trees and are as comfortable descending as ascending tree trunks and large branches, always going headfirst (more nuthatch jizz). Another cousin, the pygmy nuthatch, prefers pine needle bundles. Once these birds find your hanging tube feeder, they will scout out the hanging suet feeder too.

Several species of finches will visit the platform feeder, which is solid and closer to the ground, as well as the hanging feeder. The most ubiquitous finch throughout the West, and is found throughout the lower forty-eight states, is the house finch. This brownish bird with an orange-red headband and bib seems to know the southern boundary of Canada and generally stays south of it. It has two look-alike cousins, the Cassin's finch and the purple finch. The Cassin's finch prefers the higher mountain forests and the purple finch—uncommon in the West—may begin to appear later in the year, during spring migration.

A dramatically different-looking cousin is the American goldfinch. It is a brilliant yellow, black, and white during spring and summer, but its winter plumage is dull and muted. Most bird books show this distinction.

As the birds pick at the seed from hanging and platform feeders, lots of bits will fall to the ground, but that's good. This fallen seed feeds another group of birds that prefer to scrape around below trees and shrubs for their fare. The most widespread winter ground feeder is probably a little gray-and-black bird with flashy white outer tail feathers, the dark-eyed junco.

One rather shy ground feeder is the common song sparrow. I don't often use the word drab to describe a bird's appearance, but here I make an exception. It's dark brown with gray stripes on the head and back; dark streaks coalesce into a spot on the creamy breast. Later in the spring, when the song sparrow begins to show off its voice, I'm charmed by the music and forget its drab looks. This bird is found from the Aleutian Islands in Alaska to Baja California and throughout the United States.

Compare all these tiny birds (the chickadees and nuthatches are about four and one-half inches long and the finches and sparrows are about six inches long) to a larger, eight-inch bird that will begin skulking around under the feeders. At first glance the bird might resemble a robin, but closer examination reveals a black hood and white belly. White spots on its dark wings give it its name: spotted towhee. This bird also prefers U.S. soil, or just can't stand the wait at the U.S./Canada border crossing; it is uncommon north of the lower forty-eight.

Another ground feeder is the ten-inch California quail, unmistakable with a forward-thrusting topknot. Almost daily a covey of between eight and sixteen quail emerge from the Nootka roses to the south, peck across our back lawn, stop under the platform feeder, and then continue around the house to the blackberry bushes on the north side. Their soft clucking follows the group as they disappear from sight.

Whew, that's enough. There are other birds that stop at feeders during the winter, but they will be discussed later. For example, we'll pick up the downy woodpecker when we talk about woodpeckers in a chapter later on. The wrens and more types of sparrows are included in the chapter on the LBBs, little brown birds, discussed when we get to fall.

As soon as the birds start coming, I invite you to begin recording your life list of birds. Even Phoebe Snetzinger, who saw more than 8,400 bird species, had to start with number one. At a minimum, write down the name of the bird and the date and location of the sighting. To help you remember the bird, include something unique like "hanging from the suet feeder" or "eating the red pyracantha berries." You'll be on your way to developing the habit of noticing birds.

When the rain stops and there is a break in the January weather, venture outside for a bird walk. Carry your binoculars and a small pocket-sized notebook and wander around the neighborhood. If you see an unfamiliar bird, try making a quick sketch and later look it up in a field guide. You'll probably see some birds you already recognize, such as the American robin or the American crow. Be sure to add them to your life list. Once you have identified the basic birds, birdwatching gets much more exciting.

Winter's early dusk robs us of birdwatching hours, but there is one family of birds that takes advantage of the long seasonal nights: owls. In the next few pages we'll discuss these nocturnal creatures and how to recognize their haunting calls.

OWL-WATCHING

There was an old owl liv'd in an oak,

The more he heard, the less he spoke;

The less he spoke, the more he heard,

O', if men were all like that wise bird!

—*Anonymous*, **Punch** *(1875)*

My first memorable owl interaction occurred twenty-eight years ago in northern California, a thousand miles from here. My older son, Munro, was three years old and younger son, Alex, had just been born. We lived south of Walnut Creek, on the shoulder of Mount Diablo, where live oaks crowded the dry river canyons between open grassy fields teeming with mice and voles.

I especially remember the mice because they often shared our home. Somehow they knew it was the mid-1970s, a time of peace, love, and nonviolence. I couldn't kill any living thing, so I simply chased the mice outdoors. (I'm now a recovering pacifist; mice, slugs in my garden, and spiders in my bathtub aren't as fortunate as their ancestors were.)

The combination of grassy fields, feed scattered about for our small chicken flock, and our laissez-faire attitude drew mice to our yard like hornets to a fall barbecue. Given this banquet of nocturnal rodents, it was no surprise that a great horned owl staked its territory near our home. In the evening, it regularly perched on a low branch of the large oak tree just off our back patio. I first noticed the owl's silhouette from an upstairs window as I swayed in a rocking chair trying to lull Alex to sleep. I never saw the owl during daylight, but at dusk it flew silently through the ravine behind our house, landed in the tree, and sat quietly.

Later in the evening, well after dark and probably after the owl had consumed a mouse or two, I heard its call: from three to eight deep muffled hoots with a slightly syncopated rhythm. It sounds like "hoo, hoo-hoo, hoo, hoo," sometimes interpreted as "Who's awake? Me too." The call was soft and recognizable. Like a sentry on a rampart, the owl's presence helped me feel safe.

That owl's call was soothing, but since then I've learned that

Brushed by Feathers

owls also shriek, bark, screech, whistle, whinny, and even quack. Later on in the breeding season, after the young have left the nest and are following the parents on hunting soirees in the evening, the call of the young owls can be very alarming. Last September I cut out a police report from my local newspaper that said, "At 10:25 P.M. a Clinton resident stated she had just heard a bloodcurdling scream come from the woods near her Saska Lane residence. The woman said the scream sounded like a child in distress." I've heard that same distressing sound myself and am convinced the woman had heard a baby owl calling for food.

These unrecognizable, middle of the night sounds can be scary. When early cultures attributed the ominous sounds to owls, many stories and myths grew to explain them. For example, in the Pacific Northwest some Native American tribes believed that owls were the spirits of their deceased ancestors. In Africa, some feared that witch doctors hired owls to kill. In ancient Greece and in Shakespeare's time, the owl symbolized bad omens. Today, owls, and particularly their hooting calls, are used in adventure films to portend trouble and create suspense.

Other traditions embrace owls as a positive symbol. The bird is associated with the Greek goddess of wisdom, Mikros, and the early English believed that eating the eggs of owls would improve your vision and prevent blindness. In India, eating a healthy helping of owl was considered an aphrodisiac. In France, the call of a barn owl in the chimney meant that a pregnant woman would give birth to a daughter.

All these beliefs seemed to me like quaint ancient fables, until three winters ago. I was in Honduras, a small country in Central America, teaching local nature guides about birdwatching. (For the last four winters I've volunteered to teach nature guides with the RARE Center for Tropical Conservation.) One evening we were returning from a visit to a remote nature preserve. As the van carrying us slowly lunged up a dirt road heading back to the biological station where we were housed, I began chatting with one of my students, Yeni. An animated young woman with short hair and big dark eyes, Yeni would likely have become a cheerleader had she been born into my culture. Instead she used her charismatic energy to explain the wonders of nature to tourists. Somehow Yeni and I began talking about myths and how birds are portrayed in myths. When she shared the following story from her culture with me—parts of which she patiently repeated so I could get it word for word in my journal—her eyes widened and she became very serious.

"This is not a story, this is real," she began. "There is a woman in Comyagua (a nearby village where her husband's sister and brother-in-law lived) who becomes an owl at night. The woman goes to sleep and she becomes the owl and flies and calls around the houses. The sister of my husband had a pain in the head for one year. Then one night the owl came and the next morning the sister of my husband was dead. There was no other reason than the owl."

There is no question that Yeni and her family believed the owl was the cause of her sister-in-law's death. During the month I spent with Yeni we saw several kinds of owls, including the very common ferruginous pygmy owl which hunts and feeds during the day. I don't remember her responding fearfully to these "daytime" owls. Perhaps, in Yeni's mind, the owl-woman of Comyagua was a different species of owl or an example of one owl gone bad.

Although superstitions about owls remain deeply rooted in some cultures, in the modern world—where the owl has been studied, its eerie night sounds identified, and its unique and fascinating characteristics recognized—beliefs have changed. We now realize that owls aren't interested in humans at all. Their minds are on their next meal and how to catch it.

Studies of owls have uncovered fascinating information about their behavior and adaptations. Most owls fill a specialized niche in our environment—nighttime hunter—and have evolved physical characteristics to do this as efficiently as possible.

Owls have round heads with flat faces and large eyes. An owl sees at least two and a half times better than we do, and in a lot less light. The eyes of most birds are on the sides of their heads in order to increase their chances of seeing a predator. Owls, however, have both eyes in front, offering them binocular, or three-dimensional, vision and increasing their chances of capturing prey. Also, their eyes are huge. If our eyes were the same ratio as those of an owl, they would be the size of tennis balls. An owl's eyeballs can't move around in the socket the way that ours do, so it compensates by bobbing its head up and down and side to side. This improves the bird's ability to estimate distances.

Owls cannot turn their heads all the way around, despite what your fifth-grade science teacher may have told you. They turn their heads three-quarters of the way around then swivel it back around so quickly that it gives the impression of a 360-degree turn.

In addition to sharp eyes, owls have a keen sense of hearing. Experiments in rooms without light have shown that barn owls can catch prey by sound alone. Large facial disks around the eyes funnel sounds to the ears, which are located at uneven levels at the sides of the owl's head.

New birders are amazed the first time they actually hear the sound of a bird flapping its wings. Perhaps a crow or gull passes near enough for the bird-watcher to catch the muffled "whoosh, whoosh" as the bird's feathers push against the air to propel the bird forward. Experienced birders become accustomed to hearing this sound. Consequently, it feels eerie to experience a large bird slipping quietly past without making much noise at all, such as an owl, for example.

The leading edges of the owl's wings are equipped with comb-like bristles that break the air in such a way as to silence the wing motion. The upper surfaces of the primary and secondary wing feathers are downy soft to keep from making sound as they rub against each other in flight. With these advantages the owl can close in on prey unannounced. The owl then captures the prey with strong, needlelike talons and often remains on the ground briefly to rip the prey into pieces with its hooked bill and gulp down the meal. Later the owl regurgitates pellets of bones, fur, and other indigestible parts of the prey.

Fifteen different species of owls are regularly seen in the West, from the twenty-seven-inch, 2.4-pound great gray owl, the largest owl in North America, to the northern pygmy owl, which measures only six and three-quarters inches long and weighs only 2.5 ounces. The most common owl of these species is the great horned owl, the one I observed from my son's bedroom in California. Ninety percent of my total owl sightings since then have been of this same species. The barn owl is probably the second most commonly seen owl in the West, mainly because it roosts and nests near people in old barns or unused buildings. The short-eared owl hunts during daylight, especially at dawn and dusk, so it is also frequently observed. Glimpsing any other owl species is an iffy proposition, even for folks who spend a lot of time birdwatching.

Some Audubon groups offer Owl Prowls, nighttime field trips looking for owls. The usual goal of these searches is to *hear* owls, since seeing any bird at night is virtually impossible. In the milder parts of the West, including the Pacific Northwest, the best time to listen for owls is in January. They nest early in the year, usually in February or March. During January they move about and spend their evening courting—

hooting to attract mates and establish territory. In western Canada and Alaska, and in the colder regions of the interior West, the courting season is a bit later, when the weather warms and prey populations become available for feeding young.

Winter weather occasionally forces some owl species native to the Arctic to move south into warmer western regions in search of food. A couple of winters ago, Bill and I tracked down a great gray owl that wintered in Bridle Trails State Park in Bellevue, just east of Seattle. The largest member of the owl family, this fluffy bird prefers a low roost from only ten to twenty-five feet high. It was active during the daytime, and we watched it dodge the equestrian traffic, startling both horses and riders as it moved from perch to perch under a Douglas fir canopy.

Another occasional winter visitor is the snowy owl. Some years are bonanza years for snowy owls in the milder coastal areas of British Columbia and Washington; once, one hung out on the top of the Christian Science Church in Seattle for several weeks—perhaps looking to increase its wisdom and mystical powers.

The burrowing owl, as its name suggests, lives in underground burrows in drier areas throughout the West. If you are lucky enough to locate an occupied burrow, the birds are easy to spot since the male, looking like a football on stilt legs, often stands guard near the entrance to the burrow. To discourage predators from the nest, this owl makes a loud buzzing sound similar to a threatening rattlesnake.

Twenty years ago I wouldn't have included the barred owl in a book on common birds of the West. However, during the last two decades this eastern species has spread into forested areas of the western coastal states, perhaps taking territory from the endangered spotted owl. Today its sightings are as numerous as Elvis sightings. The barred owl has a distinctive hooting rhythm that mimics "Who cooks for you, who cooks for you, all?"

On a warm afternoon last summer, I was taking a quick walk near my home. As I mounted a slight hill, my mind miles away, two scolding robins caused me to halt and look to the side of the road. A good way to find predator birds is to take note of any small bird ruckus. A barred owl, the object of the robins' consternation, perched on a low branch of a Douglas fir tree less than twelve feet away. Its big dark eyes stared first at me, then off into the distance, unperturbed by my presence in the road or the robin ruckus encircling it. I studied the dark-brown vertical bars on the pale breast and the large facial disks. After several minutes the owl must have determined that with all the commotion no mice would venture within view, so it lifted off the branch and silently flew deeper into the woods.

I walked on, letting the robins recover their composure. Reaching the top of the hill, I wondered how many times I'd walked this road and *not* noticed the owl. It felt a bit strange now, knowing a silent "wise" bird monitored this road. Perhaps the owl ruled over a neighbor's backyard every night, as that great horned owl did to my backyard so many years ago.

Brushed by Feathers

CHAPTER TWO

February

Here, in the Puget Sound lowlands, February seems to be waiting, holding its breath. Native plants are still dormant, resident birds remain quiet, and wintering ducks and seabirds huddle in bays. Cold, rainy days, although officially lengthening according to my *Tidelog* almanac, are shortened by dark afternoon clouds. Years ago I asked my grandmother why there were only twenty-eight days in February. She said, "February is a month of waiting, so, lucky for you, it's a little bit shorter." Since I'm an impatient adult, it's likely I was also an impatient child, which helps explain her answer.

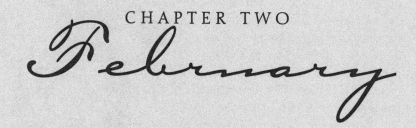

Yet February is also a month full of expectancy. Bulbs poke up through the soil and swell, although weeks will pass before they bloom. There is an exception: snowdrops, ultraearly bulbs that bloom above the leaf litter in the garden; the next day a light snowfall adds a tiny white cap to their three delicately splayed petals. And later, impatient forsythia, unable to contain itself any longer, bursts forth in golden yellow near the end of the month, breaking winter's hold and blazing the way for spring.

"Rocky"

February 25. I look out over the matte gray waters of Possession Sound, framed by maples, alders, and Douglas firs. From our house, tucked down on the island's east side away from the shipping lanes, we rarely see large boats, but today a red-striped Coast Guard cutter maneuvers back and forth between our beach and Hat Island.

The rain stops. Dry skies, along with an uncommon afternoon low tide, persuade me to drop my work and take a beach walk. As I descend the seventy-two steps of the steep ravine behind our house, damp sword ferns soak my pants. At the bottom I carefully step over slippery beach logs to reach the rocky beach. A light breeze bites my cheeks and scratches out long, rough sandpaper streaks in the flat bay as I turn and head south.

Black dots group far offshore. Through the magnification of my binoculars, the dots become buffleheads, mergansers, and scoters. These ducks and seabirds spend the summer nesting season far north in Alaska and northern Canada and retreat to warmer, ice-free bays, like ours, for the winter. Also in the mix, I spy loons, grebes, wigeons, and goldeneyes, some of the nearly forty migrant species that rest and feed on Puget Sound waters every winter. Some dive underwater to catch small fish, others nibble at the mussels and barnacles that attach themselves to pilings, large rocks, and buoy chains. Still others dabble in shallow water for small creatures hidden in the mudflats.

I stroll on down the beach until an unusual surge in the water catches my eye. I lift my binoculars expectantly. Could they be back, I ask myself? This early? A fine white spray shoots skyward as a huge, rubbery form arches just inches above the water before submerging again. A single gray whale surfaces once more, this time lifting its tail on reentry, signaling a deeper dive. "The grays are back!" I exclaim aloud to the empty beach. These forty-five-foot, thirty-three-ton marine mammals spend fall and winter in the warm Pacific coastal waters of Baja California where the young are born, then migrate up the coast in early spring. Most continue north to Alaska but, for some unknown reason, each year about fifteen behemoths take a right turn at the Straits of Juan de Fuca and settle into Puget Sound to feed for three or four months. Whale researchers began identifying our gray whales in 1991 and report that the same ones take this side trip into Puget Sound year after year. The arrival of these marine migrants foreshadows the arrival of avian migrants, which will begin to appear next month.

Northern goshawk, a rare visitor

For several minutes I watch the whale feeding, then it turns northward. Raindrops ticking against my parka hood and the incoming tide signal me to turn north as well and head back home. I trace the syncopated trail of the whale—long periods of underwater swimming, then a surfacing, followed by a steamy breath or two—until it fades into the gray rain. Reaching the steep stairs, I slowly mount them, stopping to catch my breath at each of the two bends. At the top, I notice our pigeon, Rocky, has already snuggled into his night roost on a back deck light fixture. Each morning he launches off the light fixture to circle out over the

bluff and around our meadow—morning exercise for pigeons—before returning to the bird feeder for breakfast. Most days he snoozes on the top ridge of our tile roof or the wooden trellis near the bird feeders, and occasionally he disappears during the day. I've no idea where to, but well before dark he is settled back on the light fixture.

If the bird feeders go dry, Rocky follows Bill as Bill "commutes" from the house twenty-five steps to the shed, his home office. Rocky walks along behind Bill and coos softly—merely a gentle reminder, not a demanding request—for Bill to fill the feeder. In his former life Rocky must have concluded that males are the source of food, since he never targets me as a solution to his hunger. On cold winter nights I turn on the light underneath Rocky to warm his little toes. I know this is silly, since birds have little feeling in their feet and legs, but the mother in me wants to do something to tuck him in.

Two days later, focused on my computer screen, I chance to look out the window at an alder tree edging our meadow. Halfway up the tree, a football shape sits on a branch. Why is that red-tailed hawk perching so low? As I look more carefully, I notice its long tail and upright posture.

Brushed by Feathers

*Surf, white-winged,
and black scoters*

Examining the bird with my binoculars, I realize this is no red-tailed. Light, fluffy lower-belly feathers and a white streak over the eye clinch the identification: this is a very rare raptor for this location, a northern goshawk. I run to the family room for my birdwatching telescope and carry it upstairs to a window directly across from the hawk. I set the scope and zoom in to watch as the raptor casually preens, fluffs its feathers, and looks around the meadow. Twenty minutes later the goshawk departs; evidently it was passing through and stopped for a brief rest.

The large number of raptors, including unusual birds like the northern goshawk that visited my meadow, adds a special thrill to winter birding. Each fall these birds flood into coastal river deltas and inland valleys by the thousands. The Skagit Flats northwest of Whidbey Island, the Nisqually River Delta south of Seattle, plus other flat, open fields up and down the West Coast serve up rodent, small bird, mammal, duck, and shorebird populations that provide wintertime feed for these raptors.

In this chapter we focus on February birdwatching. A virtual walk-through a western neighborhood broadens the list of local birds beyond the species that visit feeders. I offer some tricks of the trade to make birdwatching easier, such as learning about the habitats of birds and watching to see if the birds are single or in flocks. Then we begin to watch for winter raptors.

Birds introduced this month:

❏ Canada Goose *(Branta canadensis)*

❏ Sharp-shinned Hawk *(Accipiter striatus)*

❏ Cooper's Hawk *(Accipiter cooperii)*

❏ Northern Goshawk *(Accipiter gentilis)*

❏ Red-tailed Hawk *(Buteo jamaicensis)*

❏ Bald Eagle *(Haliaeetus leucocephalus)*

❏ Rock Pigeon *(Columba livia)*

❏ Mourning Dove *(Zenaida macroura)*

❏ Belted Kingfisher *(Ceryle alcyon)*

❏ Steller's Jay *(Cyanocitta stelleri)*

❏ Western Scrub-jay *(Aphelocoma californica)*

❏ Black-billed Magpie *(Pica pica)*

Brushed by Feathers

❏ American Crow *(Corvus brachyrhynchos)*

❏ Brown Creeper *(Certhia americana)*

❏ Bushtit *(Psaltriparus minimus)*

❏ Golden-crowned Kinglet *(Regulus satrapa)*

❏ Ruby-crowned Kinglet *(Regulus calendula)*

❏ American Robin *(Turdus migratorius)*

❏ European Starling *(Sturnus vulgaris)*

❏ Pine Siskin *(Carduelis pinus)*

❏ House Sparrow *(Passer domesticus)*

GANGS IN THE 'HOOD

Birds of a feather flock together.

—*Popular saying*

This thought may have crossed your mind: "Well, it's easy for Frances to notice birds; she lives in the country." Many readers, I expect, live in more urban settings, from an Idaho city to an Anchorage neighborhood, or a suburban area of greater Los Angeles. I may indeed have some advantages, but don't despair; there are birds virtually everywhere. This section focuses on the common birds that live in and around the towns and cities of the West. These birds may not frequent feeders, but they are there in your garden or hanging out in local parks. These resourceful feathered friends have figured out how to take advantage of the presence of humans; they are the birds of the 'hood.

So join me on a virtual walk around your neighborhood. Granted, we have a large geographic area to consider, but the birds we'll meet in this chapter are found in most western states. And remember, it's February, so unless you live in southern California, dress warmly and bring your binoculars and a notebook with pen or pencil.

Walk out the door. The first bird you encounter is darkly colored with a brick-red breast. This alert-looking creature stands stationary on the lawn, head up and tail resting on the grass. It flies to a shrub at our appearance. You probably learned to recognize this bird as a child. Take out your notebook, write down the date and time, and begin your bird list: American robin.

If you live in drier parts of the West, south of Vancouver, British Columbia, you should soon spot a dovelike bird—perhaps two sitting side by side—with a long, pointed tail, perched on an electrical wire. This bird has a trim, brownish body and a small head. In warmer areas, you hear a mournful call, "oowoo-woo-woo-woo," that sounds somewhat like an owl. Add mourning dove to your list.

Perhaps a dense hedge separates the lawn from the street. An insistent chattering fills the hedge. Soon a chunky, sparrow-type bird flits out of the hedge, notices you, and darts back in. The chattering continues. After a moment the bird darts out again and flies to a small tree on the corner. Two more birds follow, then five more, all communicating constantly like a group of seventh-grade girls at lunch. These omnipresent, gregarious birds—house sparrows—are found in most urban neighborhoods south of Alaska.

Back in chapter one we discussed a bird's "jizz," the way it moves and acts. So far on our virtual walk, we've barely mentioned plumage color but have focused on the bird's shape, jizz, and whether the bird is by itself or in a group. On the rest of the walk, be aware of the flocking tendency of birds. Is the bird alone, in a small flock, or part of a large flock? Is the flock loose and gangling with the birds barely aware of each other, or are the birds tightly packed, moving as one unit? Birds have sophisticated reasons for gathering in groups, a fact not unnoticed by mankind. Over the years a lexicon has developed describing birds' tendencies to flock:

A congregation of crows
A gaggle of geese
A swarm of swallows

Perhaps we can add: *A gossip of house sparrows*.

Continuing down the street, you notice a loose flock of seven large black birds flying overhead. They seem to meander through the sky, leaderless. One starts: "caw, caw," and others respond in kind. Of course these are American crows, common, easy to see, and noisy as they cluster in small groups or join large flocks of several hundred birds. When I lived in the Seattle area near Lake Washington, hundreds regularly convened in my neighbor's cottonwood trees to chat loudly and then fly south to feed somewhere, probably in a landfill.

The 'hood is home to another gang of black birds. We approach a large tree thronging with boisterous birds. Squeaks, warbles, chirps, and twittering exhale from a fairly tight group of black-speckled birds with yellow beaks—European starlings. We decide to walk around, rather than under, this heavily laden tree. The cavalcade of sound lessens as we walk by and picks up as we move on. These birds group together to protect themselves from attack. However, both crow and starling flocks have been observed turning the tables: mobbing the attacker and spurring visions from Alfred Hitchcock's movie *The Birds*.

We reach a nearby park with open ball fields and a section of trees and native vegetation. Looking across a low, waterlogged portion of the field, we notice twelve fat, brownish geese, large rumps swaying as they waddle along, long necks bent to the ground for a nibble here and a peck there. These are Canada geese, common inhabitants in parks, especially those near water. Dramatic increases in populations and a resulting abundance of bird poop have turned these birds into unwanted pests along lakes, golf courses, and large, open lawns. By the way, these are not Canadian geese—a common misnomer—they are Canada geese.

Wandering into the treed section of the park, we recognize some of our feeder friends, the chickadees, song sparrows, dark-eyed juncos, and spotted towhees. Suddenly a cloud of sixty or so tiny birds takes off from the top branches of a bare tree, swarms as one unit through the air, and lands in another tree twenty-five yards away. A sweet chorus with a harsh, descending "chee" buzzes through the tight flock of pine siskins. At this distance the birds look small and dark, though a closer investigation would reveal prominent yellow streaks along the brownish wings and tail.

Next we notice fifteen birds in a scattered flock bouncing like puffballs from bushes to low tree branches to shrubs, wandering along and happily sampling the insects and grubs. A soft chatter accompanies their antics. As we watch these small, gray, nondescript bushtits dangle upside down clinging to the ends of branches, you might wonder what drives birds to flock. Some birds flock for protection, feeding, or for migration. And some birds don't flock at all. Smaller birds are generally more likely to flock than larger birds. Most of the birds we've encountered on our neighborhood walk were found in flocks.

For most birds, hiding is one method of defense against predators; birds have developed into fast fliers for this purpose. They zip into trees, scurry into thick brush, or just get the heck out of the way. But hiding is not always an option. Thus, flocking developed as another line of defense.

This is why: a single bird must be alert to attack from all sides, at all times. If tiny tweety spends a large part of the day watching for predators, little time is left for eating. Theoretically, two birds feeding side by side can cut their watching time in half and that leaves more time to search for food. Now put the two birds into a flock of ten or twenty-five or 100 and feeding time increases exponentially. It is generally true in nature that the strongest birds survive, and the strongest are usually the best fed. So birds that flock together tend to maintain a survival edge. Presumably, shorebirds flock and migrate together for this reason. When a hungry peregrine falcon swoops down out of the sky, a single shorebird in a flock of 100, has a 99 percent chance of not being lunch. More significantly, flocks may confuse or frighten predators. Flocking can also foster more efficient feeding. The more eyes searching for rich feeding areas, the more likely those areas will be found.

Flocks of wintering or migrating birds are often comprised of different species. For example, black turnstones, birds that flip over beach litter to find prey, are often joined by sanderlings, which feed on the newly exposed substrata. Also, nearsighted gleaners, such as vireos and warblers, flock with farsighted salliers, such as flycatchers, taking advantage of the flycatcher's sharper vision. The diminutive downy woodpecker flocks with chickadees that act as sentinels announcing danger. Even birds that fend for themselves during the day may flock for protection at night.

As we turn around and head home, a fairly large, bold bird swoops into a nearby tree. It calls a series of "shack" or "shreep" notes as three similar birds swoop along behind, flashes of blue showing as they spread their wings to land. This grouping is probably a family, two parents and last spring's offspring which are now adult-sized. The loud calls and bluish tones of the feathers identify these birds as jays, either the Steller's jay of more northern pine, oak, and conifer suburbs or the western scrub jay of drier, more open areas. East of the coastal mountains of the lower forty-eight and north into Alaska, a jay cousin, the black-and-white, long-tailed, black-billed magpie, may also be seen. This large, flashy bird lives near settled areas.

Nearing your home, a new flock appears above the rooftops. Large birds, quiet except for wings flapping, circle as one unit swiftly beating the air with strong wings. They are obviously the same bird but display different colors—gray, black, charcoal, white—and some are multicolored. Most of you will recognize this final bird; the typical city pigeon properly called the rock pigeon.

Back home, count up the birds encountered on our jaunt. My tally shows twelve species, not bad for a quick walk through an urban neighborhood. (Just don't let me catch you adding these "virtual" birds to your bird list.)

There is one more point to consider before we leave the topic of flocking. It has been my observation that urban neighborhoods, towns, and cities house a higher proportion of flocking birds than more natural habitats. This must be a result of survival: birds with the protection of flocking tendencies are better able to survive the competition of human development. It seems that birds must live in gangs in order to survive in our urban areas.

Brushed by Feathers

RICHES IN NICHES

"The Birds Find Their Homes"

A long time ago on a wide, grassy African plain,
there lived a big, strong mother bird. She had many,
many children of different sizes, shapes, and colors.
One day Mother Bird realized that the plain could not feed her
large family and she decided that they must leave to find more
food. Mother Bird called all her children together and told them
they would soon begin a long journey. Some of the children
climbed onto Mother Bird's back, others snuggled into her
feathers, and some held on to her wings and tail.
Mother Bird spread her large, powerful wings and lifted
into the air. She and her children flew for many miles looking
for abundant lands. Soon the smallest birds began to tire
of clinging to her wings. The tiny barbet looked down and
saw a beautiful garden with colorful flowers. "Mamma,"
she said, "I want to live there." Mother Bird smiled,
so the tiny barbet let go and flew down into the garden.
A few miles later the little black kokodyo looked down
and saw fruit trees below. "Mamma," he said, "I want
to live there," and floated down to the trees laden with fruit.
One by one, all the birds found their own homes.
The weaver bird selected fields ripe with grain,
the pelican found olives to eat,

and the secretary bird noticed a big juicy termite mound.

Other birds found the forest, some settled near lakes.

All the birds chose a home where they could eat and

live and raise their own children.

After all her children were taken care of,

Mother Bird climbed high into the sky and

soared in great circles, just below the sun.

Today the people call her Eagle Who Announces the Drought.

That is how Mother Bird continues to look after her children;

she foretells the dry spells.

—African Myth

"Look, a *Collybia trullisatus*," exclaimed my friend Susan. Since the dark, gloomy day failed to offer birds, we had cast our eyes to the ground to search for interesting mushrooms. Susan picked up a Douglas fir cone with four sprightly white fungi springing from it. "These mushrooms grow only on rotting Douglas fir cones," she added, holding it up for me to see. It is true that many mushrooms have direct relationships with specific trees or parts of trees.

I mused: wouldn't it be helpful if birds stayed with just one tree species? Identification would be so much easier if, for example, partridges perched only in pear trees. Unlike mushrooms, birds, with their amazing ability of flight, can visit many different trees and environments. Yet birds are similar to mushrooms in some respects. Most bird species prefer specific habitats and even niches within the larger habitat where they can find food, as explained in the African myth. In the myth the bird children dropped off the mother bird when they found the right feeding niche. The barbet chose the colorful garden; the weaver bird selected the field of grain; the secretary bird settled next to a termite nest. The birds distributed themselves into different habitats, which allowed for huge numbers of species, all able to survive because they didn't compete for the same flowers, grain field, or termite nest.

Knowing a bird's preferred feeding habitat is one handy trick to increasing the enjoyment of birdwatching. For example, the brown creeper, a small, mottled-brown bird, is nearly always found on the trunks of trees. Following a distinctive trunk-foraging practice, it starts low on the trunk and probes its way upward, sometimes spiraling around the trunk to find food. After creeping up the trunk, the bird flutters down, resembling a dried leaf in color and behavior, to land at the base of another tree, then forages upward on the new tree, repeating the pattern.

Another example is the belted kingfisher, which spends its life along the edges of beaches, rivers, or lakes. The kingfisher selects a high perch, perhaps an overhanging branch or sailboat mast, where it scans the water for small fish. The bird flies into the air, hovers briefly, then dives into the water after fish. It then flies directly out of the water, without pausing to float, and returns to a perch. This behavior in this habitat makes identification a snap.

Lawns are another foraging habitat, albeit quite sterile if treated with pesticides and herbicides. Many birds peck around the edges of lawns, but a bird regularly feeding in the middle of a fair-sized lawn is likely to be either an American robin, European starling (they usually congregate in large flocks), northern flicker, or house sparrow (another flocking bird).

Deep woods, edges of woods, open fields, riparian areas, desert, and even suburban neighborhoods are examples of western habitats. Each attracts bird species that are adapted to feeding in that habitat. Some birds are highly specialized such as gray-crowned rosy-finches that feed at the edges of alpine snowfields. A few bird species, called generalists —American crows, European starlings, and rock pigeons, for example —feed in several different habitats. But many of our native birds are habitat specific and could die off if the habitat is not preserved.

Bird families often disperse over several habitats with individual species adopting different ones. Take raptors, for example. Bald eagles forage along beaches and flooded fields, red-tailed hawks search open fields, northern harriers patrol marshes and farmlands for their dinner, and sharp-shinned hawks look in woodlands. Each species focuses on a distinct feeding habitat and has physical adaptations that facilitate successful hunting in its habitat of choice.

Within these more general habitats are minihabitats called niches. A niche might be a particular part of a tree. The ends of branches of large fir, maple, or alder trees attract different bird species than the trunks of those same trees. If you spot a large bird clinging to a tree trunk, I'd bet money it's a pileated woodpecker. Small woodpeckers, the downy and hairy, also prefer this part of a tree, and the downy may travel out onto the larger limbs. But the toes of large woodpeckers are designed for clinging to wide surfaces and they can't grasp small branches.

On the ends of tree branches only the smallest birds can establish a perch, and many hang upside down monkeylike while gleaning seeds, insects, and grubs. Since hanging bird feeders mimic the ends of branches, several of our familiar feeder birds fall into this category: siskins, chickadees, and bushtits. Ruby-crowned and golden-crowned kinglets are also winter branch hangers, although they do not frequent feeders.

Wetlands also provide feeding niches. Shorebirds come with differing lengths of legs and bills, from the stubby one-inch bill of plovers to the long, curved, nine-inch bill of the long-billed curlew. The bills are designed to extract food from different layers of substrata. Even if the plover and curlew feed shoulder to shoulder, they are reaching into different niches of the soil rather than competing.

Unlike mushrooms, birds don't stay put, and we can't spread glue on tree branches to make them stay. But Mother Bird knew the best solution to keep her children from squabbling over their dinners—she separated them into individual feeding habitats and niches. One familiar with the habits and haunts of different species would know, for example, that seeing a song sparrow hanging from the end of a branch is as improbable as seeing a polar bear lounging on your driveway. Or, for my friend Susan, seeing a Douglas fir cone–loving *Collybia trullisatus* growing in a wildflower meadow.

RAPTOR, RAPTOR EVERYWHERE ...

To know the universe itself as a road

—as many roads—

as roads to traveling souls.

—Walt Whitman

Our birding guide, Wezil, jammed on his Toyota 4-Runner's brakes and he and I leaned forward to peer at the top of an electrical pole alongside the road. In the backseat, Bill craned his head against the side window as we all watched a large football-shaped bird sitting quietly on the upper crossbar. It had a dark head and creamy breast with a dark belly-band. "Looks like a red-tailed," Bill offered. Wezil and I nodded in agreement. We continued, scanning ahead to the long, regular row of poles, a skimpy artificial forest in an otherwise flat desert.

A quarter mile farther down the gravel side road in southeastern Arizona's Sulphur Springs Valley, Wezil again stopped the car. We lifted binoculars to a different pole to scan a new football-shaped bird. This bird was completely dark. "Another red-tailed," Wezil said. "We call the dark ones Harlans, but they're still red-tails." He slipped the car into gear and we drove on through the high-desert landscape, a somber brownish gray of winter dormancy.

Earlier that morning Wezil had picked us up at our bed and breakfast west of Bisbee for a day of winter birding. "We'll see plenty of raptors," he'd announced as we loaded gear into his vehicle, the temperature at the freezing mark, a weak but promising sun on the horizon. Southeast Arizona is famous for hummingbirds in the spring and summer; in winter interest switches to raptors. Knowing exactly where to find wintering raptors, Wezil had driven us east into this wide-open valley of sage, rangeland, and—where a spring or river provided water—small, cultivated fields. For good reason, local birders had tagged this gravel road "Raptor Valley."

Raptors are a general grouping of birds including eagles, hawks, falcons, osprey, owls, and kites. Most are easy to see, majestic and flashy. Birds of prey that sit atop the avian food chain, raptors eat mammals, smaller birds, large insects, snakes, amphibians, and infrequently pick off small dogs and cats. The word "raptor" comes from the same root as "robber," meaning to seize by force.

A mile farther down the back road, we spotted another football-shaped hawk. It was completely white on the breast—no diagnostic dark bellyband—with a dark back and distinctive red tail. We looked carefully, consulted the identification book, and concluded: the Fuertes variation of red-tailed hawk. One hour later, thanks to our guide's sharp eye, we'd found four different examples of the red-tailed hawk: western, Fuertes, Harlan's, and rufous-morph. They all had the distinctive football shape, but plumage ranged from light all over, to strongly contrasted, to completely dark. The bird book was correct: "plumage *extremely* variable." (Birders haven't yet standardized terms for these variations in the plumage and geography for the red-tailed hawk. Some call them subspecies; others use the term "races." Other differences are identified as color morphs. Until we get our lingo more standardized, I'll use the term "variations." Also, these variations are a source of skepticism and ongoing arguments among birders, particularly raptor experts. Becuase of this, documentation of these variations has been slow to reach the birding literature, especially on the edges of the birds' ranges as with the Harlan's and Fuertes here in Arizona.)

Southeastern Arizona offers a particularly wide selection of red-tailed hawks. One variation or another of these high-soaring hawks, with their large, chunky bodies, smallish heads, and broad wings that bulge out on the trailing edge, inhabits most open areas of the western states. Most show reddish tails, a useful field mark. Don't be fooled, however, as several adult birds and immature red-tails have no red on their tails.

At the end of the day, our tally had increased to six different species of raptors, but puzzling out the different types of red-tails remained the highlight. Wezil dropped us at the B & B with an invitation to return in the summer for a day of humming-birding.

Two weeks later Bill and I were back in the Pacific Northwest, clad in layers of fleece and shod in polypropylene booties as we prepared to launch our double kayak into the icy waters of the Skagit River for another day of raptor watching. Bill's kayaking buddy Al had organized a day of eagle watching. Al's wife, Sarah, and a naturalist friend, Larry, had joined us for a half-day paddle down the middle section of the full-bodied Skagit. Al, a professional kayak trip leader and instructor, had planned our route, checked the water flow, and promised "no real white water."

As Al readied the kayaks and Larry wandered off to examine an unfamiliar moss, I stood at the edge of the Skagit watching a belted king-fisher perched on a low branch. I needed to take a few minutes to psych myself up for this trip. Although I kayak regularly and Bill and I have taken several weeklong kayak trips on flat water, river kayaking makes me anxious. Old reoccurring dreams about getting swept under water and being trapped by the force of the river creep into my brain before every trip. Once on the water, I'm okay. The buoyancy of the kayak reassures me and the joy of moving through a beautiful wild area grabs my full attention. Later, after the trip, in the glow of the adventure, I will think this worry was all nonsense. However, at that moment my heart was pounding.

A putrid smell brought my attention to puffy shapes of rotting salmon eddying in the cove at my feet. Fall and winter salmon runs attract bald eagles to the Skagit and other coastal rivers of western British Columbia and Washington. The eagles gorge on spent salmon. Along these rivers, eagles are more common than red-tails.

The majestic eagle stands a yard tall with a wingspan of more than two yards. Mature bald eagles wear pure white head and tail plumage; the body is dark brown. Telling the similarly plumed male and female apart is difficult unless you see a pair sitting close to each other. The female is slightly larger, true of most raptors. Immature eagles lack the white head and tail feathers and appear mottled brown, sometimes with a whitish belly, which fools many novice birders and even confused Audubon himself, who thought the immature bald eagle a different species and named it the Washington eagle after our first president.

Wispy white clouds drifted low in the narrow valley, while heavy gray clouds blanketed the conifer-covered hills and held their moisture as we began our journey. I took a few deep breaths as I'd learned in yoga class and climbed into the boat. Al said the current was running about five to six miles per hour, which would take us quickly through our ten-mile trip. Bare, twiggy alder branches, trunks white with lichen, leaned over the river while shaggy, green cedar and Douglas fir crowded the rocky bends. As we rounded the first bend Bill asked, "Who's going to count eagles?" I volunteered since I'd already spotted three. Counting the eagles would keep my mind concentrated on the trees, rather than on the ominous watery depths. On this cloudy day the dark bodies of the eagles were hard to spot in the conifer branches, but the white heads shone like round balls. Sarah asked, "What do you look for?" I answered, "Golf balls in the trees."

As we slalomed down the river, fast and churning but mostly free of frothing white water, a few mergansers, gulls, and a goldeneye huddled in the shallow bends. We even identified a soaring red-tailed hawk. This, however, was eagle country through and through. Eagles lined both sides along the route, sometimes two or three in one tree. At one slow bend, where fish carcasses eddied out of the swiftly moving water, I counted seven eagles quietly watching the river, probably digesting a scavenged salmon breakfast. Tallying the eagles, ducking under branches in narrow channels, and watching Al maneuver through whitewater rapids as we took a more conservative route, my mind was absorbed in the moment and completely free of worry.

After two hours on the river we reached our take-out spot. My total had climbed to forty-eight bald eagles, and by the time the boats were loaded and we headed home my tally numbered fifty-one. Being in the presence of dozens of eagles, and now safely off the water, left me full of delightful ecstasy—a raptor rapture.

One week later, still in February, I was eating lunch in the sunroom at home. Outside the window, finches, chickadees, and juncos casually munched seeds at the feeder. Suddenly a dark flash raced past. With a burst of energy the small birds darted for the blackberry thicket to evade the attack of a small, agile hawk. At the last minute the hawk pulled up—the prey escaped—and flew to a bare maple branch across the ravine. This sharp-shinned hawk was a young bird, less adept than more mature hawks at hunting.

Sharp-shinned hawks are accipiters, a group of smaller hawks that zip through the woods rather than soar. They often hunt near bird feeders, waiting for a chance to grab an unsuspecting sparrow or junco. The West has two common accipiters: the sharp-shinned hawk and the Cooper's hawk, frustratingly similar with longish, banded tails and short rounded wings. The sharp-shinned, the smaller of the two, is ten to fourteen inches in length, the size of a large robin. Don't even try to look for a "sharp shin"; that feature is difficult to distinguish even with the bird in your hand. Instead look for a smaller head in proportion to the body and a shorter, squared tail as compared to the Cooper's hawk. Although the

Cooper's (fourteen to twenty inches in length) has more contrast between the gray back and dark crown and a more rounded tail, distinguishing these two accipiters is a difficult call, even for experienced birders.

There are other common raptors, but the red-tailed hawk, bald eagle, and sharp-shinned hawk are a good trio for the beginning bird-watcher to learn. If all the little brown birds drive you crazy, then these large, showy birds may be more to your liking. Raptors are the birds for folks like my friend Tom who says, "If ya can't see 'em without binoculars, they ain't worth looking at."

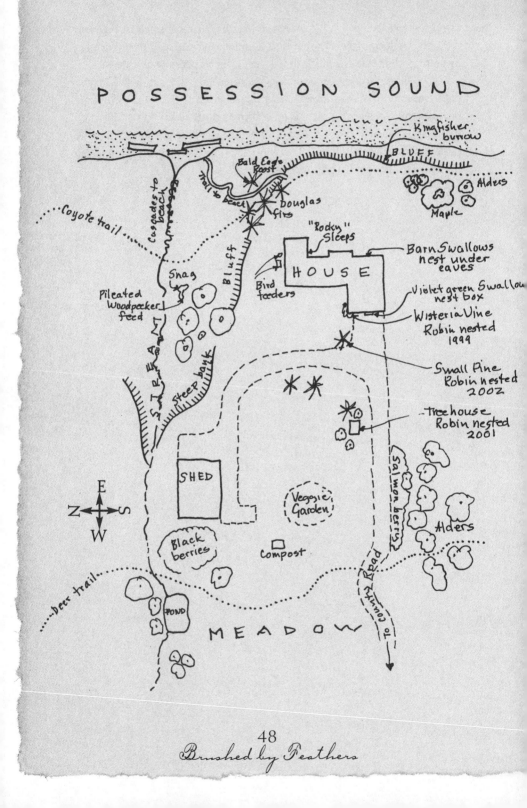

POSSESSION SOUND

Kingfisher burrow

BLUFF

Bald Eagle Roost

Coyote trail

Cascades to beach

Trail to beach

Douglas firs

Bluff

Alders

Maple

"Rocky" Sleeps

HOUSE

Barn Swallows nest under eaves

Violet green Swallow nest box

Bird feeders

Snag

Pileated Woodpecker feed

Wisteria Vine Robin nested 1999

Small Pine Robin nested 2002

S T R E A M

Steep bank

Tree house Robin nested 2001

E

N — S

W

SHED

Veggie Garden

Salmon berry

Alders

Black berries

Compost

Deer trail

POND

To County Road

M E A D O W

CHAPTER THREE

March

When it comes to avian activity, that old saying "March comes in like a lion and goes out like a lamb" is dead wrong. The month begins quietly. Alders, maples, ocean spray, and other native shrubs remain leafless and dormant; winter still holds tight to occasional freezing nights. (One March 7, five inches of snow fell, unusual for the mild Puget Sound lowlands.) Most local resident birds are tongue-tied as the month begins. But a warm, sunny day, a Chinook wind, or simply the higher arc of the sun pushes life into the swelling buds and breathes song into local birds.

March 2. Cuddled in a blanket on the sunroom couch, I notice the rising sun has inched north across the Cascades-carved horizon to emerge in full view, unscreened by alder trees. It appears at 6:50. For the first time this spring, I hear soft cooing from Rocky, our semiwild rock pigeon, still clinging to his nighttime roost on the back deck light fixture. His gentle cooing ceases in the fall and he remains quiet through the winter until spring stirs his hormones to start the cooing again.

A large, dark silhouette on a leafless alder branch spreads its huge wings and lifts off to soar along the bluff; a mature bald eagle scouting the shoreline for the night tide deposits. Suddenly, the eagle banks sharply upward, flapping urgently to gain altitude. Then I spot the cause of the dramatic change in flight—a second eagle is approaching from the south. The two spiral upward, each aspiring to the higher position. Living halfway between one bald eagle nest a mile south of our home and a second an equal distance to the northwest, Bill and I occasionally observe eagle border patrol. Each nesting pair monitors the edges of its breeding territory and reminds neighboring eagles of the boundary lines. Today the "discussion" ends casually, with each eagle soaring off in opposite directions, back toward its respective nest.

After lunch I bundle up for my daily walk. As I step outside in the damp forty-two-degree weather, a chill shimmies down my arms. Snuggling my shoulders to my ears, I pull my jacket sleeves over my fingertips and gather the sleeve cuffs together to close off the chill. I jam wadded-up fists into my jacket pockets and glance at the two-acre meadow—framed by tall, twenty-year-old alders—between our house and the county road. A soft drizzle freshens my face.

In spring and summer, Bill mows the close-in grass that surrounds our house, our well-fenced vegetable garden, four young fruit trees, and a handful of nonnative trees and shrubs. This gives the impression of lawn. He also fights invasive blackberry vines to maintain order. West of the vegetable garden the grass grows untamed and blackberry tendrils sneak in from under the alders. An unnamed, marshy stream flows along the north edge of the meadow, draining the wetland on the far side of the county road, then gathers speed and cascades down a steep ravine to join the Sound. At a low spot along the trickling flow beside the meadow, a small pond gives refuge to amphibians, offers year-round drinks for deer and coyotes, and clouds with emerald green duckweed in the fall.

Strolling down our driveway along the meadow's south side, I pass the unused tree house. Without children filling it with fantasy games and Tarzan yells, robins nest under the dry eaves and once a pair of house wrens raised young in the wooden birdhouse hanging off a support beam. I pass a row of birch trees where a bushtit couple wove a long, hanging nest, a brownish green knee sock dangling among the branches. But nest building is still a month away. Signs of breeding activity will be subtler today.

Halfway to the road I notice a salmonberry blossom peeking open in sweet cotton candy–pink. The grass is beginning to mound. A song sparrow that has been spitting out only bits and pieces of song since January comes forth with a full, strong melody. Black-capped chickadees begin a clear, whistled "fee-bee" or "fee-bee-bee"—the first note higher in pitch—a song they reserve for spring, mixed in with the

A hairy woodpecker resumes tapping

typical "chick-a-dee-dee-dee" call note that can be heard spring, summer, and fall.

As I reach the county road, a single, sharp "squeak" calls from the wetland. I stop and search the bare alders for the source. High on a branch a hairy woodpecker—a red head patch tells me it is a male—calls again then resumes a "tap, tap, tap," its strong chiseled bill dislodging bits of moss and digging into the bark for grubs. A response sounds from farther in the trees, his mate. They forage along separate paths but keep within squeaking distance. Below the bare trunks, on the marshy floor, a swamp lantern, also called skunk cabbage, resembling a lemon-yellow flame in a bright-green chalice, seems to dance with springtime promise. I inhale deeply but the rain keeps the sour "skunky" smell from reaching me. The plant emits a foul smell to attract insects that pollinate this species. I'm nearly kneeling at its base before I catch the musty scent, a smell that returns me to my childhood when I explored the bottomlands near my family home on Seattle's Lake Washington.

The drizzle turns to heavy rain, but I pull up my hood and continue to walk along the county road. Fifteen minutes later, I turn around and shake water drops off my Gore-Tex jacket. The fronts of my khaki pants are plastered against my thighs. On the way back, I loop through the meadow on a deer trail toward our pond. Well before it comes into view, loud "quack quacking" startles me as two mallards climb steeply through the trees and circle above, furious at my intrusion. They seem particularly edgy, perhaps a sign that March is warming and getting ready to turn from a lamb into an avian lion.

Spring migration, a huge movement of birds from wintering retreats to breeding grounds, begins in March, with a few species jumping the gun and showing up at the end of February. By mid-March many birds will have ventured north and arrived here in our meadow. By month's end locals will be in full song, migrants will be arriving and moving through in large numbers, and breeding season will be roaring—every whit like a lion.

This month we look for woodpeckers, showy local resident birds. Then we'll examine the amazing northern migration. One of the earliest and longest-distance migrants to arrive is the rufous humming-bird. The males stake out their territories, possibly the exact same locations as in previous years. Next the females arrive and the buzzing begins as the males chatter a "zeee-chuppity-chup" that can be heard from northern California to southern Alaska.

Salmonberry

Rufous hummingbird

Birds introduced this month:

☐ Turkey Vulture *(Cathartes aura)*

☐ Swainson's Hawk *(Buteo swainsoni)*

☐ Arctic Tern *(Sterna paradisaea)*

☐ Black-chinned Hummingbird *(Archilochus alexandri)*

☐ Anna's Hummingbird *(Calypte anna)*

☐ Calliope Hummingbird *(Stellula calliope)*

☐ Rufous Hummingbird *(Selasphorus rufus)*

❏ Acorn Woodpecker *(Melanerpes formicivorus)*

❏ Red-breasted Sapsucker *(Sphyrapicus ruber)*

❏ Downy Woodpecker *(Picoides pubescens)*

❏ Hairy Woodpecker *(Picoides villosus)*

❏ Northern Flicker *(Colaptes auratus)*

❏ Pileated Woodpecker *(Dryocopus pileatus)*

WOODPECKERS IN THE
PERCUSSION SECTION

No sooner has spring called [northern flickers] to the pleasant
duty of making love than their voice is heard from the tops of
high decayed trees proclaiming with delight the opening of the
welcome season. Their note is merryment itself as it imitates a
prolonged and jovial laugh. … By way of amusement, it will
continue to destroy as much furniture in a day as can well be
handled by a different kind of workman in two.

—John James Audubon

"That damn bird bangs on our gutter every morning!" complains my
neighbor, her tone implying I'm somehow responsible. "It wakes us up
and my husband is ready to shoot it." I try to calm her, remind her shoot-
ing birds is illegal, and explain that the bird is called a northern flicker,
our most common woodpecker.

She seems interested as I explain that members of the woodpecker family don't have particularly melodious songs. Instead, in the
spring, they drum on hollow surfaces to establish territory and attract a
mate. Each woodpecker species has its own characteristic drumming,
cadence, and rhythm. The birds use metal gutters, stovepipes, trash cans,
and even car hoods as well as hollow trees to share their message. I reas-
sure my neighbor that once the woodpeckers establish their territory, the
gutter banging will cease as the mates seek trees to excavate their nests.

"Great! Then next year we'll have more drummers," she says.
"Maybe they'll form a steel band."

The West Coast is "blessed" with six common species of woodpeckers including one sapsucker. Although some species of woodpeckers migrate, our woodpeckers are mostly residents, staying in the same
area all year. Woodpeckers begin their breeding season early in the
spring, heralded by calling and drumming.

The ability to drill holes and carve out nests inside vertical tree trunks requires specialized tools. Woodpeckers have several. The feet of most woodpeckers are large and zygodactylous, meaning two toes point forward and two toes point backward on each foot. The large claws—plus a stiff tail serving as a third point of contact with the tree—help woodpeckers cling to vertical trunks. These three points of contact offer enough leverage so the woodpeckers can rip holes in the wood with their bills. Smaller woodpeckers can easily maneuver along a horizontal branch while hanging upside down.

Another woodpecker tool is a strong, shock-absorbing skull that protects the brain while the bird pounds on wood or other surfaces. Its thick, chisel-shaped bill can chip through solid wood. Its long tongue is barbed to extract insects and sticky with saliva to retain the prey.

The northern flicker, my neighbor's particular irritant, acts and looks less like a woodpecker than the other species. Sized between a crow and a robin, it is distinguished by a black crescent bib and spotted belly; red shafts of wing feathers "flicker" as the bird flies. Unlike other woodpecker species, the flicker hops about on the lawn looking for ants, but it also forages in the trees like other woodpeckers.

The West's most dramatic woodpecker is the pileated wood-pecker, apparently the inspiration for the cartoon character Woody Woodpecker. This sixteen-inch, black-and-white bird flaunts a bright-red crest as it whacks out rectangular holes in old snags. These flashy, rau-cous birds require at least sixty- to eighty-year-old trees for nesting. As old forests are destroyed, the birds take up drumming on stovepipes and house siding, probably the best substitute available.

Two smaller woodpeckers are the downy woodpecker and the hairy woodpecker, six and three-quarter inches long and nine and one-quarter inches long respectively. Both of these similar-looking species have black backs trimmed in white; the males sport a splash of red on the back of the head. Downys share people-populated suburbs; hairys prefer less populated areas. Both often come to suet feeders. The longer-billed hairys are declining in numbers throughout their range. Blame, in part, starlings and house sparrows, introduced species that often appro-priate the woodpeckers' nesting sites.

These smaller, shyer woodpeckers can be located by listening for their calls. One day while walking in a wooded wetland near Seattle, loud peeping stopped me. Examining the trees nearby, I couldn't see any nests until finally I found the source of the noise. Inside an alder tree, downy woodpecker babies begged for food, safely tucked deep in their hollow cavity. On another day, at a different nest, I watched as three downy fledglings poked their heads and bodies out of their nest hole, complaining for food as loudly as any teenager.

From the Columbia River south to Baja California, another raucous woodpecker with a loud "waka, waka, waka" frequents oak woods. Generally found in small, noisy colonies, the acorn woodpecker is mostly black with a flashy white rump. This bird drills small, round holes in tree trunks, telephone poles, or the sides of buildings, then pounds an acorn into each hole for their winter food supply.

Undoubtedly, the most reclusive woodpecker along the Pacific Coast lowlands is the red-breasted sapsucker. A purplish red head and breast make this bird easy to identify—if you can find it. True to its name, the sapsucker drills even rows of holes in tree trunks, then waits for the sap to run. Its tongue uses capillary action to capture and drink the sap. The sap serves a dual purpose by attracting insects, which the sapsucker gobbles up.

One spring, a red-breasted sapsucker feasted on a pine tree outside my kitchen window. Off and on throughout the afternoon, I watched the bird slowly moving from hole to hole, drinking sap and munching insects. At one point it seemed to close its eyes and snooze. Hmm ... drinking, eating, and snoozing; sounds like a classic case of spring fever. I can't imagine this species disturbing anyone, including my complaining neighbor.

AMAZING MIGRATION FEATS

Everything connects

absolutely everything.

—*Hazel Wolf*

The rest of the world may associate March Madness with college basketball, but for me March madness always refers to spring migration. What could be crazier than a tiny bird—the weight of two dimes—flying from Mexico to Alaska? Not just the top fliers—the sweet sixteen, the elite eight, or the final four—participate in migration; *every* rufous hummingbird makes the trek north in March and returns south in the fall. And it's not only hummingbirds; Swainson's hawks, for example, travel from southern South America to northern Canada without a game plan, coach, workout schedule, or daily practice. Makes a couple hours of playing time on a basketball court every few days seem like pretty small potatoes.

Migrating birds congregate along aerial pathways. In the West, birds typically use the Pacific Coast flyway or the valley between the ridge of the Cascades and Sierras and the Rockies. Viewed from high in the stratosphere, a flyway resembles a huge river of migrating ducks, seabirds, shorebirds, raptors, and songbirds. In the spring the river flows north and each fall the flow is reversed. Millions and millions of birds make up the current. Some long-distance, neotropical migrants travel from South America to Alaska and back. Other species merely hop across a state or two, and some travel from lowlands to mountains and back. Many birds, like the famed swallows of San Juan Capistrano, return to the same nesting areas on a regular schedule.

Looking down from farther out in outer space, we would see two additional major flyways across the United States: the Mississippi flyway and the eastern flyway, which roughly follows the Atlantic Coast. From that perspective we would also see that some birds don't stick to one flyway or one continent but travel across oceans while migrating. For example, arctic terns, the world champions of long-distance migrants, nest in the Arctic, as far north as there is land. The terns migrate south out over the Atlantic, brush the coast of Africa, and "winter" in Antarctic waters east of Africa. They sometimes circle the

Antarctic ice pack before heading north again for an annual round-trip journey of 31,000 miles.

Even before my husband, Bill, became a birder, he enjoyed telling the story of the migration habits of a seabird, the mottled petrel. This species nests on a clump of islands off New Zealand, then migrates nearly 10,000 miles to "winter" (our summer) in the Aleutian Islands of Alaska. Quite a feat, but what most fascinates Bill is that after nesting the parents stay with their young only for a brief time, then take off for points north, leaving the young to follow a month or so later. Miraculously the young adults find their parents in Alaska and winter with them in the same locale. Bill's practical lawyer mind must have trouble trying to grasp such unexplainable feats.

Another migrating champion is the Hudsonian godwit. This large shorebird migrates from the southern part of South America over the Atlantic Ocean to breeding territory in Canada's Arctic tundra—often nonstop! Now that's March madness.

We don't need to go into space to see fascinating migration patterns. From western backyards, we can parse out the broad migration flow into separate elements, each a story in itself. The flow includes many tributaries, fast and slow currents, back eddies, and stagnant water. Some birds dribble slowly north through trees in small numbers, others swarm quickly past in huge flocks. Songbirds migrate at night, and we notice them only when they stop to refuel at specific feeding grounds.

Migration habits generally separate western birds into four categories. First are the *residents* (nonmigrants) such as song sparrows, wrens, and most woodpeckers, who remain in their territories all year long. They may wander around—even do a fall walkabout—but not in a pattern that would be considered migration.

Second are the *summer breeders*, insect- and nectar-eating birds that nest in the West, then retreat south to Mexico, Central America, and South America when food supplies dwindle. Many songbirds—warblers, tanagers, orioles, and flycatchers, as well as hummingbirds and swallows—fall into this group.

Third are the *winter visitors*, migrants that breed in northern Canada and Alaska and spend the winter in our lower forty-eight. Loons, grebes, seabirds, ducks, and some species of raptors are examples of this group. Also in this category are birds that nest in higher elevations in the mountains and come down to the warmer lowlands during the winter.

Fox sparrows and varied thrushes are two examples, as are some populations of dark-eyed juncos.

A fourth category is that of *transients*, birds that pass briefly through the western states on one or both directions of their migration routes. Many songbirds, shorebirds, and some raptors, like the Swainson's hawk, make up this category.

Bird-watchers in Anchorage experience the ebb and flow of migrating birds differently than birders in Boise or San Diego. If your viewpoint is in the southern part of the migration river, birds will arrive and pass through earlier in the spring than if you are farther north where spring arrives later. Scientists have tracked when migrants arrive at key points along their flyway, and some guidebooks include this information. I keep track myself, jotting down notes in my journal.

Here in western Washington the migration starting bell sounds when rufous hummingbirds arrive around March 12. These jewels return annually to my garden and buzz my window as if to remind me to put out the hummingbird feeder. This year I spotted an early turkey vulture in eastern Washington on March 23, while attending the Othello Crane festival. A day later, back in western Washington, I noticed swallows circling over our meadow; although they may have arrived earlier while we were away. Two swallow species come through our yard in March, the tree swallow and the violet-green swallow. The first swallows are often heading farther north and merely passing through, giving rise to the old saying "One swallow doesn't make spring."

Even so, the sighting of one swallow or a single hummingbird brings promise. It satisfies the birder's expectation that hangs over March and signifies the imminent flow of another migratory stream full of avian munificence. Northbound migration plays on through April, May, and June with early, middle, and late migrating species. Then in July, while basketball players relax on the beach or casually toss practice free throws, the huge migrant river turns and begins to flow south again.

Brushed by Feathers

THE MIGHTY PUFFBALL

The Spaniards and Portuguese call [hummingbirds]

by more poetical names, such as Flower-peckers,

Flower-kissers, myrtile-suckers,—while the Mexican

and Peruvian names showed a still higher appreciation

of their beauties, their meaning being rays of the sun,

tresses of the day-star, and other such appellations.

—Alfred Russel Wallace,
Humming-birds, 1877

It was a mild mid-March morning when Bill and I stood on our deck discussing where to plant the tomatoes this year, hopeful that we could encourage a few to actually turn red in our cool Puget Sound climate. A buzzlike chirping pulled my attention to the edge of our garden, and I announced teasingly, "Bill, you're no longer the alpha male around here."

"Where?" he asked, then followed my gaze to the salmonberry blossoms glowing bright pink. A male rufous hummingbird sporting an iridescent scarlet throat and a uniform of rich chestnut brown darted from one star-shaped blossom to the next then turned and made a beeline toward us. Bill ducked as the feisty three-and-a-half-inch hummer charged like a football linebacker right between our heads and hovered outside the dining room window. A hummingbird can decelerate from twenty-five miles per hour to a dead stop in a space no longer than the length of my index finger, so it wouldn't actually make contact with us. Even if it did collide with something, it's unlikely the impact would cause much damage since this mighty puffball weighs less than two dimes.

Bill said, "Hey, that's exactly the spot where you hang the hummingbird feeder. This must be the same male that was here last summer."

"Yep, he's just migrated back and is staking out his breeding territory," I offered. With energy-packed zest, this guy was taking control of his territory including our hummingbird feeder, summer blooming fuchsia baskets, and perhaps a half-acre of native habitat around our house.

In hummingbird land-rights terms, he owned it. Any other male hummingbird intruder would be quickly chased away.

As we continued to watch, a Douglas squirrel climbed carefully up the stucco exterior wall of our house, eyeing a possible leap to the seed feeder positioned near the window. Dive-bombing to within inches of the intruder, our alpha male sent him packing.

Before returning north to select breeding territories along the West Coast between southern Oregon and Alaska, rufous hummingbirds spend the winter in sunny, flower-filled southwestern Mexico. They arrive here in early March, around the time yellow skunk cabbage plants illuminate our wetlands and just before the alder and maple trees begin glowing with the suggestion of spring green.

For anyone who grew up east of the Rockies, your hummingbird image is probably that of the ruby-throated hummingbird, with its emerald green back and a brilliant-red throat. Of the eight species of hummingbirds commonly found in the United States, the ruby-throated is the main species east of the Rockies. This hummingbird migrates across the Gulf of Mexico in a single bound, 500 miles (and twenty hours) of nonstop flight without food or water. This amazing feat spawned a popular folktale that hummingbirds migrated on the backs of geese. Recalling my years as a mother of small children on car trips, I can't imagine any goose with enough patience to fly twenty hours with a pestering, testosterone-driven buzzbomb on its back.

Hummingbirds are the smallest birds and the smallest warm-blooded creatures. The tiniest, the bee hummingbird of Cuba, is only two and one-half inches long, including a needlelike bill. The giant hummingbirds of western South America reach eight and one-half inches long, the size of the European starling.

The majority of hummingbirds—more than 300 species—live in Central and South America. In summer, a few of these tropical species stretch up into southeastern Arizona, providing the best hummingbird watching in the United States. Interestingly, they live only in the New World; there isn't a single hummer outside North and South America.

In the West, four hummingbird species spread out along the coastal lowlands. Only the rufous and Anna's are seen north of California; California is home to the Allen's, Costa's, and Anna's. The Anna's hummingbird does not migrate, making it the only hummingbird that commonly winters along the West Coast. Higher elevations of the Cascades

62
Brushed by Feathers

and Rockies attract three more species, the black-chinned, calliope, and broad-tailed hummingbirds.

When nature writer A. R. Annons said "Birds are flowers flying and flowers are perched birds," he may have been thinking about hummingbirds. Their eye-catching iridescence is caused by tiny droplets of oil within the structure of their feathers, which refract sunlight and create the rainbow of brilliant colors. In the Tropics hummingbird names are much more expressive of their dazzling colors: starthroats, emeralds, sapphires, woodnymphs, mountain-gems, woodstars, and coquettes. Our word "hummingbird" came from the early English colonists' attempts to describe their buzzing flight. However, the Purepecha Indians of Michoacán state in Mexico were even more onomatopoetic when they named their town "Tzintzuntzan," meaning the place of the hummingbirds. Try pronouncing that word in three syllables, putting the stress on each letter "n."

Glittering like sequins in the sun as they move from flower to flower, hummingbirds precisely place their long, thin bills into the throats of blossoms to sip up nectar before backing away. They are the only birds that can truly hover, creating a figure-eight pattern with unique rotating wing joints. Their tiny wings flap a mind-numbing twenty to eighty times per second and propel them to speeds up to seventy-five miles per hour. Hummingbirds fly straight up and down, backwards and forwards, and can even fly upside down.

Later that same day I was in the kitchen preparing the sugar-water mixture for the hummingbird feeder. Bill walked in and noticed two feeders on the counter. "What's with two feeders?" he asked.

"Oh, nothing," I lied.

"I know you," Bill said. "You're going to put one feeder on one side of the house and another on the opposite side and drive our alpha male crazy trying to defend both feeders at once."

"Would I do something that mean?"

"Yes, you would."

"I'm just thinking of the female and babies. I'll reserve this second feeder just for them."

A flash outside the kitchen window caught our attention. "Look, he's begun his courtship, there must be a female somewhere in the blackberry bramble."

We watched as the male slowly buzzed higher and higher in the air. Starting forty to fifty feet above the blackberries, he dive-bombed toward the female while making a whirring noise with his feathers. Just a few feet above the bushes he arced upward, creating a huge J-shaped pattern, like an Olympic-scale ski jump. He then slowly flew back up again to repeat the performance.

The evident purpose of these acrobatics is to show off his speed and maneuverability. The female, if properly impressed, mates with the male. But that is all she gets. As with most hummingbird species, the male has no involvement in the nesting or care of the young, so he has plenty of time to defend my—or should I say *his*—feeders. His goal is to keep other male hummers away from his territory, so that his genes are perpetuated. Although we couldn't see her from our window, it is easy to identify the less colorful female, with dull green on her back and a splash of rufous (reddish) color at the base of her black-and-white tail. She builds a walnut-sized nest of soft plant material, lichen, and spiders' webs and lays two pea-sized eggs. This pliable nest insulates her young and expands as they grow.

Baby hummingbirds spend up to one month in their nests, but even with all the activity of the female tending the young, it is often very difficult to locate a hummingbird's nest. In more than thirty years of birding, I've only happened onto a hummingbird nest twice. Even when I knew I was looking exactly at the right spot it was hard to tell that the subtle bump on a limb or bit of moss in the crotch of a branch was a nest. In June the juveniles will begin appearing at feeders, looking like the female except without the flashy tail feathers. The juveniles will return to their nests to rest during the day and spend the nights. Soon after, the alpha male, exhausted from his guard duty, will leave the territory. By the end of July, most of the females and juveniles will head east to the Rockies then continue their voyage south.

I returned to preparing the sugar-water mixture. For me, hanging hummingbird feeders is a mess-free, guilt-free activity, worth all the effort. I use a practical red-colored feeder, with a flat flying-saucer design and a big red snap- or twist-off top. To keep the birds healthy, it is necessary to clean all interior surfaces. Ceramic or glass balls or tubes look attractive, but are difficult to clean and tend to drip. I replace the mixture every two or three days, sooner if the feeders run dry.

To make the feeding mixture, I dissolve one part sugar in four parts boiling water and let cool. Refined white sugar most closely resembles the natural sucrose found in flowers; honey or sugar substitutes should be avoided. Red food coloring is not necessary; instead I rely on the color on the feeder to attract the hummers. The sugar-water solution can be made in gallon quantities and stored in the refrigerator. Anna's hummingbirds (the ones that stay through the winter) don't visit my feeders, but if they visit your feeder, offer fresh sugar solution all winter because the birds may have become dependent upon your feeder.

I don't feel guilty that the feeder lures the birds away from the natural nectar of flowers. Because of their hyperactive lifestyle, hummingbirds require a large amount of high-energy food, which they obtain from plant nectar, small insects, and sap, as well as the sugar-water at feeders. Hummingbirds daily consume at least five times their own weight in liquid. I guess if I had to seek out and drink a comparable amount of sugary liquid every day, I'd be pretty hyper too.

Bill and I continue to look out the window, but all is quiet; the male hummingbird has now settled on a branch somewhere, exhausted from his courtship display. "Remember the Doubleday's hummingbird we saw last winter in Mexico?" Bill asks. "With its deep blue-and-green body and bright-red bill, it was probably the most beautiful bird I've ever seen."

I stare out the window remembering the warm day and brilliant bird. "Did you know that early Mexican cultures associated the hummingbird with love and used hummingbird feathers to decorate their love charms?" I said. "The early Maya populations carved pictures of hummingbirds in their architecture. To them the hummingbird represented a sudden burst of energy." But I was talking to the walls; Bill had wandered back outside to the garden looking for a sunny spot for the tomatoes.

Then the rufous male flew toward the salmonberry blossoms. These tiny birds provoke thoughts about aerodynamics, about strength and fortitude, about love, and even about glitter. Each time I watch these dancers-of-the-air dart and weave from blossom to blossom, spreading pollen as they sample nectar and entertain me with their high-speed maneuvers, I feel the essence of energy that they portray and an affirmation of that power settles into my soul.

My gaze followed Bill toward the vegetable garden. He looked deep in thought considering the placement of the tomatoes, but perhaps he was also trying to figure out how to reclaim his status as alpha male.

CHAPTER FOUR
April

Hungry juvenile chickadees

During the first two weeks of April, rain drenched the Puget Sound lowlands. Like electrical poles lined up along a long, flat country road, showers followed one after another with no end in sight. Finally, today, blue skies and a warmish sixty-two-degree temperature provide the first opportunity to satisfy that spring urge to spend time in the garden and dirty my hands with the rich soil. The ground is too wet to use the garden tiller, but I work one small section by hand to get the early vegetables started.

A few years ago I would have argued that a bench in the vegetable garden constituted a waste of valuable growing space. Last year that changed. Bill and I scavenged some beach wood and found a couple old planks, then he hammered the pieces into a rustic bench that we dragged inside our fenced garden. After half an hour on my hands and knees planting pea, lettuce, and spinach seeds in the moist soil, I'm delighted to have a dry spot to sit and rest. At various times the bench holds excess sweaters, shed after gardening has warmed us up; smaller tools that later in the year we're likely to misplace among the rows of vegetables; a hot cup of tea in the spring; or a cold brew in August. Now it holds me as I relax, my muscles unused to the bending and hauling of spring gardening. My lower back is complaining already.

An open-weave wire fence, tall enough to keep out deer and reinforced at the bottom to keep out rabbits, surrounds our round garden, about thirty-five feet in diameter. The folks who lived here before we moved in designed the circular shape of the garden. We've grown rather fond of it. Bill can follow a spiraling pattern as he tills without needing to lug the Troy-Built around corners. One tall, rotating sprinkler in the center reaches all parts perfectly, without neglecting dry corners.

Green fuzz dusted the alder trees in early April; now, two weeks later, verdant leaves shimmer in the breeze. The conifers move to the back of the stage while deciduous trees take the spotlight, suddenly bursting with life after five months of quiet dormancy. It's as if Irish leprechauns busily sprayed luxurious green paint one night to cover the branches with color. Big-leaf maples explode with yellow flowers hanging in cylindrical clusters that are joined by deeply lobed leaves. Blackberry vines, Nootka roses, salmonberry, and elderberry surround the meadow, all clothed in fresh, green leaves.

Relaxing in the garden, I take the chance to observe breeding activity around the meadow. The California quail have disbanded their covey, their flocking needs displaced by the drive to breed, and move in pairs through leaf detritus, pecking for tidbits. The male flutters to the top of a stump to announce his territory with "chi CA go, chi CA go." A male dark-eyed junco, a species that seems to spend its winter on or near the ground, finds the tallest Douglas fir tree from which to sing its spring song, a sweet, clear, bell-like trill.

A pair of black-capped chickadees have again claimed the nest box, which Bill and I purchased as a violet-green swallows' box and installed near the peak of the garage's eaves. The resident chickadees, ready to nest well before the migrating swallows return from Central America, get their choice of nesting cavities. I wish this pair of chickadees good luck. Last year, a week or two into the nesting season, an amazingly agile Douglas squirrel climbed the stucco wall to the box and gnawed at the small hole opening, enlarging it to nearly twice the size. The squirrel and other predators raided the nest, forcing the chickadees to move housekeeping somewhere else. Sometime later, I noticed the violet-green swallows had returned and assumed

Song sparrow

Brushed by Feathers

*Maples explode with
banging yellow flowers*

rightful ownership of the nest box. Either the squirrel gave up or the swallows were more aggressive in fending off intruders, since the swallows hatched a full batch of youngsters. The hole remains enlarged and the chickadees will have to be more vigilant this year.

A pair of robins nests somewhere around our meadow, changing locations each year. One year Mother Robin selected the wisteria vine under the eaves near the front door of the house, another year a support beam of the children's playhouse. The year our house went through major remodeling, she presumably moved across the road to quieter surroundings. Last year she selected the Austrian pine next to the garage. I'll watch to see what appeals to her this year.

The barn swallows, when they arrive later this month, will resume the same location as last year, under the eaves of our bedroom, facing east with a glorious view of the water. I expect it's the insects over the back bluff, not the view, that sells this location.

Relaxed, I shed my sweater, lean back on the bench, and close my eyes. As the afternoon sun sinks into my sunlight-deprived pores, my ears take over identification of the birds frolicking around the meadow. Papa Robin is the loudest with a perky "cheerily, cheer-up, cheerio." A song sparrow sounds three clear introductory notes, a buzzlike "towwee," then a trill. White-crowned sparrows join with a thin, whistled buzz followed by a twittering trill, which makes me think they are proclaiming, "Ah me, look at pretty me." It is a sound so familiar it will ring in my ear all summer long, like an advertising jingle I can't shake off.

There are other sounds as well. April brings a whole bushel basket of migrating songbirds. Many continue north, but some stay to establish territories and breed. Although quiet for the moment, the orange-crowned and yellow-rumped warblers were singing earlier in the morning. The orange-crowned sings a high, thin, lazy trill; the yellow-rumped croons a slow, undulating warble.

An odd sound jerks me from my reverie. I open my eyes, sit up, and follow the sound to the driveway near the house to see a big male river otter. Otters are fairly common down in the bay and I often see them swimming near shore, but it always surprises me to see one on land, especially up here on the high 150-foot bluff. This male is huge, up to five feet long, galumphing along with an arched back, broad muscular tail, and alert, rounded head. Whiskers curve out from the flat, wide snout. The dark, furry creature lopes along the side of the house, lifts his head to glance at the activity around the bird feeder, then turns around and sneaks down the steep ravine through the thick blackberry bushes. He's gone in twenty seconds.

I leave the garden, walk to where he disappeared, and circle around to the back of the house, thinking I might hear him down in the thickly vegetated ravine. The only sound is the wind wrestling through the Douglas fir branches high above me and the soft tinkling of glass wind chimes on our side deck.

The breeze also kicks at the sea, breaking the surface into tiny cups of cobalt blue. A flock of black seabirds fly low over the bay, the last of the wintering ducks returning to their breeding grounds, joining the river of migrants heading north. The bay lies empty, finished with the task of feeding and sheltering wintering ducks, geese, loons, grebes, scoters, and other waterfowl.

In April all avian activity focuses on breeding. Bird songs fill the morning air with distinctive tunes. Locals and some early returning migrants establish territories, build nests, lay eggs, and begin incubating. Other migrants continue to move through in large numbers all month. The biggest migration show occurs in estuaries along the Pacific Coast where millions of shorebirds pause for rest and food as they move in waves from South and Central America all they way up to northern tundra.

The essays for this month look at birdhouses, constructed both by bird beaks and by human hands. We'll also follow springtime ducks as they waddle upland away from lakes to find suitable nesting. And we'll travel to the New Dungeness Lighthouse to watch the waves of shorebirds flowing up the coast.

Birds introduced this month:

❏ Red-necked Grebe *(Podiceps grisegena)*

❏ Horned Grebe *(Podiceps auritus)*

❏ Wood Duck *(Aix sponsa)*

❏ Gadwall *(Anas strepera)*

❏ Green-winged Teal *(Anas crecca)*

❏ Mallard *(Anas platyrhynchos)*

❏ Northern Pintail *(Anas acuta)*

❏ Blue-winged Teal *(Anas discors)*

❏ Cinnamon Teal *(Anas cyanoptera)*

❏ Northern Shoveler *(Anas clypeata)*

❏ Hooded Merganser *(Lophodytes cucullatus)*

❏ Common Merganser *(Mergus merganser)*

❑ Ruddy Duck *(Oxyura jamaicensis)*

❑ Black-bellied Plover *(Pluvialis squatarola)*

❑ Ruddy Turnstone *(Arenaria interpres)*

❑ Sanderling *(Calidris alba)*

❑ Western Sandpiper *(Calidris mauri)*

❑ Dunlin *(Calidris alpina)*

❑ Winter Wren *(Troglodytes troglodytes)*

❑ White-crowned Sparrow *(Zonotrichia leucophrys)*

❑ Brown-headed Cowbird *(Molothrus ater)*

BIRDS' HOUSES

I have great faith that if the thing is rightly put together

in true organic sense, with proportions actually right,

the picturesque will take care of itself.

—*Frank Lloyd Wright,*
On Architecture

One dewy April morning, I watched a little brown winter wren gather nesting material. I was walking in Pioneer Park on Mercer Island near Seattle, where I grew up and later lived as an adult from 1985 until 1998, before moving to Whidbey Island. The winter wren, a four-inch, stubby-tailed, chocolate-brown recluse, is usually heard rather than seen; its cascading melodious trills filter through the dense understory of moist conifer woods. On this occasion the bird flew to a decaying log near my feet, delicately collected a small sprig of apple-green lichen in its beak, then disappeared into the salal and huckleberry shrubs. A moment later it returned for another fluff of the soft, fine nesting material.

Earlier that spring I had observed a bald eagle adding material to its nest. Unlike the dainty winter wren, the bald eagle ripped off a five-foot dead branch with a loud crack. It flew a couple blocks to deliver the prize to its mate, who promptly wove the branch into their huge platform of sticks stationed near the top of a Douglas fir.

April indeed is the month birds build homes, from the winter wren's delicate demitasse cup to the eagle's huge six-foot-diameter platform. Robins interlace sticks and twigs to build a nest tucked up on a protected ledge or limb and then strengthen it with mud that dries into a firm cup. Barn swallows use mud to construct their homes, which they line with their own soft, downy feathers. Bushtits, little grayish birds with long tails, collect dried grass and pliable weeds to weave a hanging nest that resembles an old sock dangling from a tree branch.

Some birds' nests are more simple than others'. Gulls are content with bulky nests of seaweed and kelp placed on coastal island cliffs. The killdeer, a member of the shorebird family, lays its eggs on the ground in the open. It doesn't bother with nesting materials but creates a gravel scrape and relies on camouflage to protect both the eggs and incubating parent.

One common western bird makes no nest at all—the brown-headed cowbird, a member of the blackbird family. The female cowbird lays her eggs in other birds' nests and then flies off, leaving the incubating and rearing to foster parents. Hatching before the eggs of the adoptive parents, the baby cowbirds grow quickly and demand food from the surrogate parents, often outcompeting the nest's natural babies. I once watched a dark-eyed junco parent feeding a baby cowbird. The baby, nearly twice the size of the parent, hopped around the lawn crying for food while the parent jammed insects into its gaping mouth, attempting to satisfy the cowbird's demands. It appeared that no junco babies had survived. As might be imagined, some of my most colorful expletives have been directed at cowbirds.

Nest building may take only two to four days for the smallest songbirds that create a new nest for each breeding season. They select a protected location, gather materials, and shape the structure of the nest. After that come soft lining materials such as lichen, spider webs, grass, or their own downy feathers.

Larger birds, such as the bald eagle or red-tailed hawk, construct larger, bulkier, and longer-lasting nests that they return to year after year. New materials are added each spring to shore up the nest. To sanitize a nest, raptors may add fresh green leaves as a natural pesticide to deter infestations of insect parasites such as lice.

Red-tailed hawks will reuse their nests each year unless booted out by a larger bird that doesn't construct its own nest, the great horned owl. Another owl, the long-eared owl, uses nests built by black-billed magpies. The magpies construct huge globular balls of sticks and then nest inside the ball. After one season the number of parasites in the nest forces the magpies to move away and construct a new nest. But the parasites are species' specific—they only attack magpies—allowing owls to move into a ready-made, pest-free (for them) nest.

Woodpeckers are another family of birds that construct nests later used by other species. They hollow out cavities in old trees and snags, leaving a hole just large enough for the parents to enter. Large pileated woodpeckers chisel four-inch holes into cavities. Typically, this bird nests only one season before vacating the cavity. Wood ducks, who need an opening about the same size, may take over these woodpecker cavities. Mid-sized woodpeckers like the northern flicker carve out two-inch holes to create nest cavities. These cavities later house other mid-sized cavity nesters, such as European starlings and bluebirds. Smaller downy woodpeckers construct cavities that have one- and one-half-inch openings, just right for the smallest cavity nesters including chickadees, wrens, and nuthatches.

Of the approximately 600 bird species that nest in North America, eighty-five are cavity nesters. Somehow this small percentage of birds has sparked a burgeoning cottage industry: building birdhouses. Street fairs, farmers' markets, and gift shops often display dozens of birdhouses, encouraging otherwise reasonable folks to go gewgaw over the "darling little houses for the poor little birds."

My own family members have presented me with decorative birdhouses, some with fuzzy lichen roofs, others made of wood twigs, some painted to look like dwarf houses, others patriotic red, white, and blue with flags on top. I call them cutesy houses. A problem with this great surge of birdhouse creativity occurs if we assume that the houses actually are for the birds, rather than for human enjoyment. I delightedly display my collection *inside* my house. Outside I install plain, functional birdhouses constructed to Audubon-approved specifications, which actually serve the needs of birds rather than a human craving for cuteness.

Cutesy birdhouses present several problems. Twig or dowel perches poking out below the entry hole do nothing for the nesting birds but give predators a place to perch while robbing the nest. These perches should be removed. Some houses aren't deep enough to deter the reaching beaks and paws of egg- or chick-eating predators such as crows, squirrels, and raccoons. However, the biggest problem with cutesy houses is they often encourage European starlings or house sparrows to nest, two introduced species whose populations have exploded throughout the West and are pushing out our native cavity nesters. If nothing else, be sure the entry hole on the nest boxes in your garden doesn't exceed one and one-quarter inches in order to discourage these pesky birds. Nest boxes can help our local native cavity nesters when we select or build birdhouses with the correct size and shape of entry hole, size and proportion of nest box, and placement in garden. (Bluebird populations have successfully increased when individuals or organizations have installed bluebird-specific houses along rural roads. Chapter nine describes a bluebird trail near Tonasket, Washington.)

Wrens, chickadees, and violet-green swallows nest in boxes on or near our house. These simple, unpainted houses are designed to blend into the habitat where they are installed. The last thing birds need is a brightly painted house that draws human and predator attention to their eggs and babies.

A harmless way to assist birds during nesting season is to offer nesting materials. Lint from the dryer, dog or cat hair, biodegradable yarn and string, even combed human hair from hairbrushes can be set out for birds to collect. After assembling the materials, stuff them into a cage— like the holder used for feeding suet—and hang it near where birds feed. If you don't want to collect materials yourself, local shops that carry wild bird accessories often sell a package of natural materials assembled into a ball so that birds can peck away the soft material.

Birds are out looking for nesting material this month, and it's not limited to dryer lint. Crows and jays will pick up shiny objects to add to their nests. Along the craggy coast of Baja California I saw a huge osprey nest with bright-turquoise nylon rope woven throughout. So you might want to be careful what you leave lying around, or you may make an unintentional contribution.

Large or small, with or without human contribution, a bird's nest is a construction marvel. The form and beauty are determined by and expressed in the function. As Frank Lloyd Wright stated, if the thing is rightly put together the picturesque will take care of it self.

SPRINGTIME DUCKS

"What are the mallard ducks doing on the uphill side of East Mercer Way?" asked Bill. "I almost ran down a quacking mother duck with a dozen little yellow puffballs as they tried to cross the street and get back down to the lake." Bill's encounter—we were still living on Mercer Island then—reminded me of the wonderful old children's book *Make Way for Ducklings* by Robert McCloskey. In it the mother duck stops traffic on Boston's Beacon Street as she proudly leads her eight ducklings across the street and back to the safety of the Public Garden's pond.

To understand why Bill encountered Mother Mallard and her brood up a steep hill a quarter mile from the water, we need to know some basics of baby bird parenting. Ducks, like most birds, change behavior at breeding time. The reason: to deploy innate breeding-time strategies that enable their species to survive. Throughout millions of generations, natural selection has evolved the most effective strategy of continuing the species. Birds use intricate methods of establishing breeding territory, competing for food supplies, locating and constructing nests, and protecting eggs and young from predators.

Breeding birds typically establish a territory to reserve space and food supply for themselves. Next, one or both parents build a nest, which can be simple or very complex. Once the eggs hatch, some young are on their own, but more often mom and sometimes dad work like crazy to feed the babies and give a few flying lessons, encouraging the teenagers to get out of the nest and on their way as soon as possible. (I doubt bird parents suffer from empty-nest syndrome.) Many smaller species have a second or third hatching each year.

Within this basic structure are many variations among bird species. The size of breeding territory ranges from thousands of acres for the California condor to practically no individual territory where birds nest in colonies. The clutch size can be one egg, if chances of the chick's survival are good, to fifteen eggs, if many chicks are likely to die before adulthood.

Mother Mallard's babies are vulnerable to predation so she lays lots of eggs. Losing some of her offspring is part of nature's plan. Calculating that each pair of mallards has a ten-year reproductive life, if all twelve babies lived all those years, we'd soon be knee-deep not just in duck doo-doo but in ducks themselves.

Laying a dozen eggs takes a lot of energy. Instinctually, she knows to change her diet from seaweed and aquatic vegetation—the equivalent of lettuce and popcorn in bird cuisine—to a protein-rich diet of insects, seeds, and perhaps even that lakeside delicacy, the slug. A laying female consumes twice as much protein-rich food as males or non-laying females.

The fact that rivers flood and lake levels rise in the spring is also buried deep in Mother Mallard's genetic imprint. Don't bother to explain to her that the level of Lake Washington is regulated by locks. She also knows that she needs time to lay all those eggs, one each day, and, because her chicks do a lot of their developing within the shell, she needs approximately twenty-eight days to incubate the eggs. So she waddles up the forested ravines to find a spot that is high and dry with hearty food close by.

Lakefront and view property around Lake Washington is developed with houses, many of which house dogs and cats. So Mother Mallard heads farther upland to find a safer spot to nest, even if that means crossing East Mercer Way. After the eggs hatch she needs to get her darlings down to the water as soon as possible, so the puffballs Bill saw on his way home from work probably were day-old chicks. Once on the lake, the babies can feed themselves, but at night they come ashore to huddle under their mother for warmth and protection, a practice they'll repeat for nearly two months until they can fly. Until then they remain vulnerable to attacks from cats, hawks, eagles, and members of the rodent family.

Over the eons a precious balance has been created in nature. What hasn't been factored into bird chromosomes is the huge influence humankind has had on habitat and predation during the last century. Fortunately, our Mother Mallard comes from a relatively adaptable species. She has learned to coexist in habitat dominated by humans.

Mallards are by far the most well-known ducks throughout the West; however, several other species—many as beautiful and colorful as the mallard—breed in the lakes and rivers of Idaho, Montana, Colorado, Wyoming, and parts of Nevada, Utah, Washington, Oregon, California, British Columbia, and Alberta. Other duck species have migrated north and east to Alaska and northern Canada to breed.

One of those species of ducks that is common throughout the West is the gadwall. Many people mistake this duck for a female mallard because of its grayish brown, mottled plumage. Upon closer examination, the male gadwall's soft gray-and-chestnut back and black rump give this duck an elegantly understated yet distinguished costume. The female gadwall, like most female ducks, is a mottled brown.

The colors nature saved when designing the gadwall were lavishly spent on the male wood duck, another common lake nester. It's decorated with a complete artist's palette: red eyes; orange, yellow, and green head; brown, green, yellow, black, white, and rust body; and sky blue speculum, those colorful shiny feathers midway up a bird's wing. An iridescent green crest further outfits this dandy. Rather than nesting on the ground like other ducks do, female wood ducks nest in cavities high in trees—often excavated by woodpeckers—where they lay a dozen eggs. A few hours after hatching, the downy babies jump from the nest, tumble to the ground, and skitter to a nearby lake where they huddle with nest mates around their mother.

Common mergansers nest near larger lakes and streams. Longer than the mallards by a couple inches, the males of this unmistakable bird sport long, pointed red bills; green heads; and black-and-white bodies. The females show off rusty heads with a flowing crest.

Many other duck and ducklike species decorate riparian areas of the West during breeding season. Hooded mergansers, northern shovelers, northern pintails, blue-winged and green-winged teals, cinnamon teals, and ruddy ducks—distinctively plumed males and somber, brownish females—are examples of common springtime breeders.

One summer when Bill and I were exploring a freshwater lake in South Central Alaska's Kenai Peninsula snooping out duck and seabird nesting areas, we observed an unusual interaction. We noticed a mother mallard viciously assaulting something in the water. Her days-old ducklings—we counted six—huddled in a tight knot close by. The attacker approached from underwater, sneaking up snakelike on the tiny ducklings. Momma Mallard jabbed at the intruder with her bill and beat at it with her wings, while the young scuttled themselves to safety.

It took us several moments to identify the source of her anxiety, a red-necked grebe, or "mugger," as the Kenai locals call it. This twenty-inch-long diving bird winters along the West Coast's saltwater bays, innocently feeding on aquatic insects, invertebrates, and fish. In spring it heads north to breed in western Canada and Alaska, where its feeding habits change. Earlier, on the same lake, we had noticed the grebe's nest, a floating platform of fresh and decayed reeds. The mugger was attacking the mallard ducklings to feed its own young.

Watching the mother mallard fend off the grebe reminded me of my childhood on Mercer Island. Each day during breeding season we counted the mallard babies on Lake Washington. Almost every day the numbers decreased as another chick was lost. Unlike the Robert McCloskey story, wherein all eight ducklings arrive safely at the island in the Public Garden's pond, only a few mallard babies survived on my lake.

AN INTIMACY OF ENGAGEMENT

Nature is always hinting at us.

It hints over and over again.

Until suddenly we take the hint.

—Robert Frost

Chores completed, binoculars around my neck, I carried my spotting scope and journal to a row of drift logs along the shore where the dune grass borders the driftwood. A large, bone-white trunk, acting like a duck blind, hid me from the quiet, gray waters of Dungeness Bay, smooth as a satin pillowcase. I selected a comfortable log to sit on and adjusted my scope to peer between the branches of the driftwood trunk. A thick cloud cover obscured the sun and held down the early April afternoon temperatures. Hat, gloves, and a thermos of herbal tea helped stave off the cold. (The raw numbness of sitting and waiting continues to be my least favorite part of birdwatching.) An oystercatcher, solid black with a bright-red bill, rattled the air, but otherwise the narrow beach remained deserted. I knew the solitude wouldn't last long; the late afternoon shorebird show would begin soon.

Six days earlier, Bill and I had begun a weeklong tour of duty as volunteer lighthouse keepers for the New Dungeness Lighthouse. My dream of tending a lighthouse kindled decades earlier as a young girl. In my childhood fantasy, probably ignited by a children's book, I cared for the lighthouse and protected ships from crashing onto the rocks. Now that I was an adult, the reality held a different kind of adventure.

The New Dungeness Lighthouse stands on the southern flank of the Straits of Juan de Fuca. The eighteen-mile-wide straits separate the Olympic Peninsula in the northwest corner of Washington State from the islands of southern British Columbia. Tributaries of the Dungeness River start on the high, rugged slopes of Mount Constance, Mount Mystery, and the Gray Wolf Range and cascade toward the sea, dragging down bits of those hillsides and depositing them in the Straits of Juan de Fuca. Prevailing westerly winds and water currents erode the bluffs along the shoreline, further churning and washing those former pieces of mountain, finally depositing them as sand in a graceful arm reaching north and east into the straits. Eons, gravity, and the same generous rain that created the rain forest of the Olympic Mountains formed the longest natural sand spit in continental North America, the Dungeness Spit. Five miles out near the tip is the New Dungeness Lighthouse, perched at the end like a sparkling lure caught in mid-cast from a fly fisherman's rod.

Our chores as lighthouse keepers included minding the sixty-three-foot-tall red-and-white lighthouse and wooden, two-story keeper's residence. Decommissioned several years earlier by the Coast Guard, the buildings and grounds are managed by a nonprofit group, the New Dungeness Light Station Association. The instructions for volunteer lighthouse keepers read in part:

> 8:00 A.M., hoist the Stars and Stripes; 9:00 A.M., open public restrooms; 9:00 A.M., begin conducting tours. Finish tours two hours before sunset (since it takes at least two hours for visitors to walk the five miles back to the parking lot). At closing time, lock the lighthouse front door and public restrooms. Clean the restroom and empty the trash. In the lighthouse, shine the brass in the lantern room. Sweep the lantern room, stairs, (all seventy-four) and entry. Collect and tally donations. At sunset, lower the flag. Fold the flag and store indoors.

Volunteers are also expected to answer questions about the spit and surrounding shorelines designated as the Dungeness National Wildlife Refuge. Established in 1915 by President Woodrow Wilson, the 636-acre refuge is home to 240 bird species, many of which use this area as a rest stop for spring and fall migration. Arching out into the straits, the spit collects northbound migrants flowing up the Pacific Coast as well as migrants flying the inland pathway through Puget Sound. The migrants use the spit to refuel and rest before heading north across the open water of the straits.

I'd specially requested the first week in April for our volunteer duty to coincide with the onset of spring shorebird migration. For years I had read about the flocks of shorebirds passing this point. Now I was sitting right in the middle of it.

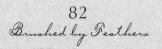

From my perch I observed a sailboat slowly motoring into Dungeness Bay, a large, protected body of water between the spit and the mainland of the Olympic Peninsula. Looking south across the bay, I focused my scope on a horned grebe 100 yards offshore, then scanned to a pigeon guillemot, both common seabirds. A fuzzy smudge appeared above the guillemot and gradually came into focus. A black-bellied plover was flying directly toward me low over the water. Another joined it, then another. Keeping the plovers in the scope, I followed them as they came closer and closer until they landed on the shore directly in front of me. I refocused on the floating guillemot and saw more plovers heading toward me. In waves of ten to twenty birds, the migrants crossed the bay to this shore.

This behavior explained why I hadn't noticed large flocks coming in. The shorebirds traveled in smaller groups and formed large flocks only when they settled for the evening. Plovers, dunlins, western sandpipers, and sanderlings piled onto the shore in front of me. Some fed voraciously, others immediately fell asleep—as much as a bird ever sleeps. A pair of ruddy turnstones landed and, without a pause, started foraging for food. I was tingling with excitement, the cold forgotten. Questions flooded my mind. How far had the shorebirds flown today? Where were they going? Only the birds themselves knew the answers to these questions.

During my week at the lighthouse, I noticed a subtle change. Each day the number of turnstones arriving grew larger. My journal confirmed it. That day I counted twenty-five of these shorebirds as compared to barely a dozen two days earlier. It was, I realized, the start of the movement of turnstones along this migration route. If I could have spent a month at the lighthouse, I would have seen different species trickle in, build in number over the succeeding days, and then fade out, looking like the bell curve of a graph.

As birds fed in front of me, I examined them carefully. These flocks were midway through their annual spring migration. They were traveling thousands of miles from wintering grounds along the west coast of North and Central America to the Arctic tundra to set up nesting territories and rear their young. And in July a reverse cycle would begin. Finished with nesting, they would return south to warmer wintering grounds along the Pacific.

Shorebirds are notoriously difficult to identify, probably because it is rare to have close examinations of these similar-looking birds. I won't begin to describe them here because whole books have been written to help bird-watchers identify the forty-two species regularly occurring along the West Coast. The best of these books is Dennis Paulson's *Shorebirds of the Pacific Northwest.*

After the shorebirds gathered, rested, and fed, the aerial displays began. Flocks lifted off, turning in tight formation, undulating as one organism, swirling in a perfectly choreographed dance—a syncopated rhythm of light and dark as their bellies then their backs flashed toward the viewer. The largest flocks were of dunlins, small dun-colored shorebirds. There were fewer black-bellied plovers, large plovers still attired in drab gray-brown winter plumage. Though most flocks were of a single species, these plovers were also mixed in with the smaller dunlins. The plovers tagged along near the back of the dunlins but knew all the flight patterns. Once landed, the flocks remained in tightly packed bunches as they snuggled up for evening in the lee of the drift logs.

I finished jotting notes in my journal, trekked back to the keeper's house, and met Bill in time to climb to the top of the lighthouse to watch the sun set. We had started this routine the first night of our duty. This being the last night, we carried a couple of beers to celebrate. Dizzy from the seventy-four spiraling steps and panting from the climb, I carefully stepped out the door and onto the catwalk. Vertigo forced me to grab the guardrail, ease down to a seated position, and shift my gaze to the horizon. The steady monotone of the rotating light hummed behind me as the sweeping beam flashed above my head on its 360-degree sweep of the horizon.

Sitting side by side, we looked west toward the Pacific Ocean. The surface was calm: the high tide pushed against the shore. Bill pointed out harbor seals poking their curious heads up while rafts of white-winged and surf scoters dove for food. A call that sounded like a squeaky hinge turned our gaze south to the Dungeness Bay where a pair of bald eagles sat on a large drift log. The shallow bay now attracted common murres and red-breasted mergansers in addition to the birds mentioned earlier. A great blue heron stood in statuesque quietness at the water's edge.

The clouds broke just as the sun, full and juicy, slid below the horizon. Bill and I watched as the departed globe painted the sky tangerine and crimson. I shivered and Bill wrapped his arm around my

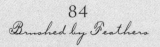

shoulders. After six days my body had begun to merge with the ebb and flow of the natural world. Sunrise, slack tide, tide change, flood tide, sunset; these became the hands and hours of my clock. My lighthouse duties had fallen into sync with the stronger pull of the universe. Like a cat rubbing against its owner's legs at mealtime, I wanted to get closer to nature. I wanted to rub against it, make friction, cling to it. I wanted to nestle in and feel like I belonged.

The clouds slowly muted to a dusky yellow and dark blood red. I removed my official keeper's cap and looked at the insignia, stroking the silky threads sewn into the shape of a lighthouse. The image took me back to my childhood fantasy. Even then, I had a sense of responsibility. I thought of the huge tankers and freighters that now pass the spit. With their sophisticated GPS systems, they hardly need saving. It's the fragile spit and its hundreds of species of wildlife that need protection. Over the years, my ships have transformed from the sailors of the sea into the sailors of the air. We descended the lighthouse steps and locked the building as instructed, although the only living beings within miles were the birds and mammals of the spit.

We fell to sleep easily on our last night at the lighthouse. A mournful song awakened me in the black of night, so I staggered to the window and looked at the lawn between the keeper's house and the lighthouse. The glow from the lighthouse revealed the sad singers. Black-bellied plovers, perhaps the same ones I had seen along the shore the evening before, were scattered about, busily feeding on some tasty tidbits in the lawn. I watched and listened to their plaintive "whee-er-eee" until the chill air sent me back to my warm bed.

The next morning, I awoke early and lay in bed motionless. It was silent, no freeway noise, no plane overhead, no bird sounds. The plovers were gone, headed north long before my day began. Bill was still sleeping soundly. At home he has a hard time sleeping and is always up before me. I quietly sneaked to the kitchen to start coffee. Electricity had been brought to the light station years earlier, so the keeper's kitchen was well equipped; it even had a microwave. As I waited for the coffee, I stepped out on the wide porch, which faced south to the quiet bay. A gull called from far away across the glassy water. I sat on the steps, closed my eyes, and felt the morning sun anoint my face.

An hour later we were packing gear when an ear-piercing whine ripped apart the morning stillness. I looked to the east and saw a

red-and-yellow-winged ultralight flying toward us. The pilot didn't veer away as he approached the refuge, but continued along the spit yards above the shoreline. Like a jet skier plowing full-bore through a duck pond, the ultralight scattered and silenced the wildlife in its wake. The pair of bald eagles took flight and headed toward the mainland. As the craft circled the lighthouse, the pilot waved and continued west. I screamed, futilely shook my fists at him, and then ran to the house to radio refuge headquarters.

Pam, the biological science technician at the refuge, knew exactly what to do. Later she explained that she had jumped in her jeep and was waiting at the local airport, rules and regulations in hand, well before the ultralight touched down. She told us the pilot had no idea he was passing through a designated wildlife area and was oblivious to his impact on the fragile spit.

By then I had calmed down and my reaction was, how sad—not only for the disturbed wildlife, but for the pilot as well. He blundered along without knowing that his flight damaged the nature he had set out to explore.

I wanted him to spend a secluded week at the lighthouse observing and learning about the natural world, not just a superficial glance from the air, but a real up-to-your-elbows-in-it visit. I wanted him to experience the waves of shorebirds that arrived each evening and were gone at the first thought of daylight. I wanted him to hear the mournful song of the plovers feeding at night. I wanted him to stay in one spot long enough to feel the ebb and flow of nature, and to learn the names of the birds and begin to create an intimacy of engagement.

CHAPTER FIVE
May

May nights are still chilly—dipping into the high thirties—and the days require a jacket, but the rest of nature says, "Welcome to May!" Apple blossoms teem with bees; sword ferns uncurl young, spiky fronds; and lettuce and spinach sprouts reach above the ground in the vegetable garden. New needles spring from the tips of conifer branches, looking like fingernails painted lime green. Violet-green swallows chatter as they zip into their nest box above the garage, while at the back of the house barn swallows natter about the exact placement of their mud nest. Heady smells of blooming lilac and azalea waft around me as I step out the door. Ivory-colored thimbleberry blossoms spill their sumptuous vanilla scent through the moist forest.

If all this isn't enough to tempt me out for a beach walk, the clincher is low tides—lowest in eighteen years according to the ticket-taker at the ferry booth a few days ago. Work, worries, and domestic duties remain atop the bluff as I descend the steep ravine to the beach. A pungent, wet seaweed smell greets me at the base of the shady bluff. Pausing to take in my surroundings, I then step out into the warm sun and look over the wide expanse of mudflats and the still, silky bay beyond. A soft haze turns water, islands, sky, and a fishing boat a mile offshore into a gauzy powder blue. To the south the two ferries that run between the mainland and the island approach each other midway across the passage between Mukilteo and Clinton. They appear headed for a grand collision, but as happens twice every hour, the illusion proves false as they peacefully slide past and continue in opposite directions. Stepping farther out onto the sandy beach I see six gulls resting at the water's edge. Beyond them a loon dives below the water then reappears fifty feet farther north. After feeding, it will take to the air to continue its northern migration on long, powerful wings.

Unlike gravel roads or concrete sidewalks, beaches leave messages about who has passed. Today the sand is free of human footprints. Gull, shorebird, and raccoon prints reveal who has traveled here since the last high tide.

Ahead is a wide, sandy area with piles of drift logs and dune grass that juts slightly into the bay. Since it doesn't warrant mention on any maps, Bill and I have tagged this area "The Point." Unlike the rest of this beach where high tides reach to the base of the bluff, The Point stays above high tide during spring and summer. As usual a pair of killdeer,

Killdeer showing
injury-feigning display

members of the shorebird family, call a loud "kill-DEER, kill-DEER" at my approach. Today their calls seem unusually piercing and purposeful. Then I spot the reason for their agitation. A baby killdeer, looking like a downy stuffed toy set on two stilts, is trapped against a large drift log in full view and only a few yards ahead of me. Despite its relatively long legs, the recently hatched youngster can't climb over the barrier to scurry back into the safety of the tall beach grass and jumble of driftwood. As I freeze in place and peer through my binoculars, the young one flings itself against the log. Instinct tells the baby it must get over the log to safety.

Unlike most shorebirds, which are migratory, killdeer live here year-round. Typical of most shorebirds, they don't build elaborate nests, but lay their eggs in an unprotected open scrape. Their strongly dappled eggs camouflage perfectly against the sand, gravel, or pasture, as does their plumage: black-and-white stripes across the face and neck and a dull-grayish back. The incubating parent will courageously remain on the nest, even if predators come close. As soon as their downy feathers dry after hatching, the killdeer chicks (usually four) are up on their long legs and out of the scrape. Both parents take up the task of keeping predators away as chicks learn to feed and fend for themselves,

As I watch the exposed baby, one parent swoops in, calls loudly, and walks along in open view in the opposite direction from the young, hoping I'll follow its noisy distraction. When this doesn't work the other parent flies in front of me, tumbles to the sand, and begins an injury-feigning display or broken-wing act. Leaning to one side, the bird drags a partially spread wing and tail on the

Sword ferns uncurl young "fiddle heads"

89

May

ground, displaying a bright reddish orange rump. The bird limps on attempting to lure me away from the young. I've since read that the killdeer's injury-feigning display effectively distracted predators in 1,012 of 1,017 observations as recorded in *The Birds of North America*.[2]

I back away and watch the baby scamper to a spot where it can scramble up the rotting log and disappear behind it. The parents are noticeably relieved and cease their piteous cries and distraction techniques. I continue on my walk, mindful of where I step, knowing there may be three more babies glued to the beach and counting on camouflage to remain unseen.

May is baby bird month. Usually my first sighting of baby birds is of mallard ducklings, downy balls of fluff lined up after their mother as she leads them out onto a lake or pond. As with the killdeer baby I saw on the beach, mallard chicks are out and about almost from birth and therefore visible to bird-watchers. These chicks are called "precocial." The opposite is "altricial"—babies that hatch featherless and are totally dependent on a parent for food, warmth, and protection. Robin young, for example, are altricial. Although I've already picked up sky blue

Mallard and her ducklings

2 *The Birds of North America*, Number 517, 2000 by Bette J. D. Jackson and Jerome A. Jackson.

eggshells dropped by robins cleaning their nests, which indicate the chicks have hatched, I won't see the robin babies outside the nest for another two or three weeks. Inside the nest the altricial babies develop from featherless, blind, helpless babies to alert, adult-sized fledglings.

Many of the migrant birds that have arrived here from points south are still looking for nesting spots and industriously building their nests. Last week, while out birding near a freshwater lake about five miles from our house, I watched tree swallows fluttering around a boat launch, obviously scouting for nesting sites. Knowing this species is a cavity nester, I examined the area for old snags with woodpecker holes. However, the only trees here were young willow and alder. The swallows began darting around the parking lot, and then I noticed one land on the tailpipe of a fisherman's SUV. It poked its head into the perfect-sized hole then chattered at the other swal-

Baby killdeer trapped against drift log

lows that came by for a look, acting as if they had found the perfect nest cavity. May is late for tree swallows to be looking for a nest site, perhaps these were just late arrivals. Or perhaps the competition for the few natural nesting cavities is keeping this species from nesting on schedule.

This month we'll learn more about the migrant birds that move into and across the western states in May. We'll struggle to get up at daybreak to experience the dawn song, the amazing early morning chorus of breeding songsters. Also, we'll attempt some warbler-watching. Our five common warblers are easy to identify, even for the novice. Here in the West watching warblers is benign and fun, rather than the drive-you-to-drink sport it is in the eastern United States, where there are dozens of look-alike species. Next we will venture across the Cascade Mountains for a kayaking trip along the Columbia River in the dry interior, where we learn about Wowshuxkluh, the messenger bird of the Wanapum Indians.

Birds introduced this month

❑ American White Pelican *(Pelecanus erythrorhynchos)*

❑ Great Egret *(Ardea alba)*

❑ American Kestrel *(Falco sparverius)*

❑ Prairie Falcon *(Falco mexicanus)*

❑ Killdeer *(Charadrius vociferus)*

❑ Caspian Tern *(Sterna caspia)*

❑ Forster's Tern *(Sterna forsteri)*

❑ Warbling Vireo *(Vireo gilvus)*

❑ Tree Swallow *(Tachycineta bicolor)*

❑ Northern Rough-winged Swallow *(Stelgidopteryx serripennis)*

❑ Bank Swallow *(Riparia riparia)*

❑ Cliff Swallow *(Petrochelidon pyrrhonota)*

❑ Orange-crowned Warbler *(Vermivora celata)*

❑ Nashville Warbler *(Vermivora ruficapilla)*

❑ Yellow Warbler *(Dendroica petechia)*

❑ Yellow-rumped Warbler *(Dendroica coronata)*

❑ Townsend's Warbler *(Dendroica townsendi)*

❑ MacGillivray's Warbler *(Oporornis tolmiei)*

❑ Common Yellowthroat *(Geothlypis trichas)*

❑ Wilson's Warbler *(Wilsonia pusilla)*

❑ Western Meadowlark *(Sturnella neglecta)*

❑ Red-winged Blackbird *(Agelaius phoeniceus)*

❑ Bullock's Oriole *(Icterus bullockii)*

WARBLER-WATCHING

Objects are concealed from our view not so much because they
are out of the course of our visual ray as because we do not
bring our minds and eyes to bear on them, for there is no
power to see in the eye itself, any more than in any other jelly.
… The greater part of the phenomena of Nature are for this
reason concealed from us all our lives. …
There is just as much beauty visible to us in the landscape as
we are prepared to appreciate—not a grain more.

—Henry David Thoreau

Every year about this time I get my first attack of "warbler neck." The neck stiffness and pain results from bending my head back to look straight overhead at migrating birds—especially warblers—filtering through the tops of trees. Holding up binoculars to identify species only aggravates the symptoms. Yet it's worth the pain. The fun and challenge of watching and identifying these brilliantly colored birds has me hooked. I just schedule more frequent neck massages.

Warblers are small, nervous birds constantly flitting from branch to branch. Usually these birds won't alight on seed feeders, but instead eat insects and grubs at the tops of trees—evidently the most delicious— challenging even the most nimble binocular-wielding hands. Why do birders strain for a glimpse of these five-inch, fast-moving birds that often stay high out of sight? It is probably a similar motivation to that which leads people to risk life scaling mountains. The birds are there and represent a challenge to be conquered. To birders, that means a challenge to identify them.

These frustrating but tantalizing daemons dressed in feathers are now returning from wintering grounds in Latin America. Some pass overhead or pause momentarily before they continue farther north or to higher elevations to breed. Others drop down to spend the breeding season.

Serious warbler-watchers travel to warbler "migrant traps" or "hot spots," such as Point Pelee in eastern Canada or High Island in

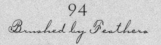

Texas, and hope for a good fallout day, a day when migrating birds are present in such large numbers that they seem to be falling from the sky. The songs of the migrants are music to the ears, and flashes of brightly colored plumage are candy for the warbler-watcher's eyes. Or so I've been told.

I prefer to stay away from those popular hot spots, which attract throngs of people as well as birds. I stay closer to home, choosing a six-mile drive to Lone Lake, a quiet freshwater lake about half a mile wide surrounded by reeds, willows, alders, and a couple dozen houses. My destination: a small, county park at the back of the lake. The migrants aren't falling from the sky, but plenty of warblers flitter through the trees, and the shorter willows encourage some warblers to come closer to earth, providing us flightless mortals with half a chance to see them.

⌣•

On one near-perfect morning in early May, I met up with Steve and Martha Ellis for a Whidbey Audubon–sponsored bird trip at Lone Lake. Steve, a custodian at the local high school, has crammed more bird knowledge into his brain than can be found in a whole shelf of field guides. Martha's bird knowledge almost equals her husband's, but she didn't stop there. She's now well into learning about plants. Each time I go birdwatching with Steve and Martha, I learn something new.

As we stepped from the car, warbler songs greeted us. The six other Audubon members on the trip scribbled notes as fast as Steve and Martha spoke. Three yellow-rumped warblers, the most common western warbler, skittered through a fifteen-foot-tall willow by the boat launch. This distinctly colored warbler is easy to spot since they are equally at home in low bushes as well as the stratosphere of tall tree-tops. The bird's dark-gray and white body is accented with five yellow patches: one on the rump, two on the sides near the shoulders, one on the crown, and one on the chin. Don't get confused by the yellow on the chin patch; it is white on some birds. The yellow-chinned variety is a subspecies called the Audubon's warbler, and the white-chinned sub-species is the myrtle warbler. Steve referred to them all as "butter butts."

I asked Steve, "Help me with the song, the many variations always confuse me."

"Just think of it as the 'deedle, deedle' bird," was his simple reply. He was right; the song does have a 'deedle deedle' quality I'd never noticed before.

Walking along the row of willows, we identified three more warbler species. A pair of yellow warblers, canary yellow with black, beady eyes, popped in and out of view. A few minutes later I spotted a Wilson's warbler, bright yellow with some olive on the back and a black skullcap. In the same grove of willows we found an orange-crowned warbler. The chances of seeing that orange crown on its head are one in a million, unless you happen to be an orange-crowned warbler of the opposite sex. We humans have to rely on recognizing the dull, Dijon mustard plumage on the remainder of the bird. Within the birding community, this species is unique in that it has no distinguishable identification characteristics. Not very helpful, but true.

One common warbler we didn't see that day is the common yellowthroat. The bird is bright yellow—like the mustard you put on hotdogs—with some olive on the back and a jet black, Zorro-like mask.

Two weeks later I visited Lone Lake again. This time I was alone and the boat launch was deserted of humans. The yellow-rumped warblers weren't present when I arrived; probably the ones we'd seen earlier had migrated farther north. Then I heard a soft "deedle, deedle" and remembered Steve's words. Deep in the branches of the willow, two male butter butts—also probably migrating through—fed ravenously. I wondered if any of them could possibly be the same birds I saw last February in Oaxaca, Mexico.

A male yellow warbler sang loudly. After a few minutes, I saw the female carry a bit of dried grass to her nest in a blackberry mound about eight feet off the ground. Wilson's and orange-crowned warblers were present and vocal but, again, no common yellowthroats. I decided to look in a more marshy location to find that species.

I continued my walk around the grassy picnic area and back to the car, where a new species caught my eye, a warbling vireo. Plain grayish with a white eye stripe, the vireo looks and acts much like a warbler but belongs to a different family of birds. As I sat in my car making notes of my sightings, a sudden May shower moistened the windshield and silenced the songsters.

Warblers are *relatively* easy to spot when they frequent willow trees, much more difficult when they hover in the top branches of alders,

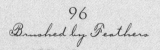

maples, and conifer trees. It's tough to identify any warbler while looking straight up at two legs and a belly. Bird books don't illustrate this
view. To overcome this impediment, more advanced birders have
learned to identify warblers by their songs. Actually, only a few warblers
warble; others buzz, trill, whistle, chirp, go "cheee," "ta-wit," "tseet,"
"witchity-witchity," etc., creating infinitely unique combinations of
melodic verses that they belt out at the tops of their little syrinxes.

The five common western warblers have distinctive songs. Here
are some simple clues to help you identify them by song.

> Yellow-rumped Warbler: "deedle, deedle, deedle"
> Yellow Warbler: "Sweet, sweet, a-little-more, sweet"
>   (sung very fast)
> Wilson's Warbler: "chu, chu, chu, chu, chu"
>   (slower and lower at the end)
> Orange-crowned Warbler: A high-pitched descending
>   staccato trill
> Common Yellowthroat: "witchity, witchity, witchity,
>   witchity"

Though these five are the most common warblers throughout
the West, several other warbler species can be found here. Higher elevations, particularly conifer forests, have three more yellow-bodied
species. The Nashville warbler has a gray head and bright-white ring
around the eye. A close cousin is the MacGillivray's warbler with a gray
head and white crescents above and below the eye. The Townsend's
warbler, which ranges from the Pacific Northwest north to southwestern
Alaska, shows a yellow-and-black patterned head.

After familiarizing yourself with these warblers, you can seek
out the additional less common warblers in the West. If that isn't challenging enough, try warbler-watching in the Mississippi flyway or along
the East Coast, where more than three dozen different species of warblers, some amazingly similar in both plumage and song, fill the sky.
Maybe someday, when I get tired of Lone Lake, I'll venture farther afield,
even as far as Point Pelee or High Island. I'll be the warbler-watcher
wearing a neck brace.

DAWN SONG

The birds begun at four o'clock—

Their period for dawn—

A music numerous as space

And measureless as noon.

I could not count their force,

Their voices did expend

As brook by brook bestows itself

To magnify the pond.

—Emily Dickinson,
The Laurel Poetry Series, Poem number 63 *(excerpt)*

Most bird-watchers can point to a particular species that opened the door to this wonderful hobby of birdwatching. Bill has such a bird, the painted bunting.

On our first trip to Mexico I arose early each morning for a bird walk. Bill, not interested in birds at the time, chose to sleep in. We were still in the courting stage of our relationship, so after a couple mornings of catching up on his sleep, he decided to join me. We were walking along a dusty road framed by tired green tropical foliage when a multi-colored bird, a neotropical migrant that breeds in the southeastern United States and winters in Mexico, landed in front of us. If I'd planned this for months, I couldn't have choreographed for Bill a better intro-duction to birdwatching. I knew the bird, called *sietecolores* (seven colors) by the locals, would dazzle him with its palette of gaudy colors. I handed him my binoculars for a brief but close-up look before it took off. It was a moment we will remember forever. Bill stood still, awestruck. Then this six-foot one-inch, well-seasoned attorney began to dance around like a nervous poodle. "Did you see that bird? Bright-blue head, green back, and a red belly; it was so cool! Awesome. it was unbelievable!" For months I'd been trying to convince Bill that bird-watching was fascinating, but it was only when he saw this special bird

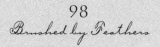

that he finally understood my excitement. That five-second glimpse changed his life—and perhaps mine as well, since I might not have married someone with no interest in birds.

I'm often asked what made me a bird-watcher. That's a hard question to answer because I don't have a touchstone bird like Bill. As a child I remember lying in my bed during afternoon nap time on warm spring days and hearing a robin singing in the tree outside my window. Later when I joined Camp Fire Girls, I selected "Robin" as my animal name. But those early life experiences didn't turn me into a bird-watcher.

For me, the process of becoming a bird-watcher evolved over time, having more to do with hearing rather than seeing them. That conversion happened during an ornithology class at Principia College near Alton, Illinois. The class required early morning bird walks through deciduous trees along the Mississippi River bluffs. On my first walk, the sound of singing birds overwhelmed me. Hundreds of birds, all singing together, filled the air with trills, warbles, and calls. I couldn't believe there were so many different, yet lovely bird sounds. Although I'd been in college for three years, I'd never been up early enough to hear this morning symphony. Once I'd experienced it, I was motivated to learn more about the feathered creatures that produced such awe-inspiring sounds. Like sailors of ancient Greece lured by sirens, I was now under a spell strong enough to persist for the past thirty years. I trust that such an epiphany justifies focusing on bird songs for the rest of this chapter.

Male birds sing for two purposes: to advertise that they are looking for a mate and to announce to other males of the same species that this territory—this section of trees, meadow, or garden—is already claimed. The average breeding male songbird sings its song 1,500 to 3,000 times each day. The star songster species is the red-eyed vireo, which can give voice to its song more than 22,000 times between sunrise and sunset. Different species may coexist in overlapping territories, so many birds sing at once. Each morning throughout spring and into summer, the males mark their territories by moving from tree to tree and at each new position exploding into song. Judging the competition are females, listening for the loudest and best singers and checking out the advertised territory. This frenetic competition to establish and maintain a breeding territory, this early morning cacophony of bird voices, is called the dawn song.

Most any wooded lot or tree-filled park will offer a dawn song.

Atop our bluff here on Whidbey Island, the robins open the performance with a clear "chirrup, cheerilee, chirrup, cheerilee," then the song sparrows join with "sweet, sweet, sweet" followed by a buzzlike "tow-wee." Black-capped chickadees call their names, "chick-a-zee-zee-zee." Their cousins, the chestnut-backed chickadees, joust back with the same song delivered twice as fast and higher in pitch. The melody is carried by the winter wren's bubbly cascade consisting of more than 100 notes and lasting a full fifteen seconds. Two-note tin-horn sounds are added by red-breasted nuthatches, and the bushtits offer continually insistent high "tsits" and "lisps." Northern flickers staccato a "flick-a, flick-a," while crows "caw, caw" and woodpeckers beat out the percussion. At the top of the scale the dark-eyed junco crowns the crescendo with a bell-like trill. For a birder, this is similar to the New York Philharmonic playing Beethoven's *Fifth*.

This ability to produce song has long intrigued professional ornithologists as well as amateur bird-watchers. Birds create their songs using a complex muscular organ called the syrinx, the avian equivalent of the human larynx. The syrinx allows the bird to croon several tones at one time. Also, it lets the bird breathe while singing, freeing the birds to belt out long, complex songs without pausing for air. The part of a bird's brain used for vocalization, especially for singing, enlarges in the spring when it is needed for courtship and defending territory. It then contracts in the off season when not used.

Recent studies show that in many species of songbirds it is the males with the loudest songs who have the most success attracting females. We might hypothesize that the best singers tend to be the strongest birds in the area and, in turn, they produce the largest and strongest offspring. I think of reactions to Elvis or Frank and wonder if human behavior is that much more advanced.

Some birders enjoy the dawn song performance without feeling any compulsion to identify each bird's song. I can't. I need to know which musician is producing each part of the avian symphony. So over the years, I've learned to identify most birds by their songs. I've also learned that unless you are unusually gifted in listening and remembering what you hear—folks who easily learn new languages have this gift—the identification process is slow and difficult.

The key is to start with a few common birds and then slowly, song by song, add to your repertoire. I wouldn't begin with the dawn

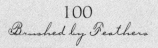

song—the chorus can be so overwhelming it is difficult to break out the separate voices. Instead, start with the soloists that sing on and off during the day. If possible, begin your education in March when the songsters are limited to the resident birds. During the succeeding months as the warblers, swallows, flycatchers, and other migrants arrive, you can add them to your data bank, one by one.

When you hear an unfamiliar birdsong, write down a pneumonic such as "chick-a-zee, zee, zee" or a description—soft metallic monotone, one long, clear note—or make a diagram of the undulating notes to help remember the song. If you can see the bird, include a description of it so you can identify the bird and attach the song to it.

Audiocassette tapes or CDs are excellent tools for learning bird songs. Look for tapes or CDs with calls limited to your geographic area—the closer to home the better. As with human speech—such as a Texas drawl or a Boston accent—birds from one part of the country may sound different from the same species in another area. Most of a bird's songmaking capability is inherited, but, in some species, inflections and rhythms are learned, thus giving rise to regional variation and even variations from one valley to the next. We may have a hard time discerning the difference, but studies have shown that birds can certainly tell who is an outsider and who isn't.

To catch a live performance of the dawn song, set your alarm for 5:00 A.M. and find a seat just as the early morning light extinguishes the distant stars. Often a chair on your deck or a bench at a nearby park will offer good listening. Most songsters breed in trees, so wooded or riparian areas are best. My favorite way to experience the dawn song is by camping overnight in a natural setting and listening to the morning sounds from inside my tent. The music lasts through sunrise and into mid-morning.

Be warned: listening to birds can change your life. The change may be dramatic or subtle. One day you'll detour on your way home from work to visit a wetland. On hiking trips you'll find yourself stopping to "check out a bird." Bird books will appear on your birthday lists, and binoculars will find a spot in your car's glove box. A five-second encounter in an otherwise well-ordered life may work its magic and change your life forever.

THE WHISPERING BIRDS

Dawson [in 1896] tells of the capture of a fledgling Bullock oriole, which was rescued from the water. Some 2 weeks later another nestling oriole was secured, and put in the cage with the older bird. The newcomer had not learned to feed itself but opened its mouth and called with childish insistence. The older bird, itself a fledgling, began to feed the orphan with all the tender solicitude of a parent. This is said to have become a regular habit, being still followed when the older bird had attained to flycatching.

—**Stanley Jewett,**
Birds of Washington State, *1953*

At dawn, bird songs filtering through the leaves and into our tent told me we weren't the only beings spending the night within the shelter of this locust grove. Quietly stretching my head out the tent flap, I counted ten Bullock's orioles tending carefully woven hanging nests in celadon green branches. The boldly colored orange-and-black males and muted females flew off to forage for food, then returned to stuff their heads down into dangling nests to nourish their young. As Bill and I tended to our own breakfast, broke camp, and packed our double kayak, the orioles filled our ears with whistles and harsher avian chatter. We pushed off and paddled out into the strong current of the free-flowing Columbia River to continue our two-day paddle down fifty-two miles of southeastern Washington's Hanford Reach.

One month earlier in the spring of 1996, Bill hatched a plan for this overnight kayaking trip. From the very beginning I was against it. This stretch of the river, running through the Hanford Nuclear Reservation, was not officially open; we had no maps to help us sort out the various river channels formed by gravel and willow islands. I'd read about sirens blasting as boats ventured too close to restricted Hanford sites and

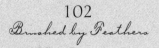

helicopters hovering to escort intruders away. I was sure the water would be "glowing" and expected to see radioactive waste mounded along the shore.

Bill had learned about the proposed trip from friends who lived in Richland, a good-sized city at the lower end of the Reach, which, Bill kept reminding me, obtains all its drinking water from the Columbia. Our friends had agreed to meet us at the put-in spot at Vernita Bridge and ferry our van to the take-out point, their neighbor's dock in Richland. "Think of all the birds along the river," Bill offered as a teaser. (I actually wondered if their colors would be brighter.) I still hesitated, but when it became evident that Bill would go with or without me, I reluctantly consented.

The first day had been full of challenges: strong, gusty headwinds, confusion about which channel to take around long islands (the only "map" we had was a page removed from the DeLorme *Washington Atlas and Gazetteer*), and foreboding warning signs near the reactors. As we launched our kayak into a small cove at the edge of the mighty river, I looked up into the huge concrete structure of the Vernita Bridge fifty feet above me. Perhaps 100 gourd-shaped nests wedged into corners of the structure. Cliff swallows, recognizable by buff-colored rumps and bright-white foreheads, swarmed around the nests made from bits of mud skillfully piled together. Swallows don't really sing, but produce a series of chatter, creaking, and rattling sounds. Occasionally one swooped over our heads and emitted a soft, low "veew," its alarm call.

We gingerly paddled into the immense body of the river, then the current grabbed our boat and swiftly but benignly pulled us along. I looked out over the Columbia River that starts in British Columbia and discharges into the Pacific. Here the river diverts from its generally southern path to flow first east and then north, rounding a horn, before resuming its southerly direction and, farther south, creates the border with Oregon. The other 700 miles of river in Washington, both upstream and downstream, are chopped into a series of lakes by seven dams, but for these fifty-two miles the flow remains unchecked.

Beyond the far shore lay stark country: flat, open sage lands, barren hills, basalt outcroppings, and shifting sand dunes—a raw geology lacking any gentrification provided by green forests and rich meadows. I'd read that the Reach passes through some of the most polluted and most pristine habitat in our country, polluted with hundreds of underground nuclear waste storage tanks but pristine in many ways because the 540-square-mile Hanford Reservation was closed to any form of trespassing or development since the early 1940s.

Within an hour of launching we came upon large, ominous, gray reactor buildings, the first of nine nuclear reactors bordering the south bank. In a natural reaction to lean away from something nasty, we hugged the opposite shore. No sirens greeted us, no helicopters broke through the quiet air. Built to produce plutonium for atomic bombs that were dropped on Japan during World War II, the reactors have been deactivated over the years, and recently the area was declared a superfund site facing immense clean-up efforts. Uncontaminated structures are in the process of being removed, and the contaminated cores of the reactors are being "cocooned" to seal the radioactive material for 1,000 years. Or so the scientists hope.

Safely past the first reactor, I began to relax. At times I wanted to put on the brakes and take a better look at the tall, white great egrets standing in the shallows or listen to the songs of breeding warblers, but the slowly moving freeway kept pulling us along. The steady rhythm of dipping paddles and rotating arms lulled me into a quiet meditation and I found myself absorbed with the gently moving river, its grassy willow shoreline, its birds, and the vast, open sage land beyond.

Continuing downriver, we approached a low gravel island separating the river into two channels. A family of American white pelicans, snow-white bodies with ink-black wing tips and huge throat pouches, stood on the island's upstream prow. Breeding adults sported tangerine orange bills with fibrous plates jutting from them like a rhinoceros's horn. Dusky head and wing markings separated the immature pelicans from their parents. On the same gravel spit, large twenty-one-inch Caspian terns rested alongside their smaller fourteen-inch Forster's tern cousins. Watching the birds distracted us, and before we could check our "road map" the river claimed our fate, sending us down the left channel toward the one landmark I'd wanted to avoid, Coyote Rapids. The shy, elusive coyotes along the bank—more curious than wary—did not concern me, but the "rapids" did. My strictly flat-water kayaking experience didn't prepare me for anything even slightly frothy. I silently fumed, knowing we could have taken the other channel and avoided the rapid, if we'd known more about the river or had been paying attention instead of watching the pelicans. In my mind, it was all Bill's fault.

Brushed by Feathers

A gust of wind pushed back the rim of my sun hat, forcing me to squint into the blinding reflection off the wind-chipped surface; ahead I heard the sound of cascading water and felt the current pick up speed. For the first time since we'd launched, I saw rocks slipping by under the surface. Then bubbling ripples and rushing water surrounded us as we scooted over shallow-water rocks. However, I could see smooth water ahead—the high water covered any obstructions or dangers—and knew we were safe. I let out a yelp and actually enjoyed the final few moments through the churning water. Bill was forgiven.

The loud "kon-ka-REE" of a red-winged blackbird sounded from the willows along the left bank. Then two mallards burst from the shady riverbank. A flock of eight common mergansers flew upriver and circled low over us, probably trying to understand this strange, colorful log floating downstream.

After lunch and a brief walk to shake out our legs, it was time to move on. Back in the boat, we drifted close to the 600-foot-high White Bluffs to view the large colonies of bank swallows, which burrow into the softer layers of sandy bank. Around the perimeter of the colony, northern rough-winged swallows have moved into vacated bank swallow burrows. Further along, hundreds more cliff swallows twittered around their mud nests; later, a prairie falcon glided on the thermals above us. We slipped past a common raven's nest constructed on a narrow ledge six feet above the river. When Bill mimicked the raven's call, four small, bald heads peeked above the rim of the large stick nest.

The ten miles of tall bluffs on our left and the continuous line of big "No Trespassing" signs on our right forced us to paddle into the evening searching for a place to pull off and camp. Just before darkness filled the sky the bluffs receded and a grove of locust trees invited us into a marshy bay. We hauled the kayak up a bank and set up our tent on the edge of a grassy meadow, an oasis where Native Americans must have camped for centuries. (Later we learned that camping along the river was illegal.) That night coyotes howled at the moon and seconds later the young coyotes yipped back. Yet I felt protected under the sheltering locust trees and was filled by a strange sense of optimism as the orioles called to us in the morning.

The second day was a marked contrast to our first. With no wind we settled into an easy, almost mystical, quietness. The sparkling blue river meandered through big lazy bends, then straightened and poured its voluminous weight south. We passed close to the small cluster of houses at Ringold where a western meadowlark belted out its bubbling, flutelike song from an electrical wire. On the same wire, an American kestrel, a small, colorful raptor, eyed a grassy field looking for its next meal.

The day practically passed without incident. However, near the end another island caught us off guard. We needed to take the right-hand channel to reach the designated take-out point but found ourselves being swept toward the left-hand channel. Five minutes of frantic paddling across the current wasn't enough, and we saw the gravel prow of the island slipping past on our right. We struggled on and landed on the island, then waded and pulled the kayak back around the gravel prow to the right-hand channel and set off again, landing easily on the dock as planned.

Driving home Bill and I pooled our knowledge about the Reach. We'd read that the future of the area was up for grabs and that local politicians were lobbying to open it for agricultural development. Chagrined to think this last remnant of a natural ecosystem could be lost forever, we vowed to do what we could to support a fledgling group dedicated to "Save the Reach." Over the next few years we attended public meetings, wrote letters, gave talks, showed our slides, wrote articles, and organized large groups to travel down the Reach, to raise money and publicize our cause and to let others experience the river as we had. Our small contribution combined with huge efforts by many others was rewarded. In the fall of 2000 President Bill Clinton declared the area a national monument. With that announcement a huge sense of relief overjoyed us knowing that this free-flowing section would likely remain wild and free.

•⤳

A couple years later, Bill and I were preparing for our sixth paddle down the Reach. We were shepherding a group of thirteen kayakers on a day trip through a twenty-two-mile stretch beginning at Vernita Bridge and ending at White Bluffs Landing, near the locust grove where we had camped years before. This trip included a program lead by historian and naturalist Jack Nisbet on the social, political, and natural history of the area. Bill was in charge of planning and logistics; my only task was to point out and identify birds.

By then, I'd fallen deeply in love with this river, so wild and free and full of contrasts. It was like an old friend: I relished its familiarity without any fear of surprises. This trip we purposefully passed by Coyote Rapids to enjoy the rush of the current over the rocks. I watched for familiar birds and delighted at seeing new ones.

The morning hours passed quickly.

To stop for lunch, we angled out of the stronger current in the center of the river to the eddy line, the slow lane, and then watched for a slight bay or protected spot to find quiet water, our off-ramp. We hauled our boats onto the sand and sat down to open our lunches. The sun warmed my wet feet, but a light breeze and a cool sixty-seven degrees kept the zip-off bottoms of my convertible pants in place. The whine of a powerboat far downriver broke the quiet. Several moments later, straining against the same current that we found so helpful on our downriver paddle, the boat passed. What a contrast compared to struggling against the river or flowing with it, in a kayak. The driver, the only other human we would see on the trip, offered a gentle wave.

Jack stood up. A half-eaten, cream cheese–smothered bagel lingered in one hand as he told the story of this majestic section of the river. He shifted way back in time to Kennewick Man, one of the earliest human remains ever discovered, which were found just thirty miles farther downstream. Jack turned and pointed to the White Bluffs behind us. He explained that these cliffs were rich in vertebrate fossils, including the remains of camels, bison, mastodons, and even a small, raccoonlike panda.

A Caspian tern, white bodied with a back Mohawk, circled above us, dropped from the sky, and plummeted into the river, emerging a split second later with a wriggling fish in its mouth. We gasped and Jack turned to watch the show behind him until the tern disappeared downstream. He continued the history of the Native Americans who lived nearby and fished these waters. The very spot where we lounged was once an encampment for fishing and meeting, and archeological evidence was all about us. Then Jack began a story new to me, the story of Smowhala, the spiritual chief of the local Wanapum Indians. This story came from Click Relander's book *Drummers and Dreamers*.

The chief lived in the mid-1800s, a time of great change for the Wanapum. Faced with explorers and settlers moving onto his land, Smowhala and other leaders were searching for inspiration. Smowhala sought the advice of his spirits by retreating to the top of Mount LaLac. There he fasted and abstained from drinking water. As the days passed, every rustle of the wind or chirp of a bird spoke to him. One particular bird, an oriole, became a messenger for Smowhala and he named it Wowshuxkluh. This bird messenger whispered in Smowhala's ear, predicting the fate of his people with the increasing presence of white people.

Later I picked up Relander's book and read that when Smowhala returned from the mountain he carved a wooden replica of Wowshuxkluh. A picture of the carving shows a realistic little bird with large brass tacks for eyes. The bird was painted yellowish orange, as are real orioles, and a sprig of feathers was attached to the bird to form the tail. Smowhala displayed the wooden bird in a place of honor atop a tall pole, facing east. From there the bird continued to whisper to Smowhala and give him direction. Years later, after Smowhala had passed on and his shaman role transferred to his nephew, the nephew was asked to identify Wowshuxkluh. He slowly paged through an early book on Washington birds by William Leon Dawson and finally found a picture of the bird, a Bullock's oriole.[3]

As Jack sat down and resumed eating his bagel, I looked through the list of birds I'd scribbled in my journal. Mostly local residents and a few early migrants had shown themselves on this cool May 18th morning. Evidently, Smowhala's oriole, sometimes called the late bird, was smart enough to wait for warmer days.

We launched the kayaks and continued along the ten miles of White Bluffs, then the river widened and slowed, giving us time to reflect on the day of paddling, birdwatching, and contemplating the unique juxtaposition of man and nature on this wild river. Finally, I could see in the distance the grove of celadon green locust trees signaling our take-out point a mile ahead. I thought back to our first river trip when Bill and I awakened to the whistles and songs of the Bullock's orioles. Reflecting

[3] Retold from the story of Wowshuxkluh as described in *Drummers and Dreamers* by Click Relander.

on Jack's story of Wowshuxkluh, I realized that the birds Bill and I enjoyed could have been offspring, generations later, of the messenger bird of the Wanapum that whispered into Smowhala's ears. It seemed as if the birds had also been whispering into our ears on that first trip, sending a message that the river needed protecting.

Jack sprinted ahead to find and signal the best take-out spot. We all landed safely and hauled the boats to the parking lot. As the men loaded the kayaks atop the vehicles, I looked toward to the celadon green locust trees. A brilliant orange-and-black oriole landed on a branch then disappeared into the leaves. I walked closer and listened. The messenger bird of the Wanapum wasn't singing. Evidently at the moment, there were no messages needing to be told.

CHAPTER SIX

June

It is June 21, the summer solstice. On this longest day of the year, the tendrils of light streak above the jagged horizon at 5:11 A.M. Over the months, the rising sun has inched its way north along the Cascade skyline, passing the end of Hat Island, to emerge at its most northern point, behind Whitehorse Mountain.

Rocky is up nearly as early, sailing off the light fixture a few minutes before six. Poor bird. Being single (we don't know Rocky's gender but have guessed he's a male) must be bothering him. During June, he perches atop the roof, rather than down under the eaves. He coos insistently, then prances back and forth strutting his iridescent body, pausing to preen, then strutting again. Neither the cooing nor strutting pulls in any other rock pigeons to our property. His only audience is me and, although I take pity on Rocky's futile attempts to find a mate, I prefer just one "pet" pigeon. A flock to feed and clean up after wouldn't be as welcome.

"Rocky" strutting his iridescent body

In June populations of birds and mammals swell as young ones are out and about exploring their world. Last week Bill noticed a small, gangly legged newborn fawn huddled at its mother's side as they rounded the side of the house. Then yesterday our other resident doe brought her twins to the blackberry bushes, just outside the kitchen window. On quiet mornings as I walk through the meadow between our house and the county road, I often spy two oval ears and a wet nose just visible above the waist-high grass.

Baby bunnies have been scampering across our lawn for a couple weeks. Instinct tells them to freeze in place when danger approaches. This works to their advantage in the tall grass, but causes jangled nerves as I drive out the driveway. Instead of darting out of the way as older rabbits do, these non-streetwise youngsters freeze into fearful mounds, forcing me to slam on the brakes and come to a dead stop. They are cute now, but next fall I'll be singing a different tune when they sneak into the vegetable garden to feast on my carrots.

Today I begin my walk early along the county road, knowing the day will warm into the high eighties. White, cup-shaped blackberry blossoms reach through the elderberry branches that drip with clusters of blood red berries. Farther along the road, the soft, creamy blossoms of ocean spray look like foamy clusters of vanilla whipped cream. The pink blossoms of wild Nootka roses that thicken into large drifts along the bluff and mix with other plants in open woodlands give off an unmistakable, sweet fragrance. Blindfold me and I would still know it is June.

I listen for morning bird songs and note that the morning chorus is less intense this month than during May, since many birds are otherwise occupied feeding young. Flycatchers, among the last bird species to migrate north, add a few new voices. Their simple vocalizations— the willow flycatcher's sneezelike "fitz-bew,"

Swainson's thrush

Pigeon guillemots

the Pacific-slope flycatcher's up-slurred "psee-yeet," or the olive-sided flycatcher's clear "quick-three-beers"—are hardly a substitute for the melodic warblers, wrens, and sparrows. One new voice, a late migrant's clear, upward-spiraling, flutelike song, emerges from the moist woodland and takes center stage. Difficult to see, but recognizable by song, a Swainson's thrush fills the diva's role, its lilting vocals serenade into the twilight telling us that summer is here and announcing how happy the songster is to be back from Ecuador. A high, thin, trilled whistle directs me to look near the top of a cedar tree where a cedar waxwing shifts on a branch displaying its black mask and yellow-tipped tail.

As I continue my walk, a tapping draws my eye to a maple tree's dead branch. Gazing through foliage I see two hairy woodpeckers. The first, a male, hops along pecking at the dead bark. Behind it a juvenile mimics the action. When the male successfully locates a bug or grub it turns around and feeds it to the young, which gobbles it down. The pair continue along the branch, father and offspring out hunting together.

After a twenty-minute walk, I pass the tall alder tree on the edge of the bluff that holds a bald eagle's nest. Typically eagles select conifers for their nest sites, but this section of the bluff lacks conifers and the eagles have managed with a less-sturdy alder. Looking up into the tree I can see only the bottom of the nest. The male perches nearby, a sentry guarding the nest. All is quiet. I assume the female is deep in the nest incubating eggs, although from this ground-level view, I can't see her. Within weeks the aerie will be busy with both parents tending one or two young.

A quietly moving shadow draws my eyes to the low branches of an adjacent tree. A spotted towhee flies off, mouth jammed full with dried grass, on its way to building a second nest. Later I see a robin, also carrying nesting material. Many of the smaller resident birds—including wrens and sparrows—and some migrants, as soon as their babies are fledged and off on their own, begin a second nest and then go through the whole breeding process again. I turn around and retrace my steps along the road.

Returning down my driveway, I follow the deer trail to the vegetable garden. I slip several ripe, juicy strawberries into my mouth, pull a few weeds, and pick a bouquet of romaine, red leaf, and Bibb lettuce for lunch. A song sparrow that nests deep in the raspberry bushes pops out and scolds me, so I carefully close the gate and leave.

Coinciding with the summer solstice, the long, protracted spring migration that began in early March as the first warblers crossed the Mexican border into Arizona now comes to a close. During the past four months ducks, shorebirds, waterfowl, raptors, and songbirds have traveled north along several migration routes across California, Utah, and Colorado, then through the Pacific Northwest into Alberta and British Columbia. Finally, in June the last of the migrants arrive in Alaska. Then, like a pause at the end of a long inhalation, migration ceases. But only briefly because early arrivals, which have now completed their nesting, will soon begin traveling back to their southern wintering grounds. Starting in July and continuing through the fall, migrants will trek south in small or large flocks.

This month we explore bird activity in three water-related habitats. First we watch the loveable pigeon guillemots play near their saltwater-bluff colonies. Next we muck around in a coastal wetland. Finally, we travel to the largest freshwater marsh in the western United States, eastern Oregon's Malheur National Wildlife Refuge.

Soft, creamy ocean spray blossoms

New birds introduced this month:

❑ White-faced Ibis *(Plegadis chihi)*

❑ Northern Harrier *(Circus cyaneus)*

❑ Virginia Rail *(Rallus limicola)*

❑ Common Snipe *(Gallinago gallinago)*

❑ Long-billed Curlew *(Numenius americanus)*

❑ Willet *(Catoptrophorus semipalmatus)*

❑ Franklin's Gull *(Larus pipixcan)*

❑ Pigeon Guillemot *(Cepphus columba)*

❑ Common Nighthawk *(Chordeiles minor)*

❑ Olive-sided Flycatcher *(Contopus cooperi)*

❑ Willow Flycatcher *(Empidonax traillii)*

❑ Pacific-slope Flycatcher *(Empidonax difficilis)*

❑ Western Kingbird *(Tyrannus verticalis)*

❏ Marsh Wren *(Cistothorus palustris)*

❏ Swainson's Thrush *(Catharus ustulatus)*

❏ Cedar Waxwing *(Bombycilla cedrorum)*

❏ Bobolink *(Dolichonyx oryzivorus)*

A FRENCH LOVE AFFAIR

While often seen on open water, guillemots prefer quiet bays,

and at mid-day, when not frisking about in the water, they

often congregate in picturesque groups on outlying rocks just

above the surf. Here it is easy to imagine the guillemots hold-

ing some sort of meeting, for they dance about to the accom-

paniment of coarse grunts almost mammal-like in tone.

Stanley Jewett,
Birds of Washington State, *1953*

For the first time in my life, I've become smitten by a bird. I used to think it wasn't right for me, a proclaimed lover of birds, to have one preferred species. It would be, I reasoned, somewhat like choosing one child as a favorite, slighting the others. My upbringing in fairness discouraged partiality, bias, or "species-ism."

I wasn't looking for a new love, just minding my own business surveying breeding birds on the west side of Whidbey Island for the Island County Breeding Bird Atlasing Project, when my epiphany occurred and my impartiality evaporated. I now readily confess to having a favorite bird—the pigeon guillemot.

A what? You may be asking.

Though the name sounds French—and a bit sexy—the pigeon guillemot is a seabird common to the North Pacific. Chubby and pigeon-like, this ten-inch dark bird is often seen from the ferries or around docks where it floats on the water, dives to catch small fish—mainly sand lance and herring—and gleans invertebrates from the rocky bottom. It prefers protected bays along the West Coast from California to Alaska, up and around the Bering Sea, and south along the coast of Russia almost to Japan. In flight, the bird usually flaps along a yard or two above the water. So far not very exciting, I'll admit.

Like I said, I was busy surveying breeding birds. Several other experienced birders and I were investigating all of Island County, which includes both Whidbey and Camano Islands, to record breeding activity for the seventy or so bird species that nest here. It was June, my second month of spending mornings with binoculars and clipboard listening for males singing and watching for signs of bird courtship, nest building, carrying food to young, and other indications of breeding. As bird activity in the forest subsided during the late morning hours, I headed to the beaches to continue my research.

On the day I compromised my impartiality, the waters of Admiralty Inlet rested dead calm, a soft, powder blue satin, the lingering moisture of a disappearing morning fog still cooling the air. The slow grinding of a small fishing boat far across the water to the west and the intermittent calls of kids playing a mile down the crescent bay, noises usually smothered by the slightest movement of the water, bounced gently on the smooth surface. On quiet, calm June days I'm ripe for the plucking. It is exactly this kind of morning that has lured me back to Puget Sound each summer, even when I lived across the continent or as far away as England, and pulled so hard that I finally moved here permanently.

I wanted to walk a section of beach that was difficult to get to because the access was privately owned. On this island, walking the beach is considered "legal," but crossing private property to get there is not. However, Marge at the post office had told my friend Susan of an unmarked road end that offered public access near the cliffs I hoped to explore. She was right. Walking the rocky beach in front of modest homes, I recorded pairs of American goldfinches at seed feeders and spied barn swallows swooping into open porches. Abruptly the houses ceased and the land rose into high cliffs with visible layers of glacial till and outwash. The beach soon emptied of any vestige of human habitation.

A soft, alluring trill drew my attention out past half-submerged boulders into deeper water fifty feet off shore. The trill settled into one long, clear note, and a second tone joined the first, cascading into a modulated duet. From farther out came a high-pitched whistle, and I raised my eyes to see eight pairs of pigeon guillemots. After dutifully recording the sighting, I put down the clipboard and settled in to watch the performance of their water dance. Through my binoculars I saw the big, white patches decorating their black wings, and it looked like someone had painted their legs and feet fire-engine red. The frolicsome birds lifted up as if on hind legs, flapped their stubby little wings, then dropped down and dunked their heads under the water two or three times. One lunged at another teasingly; the other raced away as if playing tag. A second pair, one after another, fluttered forward then dove underwater, playing a type of leapfrog—or leap duck. A third pair took to the air to continue their antics in large loops and swirls. These games and songs were establishing and reinforcing pair bonding, which is an important part of the bird's courtship and procreation.

One bird took off from the water in a big, flat semicircle, first flying away from the land and then making a wide circle back toward the bluff at breakneck speed. I held my breath, thinking that the bird would surely crash into the sheer face, but at the last moment it folded its wings and disappeared into a hole two-thirds of the way up the cliff. While waiting for the bird to come out, I counted a dozen other nest burrows in the bluff.

I pulled a sandwich from my backpack and settled down to watch; any further work that day could wait. The sun warmed my head as I lolled on a drift log for more than an hour and succumbed to my new infatuation, sketching their antics in the margins of my research cards. Why, I wondered, was I so enamored with these birds? Then I realized the actions brought to mind the playfulness of my own two boys, now grown, and I was transported back to the fun and joy of their childhood. I smiled as I watched one pair of guillemots hunch their heads forward and back exactly as my son Alex did while playing the bass guitar in his rock band. These avian clowns began to awaken a dormant playfulness deep inside me. First I mimicked the head bob, then got to my feet and checked to make sure no beachcombers had wandered within sight. I didn't want an audience for any real silliness that might happen. I shed my jacket and tried a little dance of my own. It didn't resemble the guillemots, but looked more like the 1950's twist. Then I listened for the guillemots' trill, and my dance changed into a soft, flowing ballet. When I sensed my activity might disturb the birds, I gathered my pack and started back to my car. On the way I vowed to stop taking myself so seriously, lighten up, and have more fun, just as the pigeon guillemots seemed to be doing.

Driving home it hit me that I was hooked; never had I been so captivated by one species. The old saying that people choose pets that match their personality did give me pause, particularly when I thought that the antics on the breeding grounds suggested the guillemots might

June

be promiscuous. The moment I returned home I researched these birds, and that quelled my fears—pigeon guillemots mate for life. The birds stay in the same general area year-round, although in the winter they disperse from their breeding colonies to find food. During these nonbreeding months, from October until March, their wings retain the black-and-white pattern but their body and head feathers molt into white with flecks of black. In the late spring they return to the same breeding colonies. Good, I thought, there's the potential for a long-term relationship.

Pigeon guillemots, members of the family of seabirds called alcids, typically select rocky crevices on protected islands to make a simple nest and lay two eggs. Colonies range from a dozen to more than 100 pairs. Two other guillemot species besides our local species exist; the black guillemot, also called "tystie," lives in the North Atlantic and Arctic seas, and the spectacled guillemot resides on the coastlines of Japan and parts of eastern Russia.

Later that evening when Bill came home, I was a bit shy about mentioning this new infatuation. However, I felt less reticent upon learning that the name "guillemot" comes from a pet form of "Guillaume." Derived from the Old French name Willelm, guillemot means "little William." My research suggested that the bird was named after a playful child. My William seemed pleased when I told him.

In my home office, a framed poster by Alaskan artist Rie Muñoz titled *Guillemot Legend* hangs on the wall. The poster, a fanciful depiction of brightly clothed Eskimo children waving their arms and flapping up into the sky to become guillemots, now seemed to leap from the wall. Fascinated with the depiction, I was desperate to learn the legend. I couldn't find it in any book, on the Internet, or even from a reference librarian, but I did discover the phone number of an art gallery specializing in Muñoz's work. I called and shamelessly begged for help. The kind owner located the legend in her collection of writings about the artist's work. A couple days later she faxed it to me.

In an Eskimo village there once was an evil Shaman who detested all the noise and racket from the local children as they played. One day the Shaman turned all the children into a cliff.

The villagers mourned their loss until the next summer

when a good Shaman happened through. They explained what had happened and asked the Shaman if he could help.

They all went to the cliff where the children were still trapped inside. The good Shaman studied the cliff and said, "This is very strong magic, and I cannot reverse it. I can bring the children back, but they will turn immediately into guillemots. You won't have your children, but they will have their freedom." And that is what was done.

What a beautiful explanation as to why the pigeon guillemots are so playful and loveable—and my favorite.

MUCKING AROUND THE MARSH

Beauty is before me,

and beauty is behind me,

and above me and below me hovers the beautiful.

—*Navajo saying*

Tired of standing, I leaned back against the trunk of an alder tree. Black-berry vines were mounded around me as I stared blankly across the marsh, which flowed away like a patchwork of horizontal stripes in rib-bons of green, ochre, and beige. Red-winged blackbirds sporting scarlet epaulets lifted from the cattails then dropped with a liquid, gurgling "konk-a-REE," followed by a trill. A song sparrow dressed in drab brown popped up from a tangle of rushes, gave a loud buzzlike "tow-wee," and hid again. The warbler species I failed to find at Lone Lake in May, a common yellowthroat in yellow finery with a black mask, momentarily took center stage, snatched an early-season dragonfly, and soundlessly disappeared back into the tall grass.

On that misty June morning I was stationed on the edge of a Whidbey Island marsh to assist Jack Bettesworth with a study of north-ern harriers. Jack, positioned on the far side of the 600-acre marsh, was in the seventh year of a project to band and monitor northern harriers, a mid-sized bird of prey. (Not surprisingly, this species formerly was named marsh hawk.) Fifteen percent of male harriers are polygamous: this marsh hosted one such nesting arrangement. We had determined that one male harrier supported three females in separate nests in this section of the marsh, but we hadn't located the nests.

Unlike bald eagles or red-tailed hawks, whose large, showy tree nests are easily located and studied, harriers nest on the ground in the most inaccessible parts of a marsh. Harriers don't nest in the same spot or even the same marsh each year, so Jack needed help locating this sea-son's nests. This year he hoped to monitor thirty different nests, once he found them. Females incubate the eggs and care for the young. The male's main duty is to bring food to the females. When the male has prey, typically a vole or small rabbit, he flies over, calls the female, and the two perform a midair transfer of prey. He then flies off for more hunting and she returns to the nest.

Harriers fly low over the marsh, sometimes hidden by the tallest brush rows or small trees. When the female approaches the nest, she gives no warning, but suddenly drops out of sight and may travel on the ground a distance before approaching the nest hidden in thick reeds or cattails. Spotting a nest site entails hours of hanging around watching and one brief moment of extreme concentration. Jack hoped to triangulate the location of the nests so later, clad in hip boots, he could go to the nests to band and shoulder tag the young. The damp weather must have been keeping the females on their nests; we waited and waited.

My eyes dropped to the shallow, marshy water fifty feet in front of me. A slight ripple caught my attention. Without sound a Virginia rail delicately stepped into view. Lifting its long-toed legs to reach over dead cattails, the bird exposed its long orange bill, gray head, and chestnut wings. Then, just as quickly, it disappeared back into the thick foliage. A rail sighting was fairly rare, so tingling with excitement I pushed the button on my two-way radio to spread the news to Jack.

Time dragged and my ears searched for more marsh sounds. The unending chugging of the marsh wren reminded me of an old fashioned sewing machine. The faint, two-syllable call of the common snipe high above the marsh carried across the quiet acres of reeds, grasses, and low willows. The beauty and sounds of the marsh kept me there, pushing away the nagging thoughts of my undone duties at home.

Looking over the marsh, I identified the ochre band as reed canary grass, an introduced weed, and was reminded of human intrusion on this wetland. In other marshes purple loosestrife and spartina posed significant problems by filling in ponds and marshes and displacing native vegetation. An even greater problem for our wetlands is destruction. In this state only 30 percent of the pre–European settlement tidal wetlands remain. Former wetland habitat has succumbed to ports, cities, resorts, golf courses, and housing developments.

Wetlands not only provide habitat for birds and other wildlife, they also help our planet absorb and hold fresh water. Like human kidneys, wetlands filter pollution and capture nutrient runoff. They control erosion and prevent floods. Today we understand the precious value of wetlands and the cost of re-creating those that were lost. I wondered how long this marsh would survive.

Jack's voice on my radio broke the stillness, "The female harrier is headed south toward the dike." I picked up the bird through my binoculars. She was flying low, wings held at an upward slant, beautifully adorned in shades of brown and beige. She patrolled down one side of the fence and circled back—flashing a white rump—heading my way. Closer, closer, and within a blink of my eye she raised her wings and dropped from sight. I fixed the point with a sighting off a distant fence post.

"Did you see her drop?" Jack asked anxiously.

"Bingo!" I replied.

BIRDING AN OASIS

To hear the evening chant of the mosquito

from a thousand green chapels, and the bittern begin to boom

from some concealed fort like a sunset gun!

Surely one may as profitably be soaked in the juices of a

swamp for one day as pick his way dry-shod over sand.

Cold and damp—are they not as rich experience

as warmth and dryness?

—Henry David Thoreau

It was a warm June morning when Duncan Evered, Bill, and I stood on a sandy, sage-dotted knoll 100 feet above the headquarters of southeast Oregon's Malheur National Wildlife Refuge. All around us stretched a flat beige valley—a monotone of warm brown—that formed into low hills on the horizon. The only relief was the Steens Mountain, displaying a patchwork of glimmering white snow thirty-five miles to the southeast. In front of us, the heat shimmered above 45,000-acre Malheur Lake, creating a wavy, other-worldly sensation that reminded me of the alien planet's desert landscape in the movie *Star Wars*. Through the heat waves, the lake and surrounding wetlands appeared as an undulating blue-green line across the vast valley. Beyond the lake, spread as far as we could see, was ancient, naked geology, unaltered by trees, underbrush, or human intervention.

Duncan, director of the Malheur Field Station, was escorting Bill and me around the 186,500-acre refuge, located about thirty miles south of Burns, Oregon. Shaped like a fat "T," Harney and Malheur Lakes stretch across the forty-mile top of the refuge while the Donner and Blitzen River, which flows in from the south, makes up the thirty-mile-long vertical base.

Established in 1908, Malheur National Wildlife Refuge is near the northern edge of the vast, dry Great Basin Desert region. The basin covers a significant section of the West, extending west to the Cascade and

Sierra Mountains, south to the Mojave Desert, and east past the Great Salt Lake. Where we were standing, at an elevation of 4,000 feet, the dry landscape supports desert shrubs and juniper, occasionally broken with rimrock. Little apparent fauna lives in the Great Basin except in select pockets like this oasis, where millions of birds pause on their spring and fall migrations and many others stop to breed. It was this multitude of breeding birds that lured us to Malheur and more than compensated for the nine-hour drive from Seattle.

As the three of us looked across the lake and empty land beyond, Duncan began to explain the ancient geology. "It all seems very primordial," he said, pointing to a long finger of land jutting into the broad valley. "Four point two million years ago that was a river valley. Then a huge lava flow filled it. Over the eons, the land around the lava flow eroded away, leaving a lava cast of the valley."

After Duncan's overview of the refuge, we descended the knoll to the irrigated green oasis around the headquarters' buildings. He then told us about one of the stranger occurrences during his seven-year tenure at the refuge. "The craziest day was the afternoon it rained fish. About forty four-inch fish landed around the buildings of the field station. One or two I could attribute to osprey, but forty needed more of an explanation." As Duncan gave us a moment to ponder his comments, birds called from the tall cottonwoods and I swatted at mosquitoes, wishing I had applied repellent that morning. He then continued in his Bristol-born, Oxford-influenced English accent. "Must have been a whirlwind that spun out over the lake, picked up the fish, and then dropped them three miles away over at the field station."

Duncan pointed up to cottonwood trees planted in the 1930s and began explaining the oasis effect. Birds—regular migrants plus significant numbers of eastern vagrants—pick out the tall trees from miles away and flock to this wetland. Birders call these spots a migrant trap. The Malheur Refuge, the largest freshwater wetland in the West, is one huge migrant trap.

The lakes and surrounding wetland, the heart of the refuge, are sustained by springs and snowmelt-fed rivers. Lush ponds are lined with cattails, rushes, and willows teeming with insects, fish, and invertebrates —all food that birds relish. Sparingly scattered throughout the Great Basin, oases like Malheur offer feeding and resting stops for migrating ducks, waterfowl, shorebirds, warblers, and raptors. Back in 1976, according to Carroll Littlefield's *Birds of Malheur National Wildlife Refuge, Oregon,* between 1 and 1.7 million northern pintail, 250,000 to 900,000 snow geese, 400,000 to 650,000 American wigeons, and 66,000 to 150,000 green-winged teal stopped at Malheur during spring migration. Other birds remained and bred here including sandhill cranes and white-faced ibis. More than 350 additional species have been recorded on the refuge.

After a walk around the headquarters, the three of us climbed into our van and drove into the eastern section of the "T," passing through a raptor-rich habitat of grass fields and farmland. Near Diamond we stopped to watch a nesting colony of Franklin's gulls and white-faced ibises. While the small, ternlike gulls hawked the air for insects, the long-legged, bronze-green ibises probed the marsh for food with their long, downward-curving beaks.

Around 1:00 we dropped Duncan back at the field station. Then Bill and I drove on our own to explore the southern reaches of the refuge. Bill wanted to find a bobolink, a new bird for him, although I'd seen them several times on the East Coast. A member of the blackbird family, the bobolink's black plumage is broken with a bright, buff-colored hindneck and white wings, bars, and rump. We braved swarms of mosquitoes—by now I was lathered in repellant—to search the area near the "P" Ranch. Just north of the ranch, exactly where Duncan had suggested, Bill's bird list grew by one when he spied a gorgeous male bobolink sitting atop a low willow crooning his loud, bubbling "bob-o-link" song.

We continued north along the dusty, washboard Central Patrol Road to Knox Pond, where we scouted for ducks. The afternoon sun broke through western clouds to spotlight a cinnamon teal—a bright, rusty red—before it paddled into the rushes. We observed many common ducks, even a green-winged teal. As the afternoon wore on, the mosquitoes thickened even more. We again ventured from the van when we reached the edge of Buena Vista Pond. After a few minutes I noticed the back of Bill's mustard-colored shirt, realizing I could kill a dozen of the pesky insects with one slap of my palm. Besieged, we jumped in the van, closed the windows, and retreated to the field station. Along the road, we saw a western kingbird, a flycatcher with a gray head and lovely soft-yellow belly. As we neared the station a long-billed curlew flew close over the van and called its loud, ascending "cur lee, cur lee, cur lee," probably protecting a nearby nest.

The buildings that house the field station were built as a training center for the Job Corp in the 1960s. Now used for a variety of educational programs, they have more than 250 beds open to the public. We weren't at the Hilton, but the simple accommodations suited us fine. Our trip coincided with a break in the programs and the station was empty except for two researchers, Molly and Stephen, from Reed College in Portland, Oregon, who were recording songs of Brewer's sparrows and American robins to analyze geographic variations in their songs.

That evening we enjoyed a mosquito-free dinner inside the well- screened guest quarters. Molly and Stephen had already eaten; their early morning recording sessions forcing them into a daily schedule that ran about two hours ahead of ours. For us, Bill cooked up an Indian curry, one of our favorite camping meals prepared from packaged sauces. The taste of lentils, rice, and a spicy tomato sauce brought back images of eating this same meal while kayaking along the eastern shore of Baja California Sur and another adventure on the west coast of Vancouver Island.

As the sun set through darkening clouds, we chatted with Molly and Stephen about their recording project. The next night they were headed down to camp near "P" Ranch, and I silently admired their willingness to endure the swarms of mosquitoes. Suddenly an unfamiliar whooshing sound sent us out to the deck hoping to discover the source. A common nighthawk, a black-and-white speckled bird with long pointed wings, which had spent the day snoozing on a split-log railing near the dorm, was performing a courtship display. Flying high into the air, it then plunged toward the ground, making a hollow, booming sound as the air rushed through its wings. "Just like a big fart," Molly chuckled, as the bird circled back up and repeated the display before flying to a power pole and settling onto the crossbeam. We didn't try to locate the female given the fading light and knowing her ability to camouflage perfectly with the gray-brown landscape.

That night a rainstorm passed through, bringing gusting winds. I tossed in my sleeping bag, disturbed by our room's hollow-core door rattling in the doorframe. Molly and Steven had said they would be up and gone by 4:20. By then the wind had stopped and I was sleeping soundly. I never heard them leave.

A couple hours later a loud, piercing "pill-will-willet, pill-will-willet, pill-will-willet" awoke me. I sat up delighted to have the willet, a gray-speckled shorebird that breeds in this wetland, as my alarm clock. I looked out the window at the still, blue sky and reveled in the luxury of knowing I had one more wonderful morning of birding in this amazing wetland. I doubted I would see any new species. Instead, my joy would come from watching familiar birds in an almost pristine environment. The ducks, ibises, herons, and avocets that live on or near the water as well as the meadowlarks, curlews, grosbeaks, flycatchers, and raptors that inhabit the surrounding grasslands maintain large, healthy populations here. Deep in the refuge where access is forbidden to humans, birds in numbers beyond our ability to count still follow ancient rhythms. Duncan's descriptive use of "primordial" seemed particularly apt. Malheur's bountiful feast exists in sharp contrast to the dwindling wetlands in the more populated areas of the West.

The plan for the day was to drive back down Central Patrol Road along the miles and miles of marshy ponds, stopping along the way so Bill could photograph birds while I added more watercolor illustrations to my journal. After lunch we would head home again. The first fifty miles of our return journey would take us through endless dry, open sage land. Like birds migrating north, we would have a long stretch before the next watering hole.

June

Brushed by Feathers

CHAPTER SEVEN

July

As a child, my July 2 birthday was often observed on the Fourth of July when the extended family gathered to celebrate the holiday. I must have been five before I learned that the fireworks displays weren't just for my birthday, but the country's as well. That realization didn't dim my conviction that a July 2 birthday was perfect. School was out, the warm weather encouraged my favorite outdoor activities, and everyone was in a celebratory mood. Halfway around the calendar from Christmas, a July birthday gave me a chance to satisfy my present wish list at equal six-month intervals.

Today, Bill makes an especially nice birthday breakfast and we sit on the deck in the warm sun to enjoy it: fresh squeezed orange juice, a mound of strawberries and raspberries freshly picked from our garden, and scrambled eggs with Walla Walla sweet onions wrapped in a fresh tortilla. Midway through the meal two great blue herons fly toward us from the south, make a do-si-do around each other in the air, and then continue on. "The herons are wishing you happy birthday," Bill announces.

A dull brownish willow flycatcher

I work in my office the rest of the morning and after lunch embark on a two-hour bird walk. My plan is to walk south following the county road along the bluff, then drop down to the beach and return north along the shore before climbing the bluff back to the house. An especially low tide will allow plenty of time on the beach to look for birds.

Wilson's warbler

Heading toward the county road, I detour through the vegetable garden to nibble raspberries. Stepping around tall broccoli plants, I notice a fluffy mouselike scurrying near my feet. Looking down, I spy a tail-less baby song sparrow duck under some radish leaves. It freezes in place, like an ostrich with its head in the sand thinking it can't be seen. The baby sparrow's head is hidden, but the short stumpy wing feathers folded across its back are clearly visible, as is the downy fluff that fills the spot where a tail will soon emerge. Momma Sparrow begins scolding from atop the garden fence, so I quietly slip away. Next winter when I prune back the raspberry canes, I expect I'll discover a well-used song sparrow nest.

When I reach the county road I turn left and approach the fenced pasture on the other side. I whistle to the chestnut horse grazing in the pasture, which lifts her head and snorts, but then resumes eating. After just a few encounters this horse has figured out that I don't carry treats and that a trip to the fence to greet me isn't worth the effort. Over the pasture float white-crowned and Savannah sparrow songs; the songsters are hidden in the grass. An American goldfinch dances through the air to the tune of its own sweet call, "potato chip, potato chip, potato chip." From a low alder branch, a dull-brownish willow flycatcher spits out its sneezy "fitz-bew, fitz-bew."

As I follow the road through a shady alder and hemlock forest, a Wilson's warbler's rapidly descending "chee, chee, chee, chee, chee" greets me. I lift my binoculars and watch this bright-yellow bird with black skullcap flit through the alders pecking at insects, then head to its nest. A melodious warbling phrase signals that a warbling vireo is also feeding in the alders, up near the top. This vireo is hard to spot and the

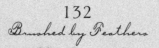

only reward is a greenish gray body with a muted eye stripe. So I continue along, as the lilting song of the Swainson's thrush fills the forest.

Descending to the beach on a private road through thick cedar and maple, I hear a small brown winter wren send out its finest birthday wish, a long bubbly series of musical tones. At the bottom of the hill a honey-colored "Lassie" ambles out to sniff me and quickly decides my familiar scent isn't worth a bark.

The north wind brushes my cheeks as I step onto the sandy beach. Above me a rich delphinium blue fills the sky from the bluff all the way to the tops of the Cascade Mountains. The same blue spreads across the water, shattered by the wind into a million silver flecks. After a fifteen-minute walk, I turn to look up at the eagles' stick nest perched high atop the bluff above me. Blinking into the sharp, mid-afternoon sun, I see two dark silhouettes stretching above the sticks. Two fledgling eagles are making their debut. One opens its wings, flaps up to stand on the nest's rim, looks down at me, and practically offers a happy birthday salute. I dance a little jig on the sand and wave my hands in gratitude.

Two fledgling eagles

Passing under the black skeleton of a derelict dock, I catch a salty whiff from exposed barnacles and other sea life clinging to the pilings. The cool shade provides a brief but welcome break from the glaring sun. Round The Point, I slow my pace knowing a killdeer family lives in the area. Stepping carefully I still startle two killdeer that burst from their camouflaged stations amid the cobbles. "Keer, keer, keer," their pleading voices beg me not to trespass, but I carefully walk past, no babies in sight.

Ten minutes later, I step into the shadow of the bluff and climb the seventy-two stairs back to the house. Up under the eaves outside of our bedroom four fat swallow babies look ready to launch into flight.

Later that afternoon, I notice a pair of adult California quail on the back lawn at the edge of the Nootka roses. Nearly hidden by dandelion blossoms, eleven tiny day-old chicks—precious beyond description—cluster between protective parents, my final avian birthday gift.

I realize the birds are not wishing me happy birthday. Just as the fireworks displays on the Fourth of July have nothing to do with honoring my birthday, the birds are performing normal bird activities, without any awareness of me. Dancing herons, bird songs along the bluff, a fledging eagle flapping its wings, and day-old quail can occur any day of the year, not just on one's birthday. The first migrating swallows usually arrive on my son Alex's March 20th birthday. The returning flycatchers often mark my son Munro's early June birthday. Even Bill's November birthday is celebrated by searching for fresh chanterelle mushrooms in the forest while observing late-arriving ducks on nearby ponds. Like agates on a beach, nature's gifts are ready and waiting for us to notice and cherish. Taking time to enjoy these gifts on one's birthday makes them even more special.

This month we examine two species of land birds that depend largely on fish for their food, the great blue heron and belted kingfisher. Then we take a trip to Kenai, Alaska, to observe birds that migrate north to breed.

Fat barn swallow babies look ready to launch

Birds introduced this month:

☐ Common Loon *(Gavia immer)*

☐ Sooty Shearwater *(Puffinus griseus)*

☐ Great Blue Heron *(Ardea herodias)*

☐ Green Heron *(Butorides virescens)*

☐ Sandhill Crane *(Grus canadensis)*

☐ Parasitic Jaeger *(Stercorarius parasiticus)*

☐ Black-legged Kittiwake *(Rissa tridactyla)*

☐ Common Murre *(Uria aalge)*

☐ Horned Puffin *(Fratercula corniculata)*

☐ Tufted Puffin *(Fratercula cirrhata)*

☐ Gray Jay *(Perisoreus canadensis)*

☐ Boreal Chickadee *(Poecile hudsonicus)*

❏ Savannah Sparrow *(Paserculus sandwichensis)*

❏ Common Redpoll *(Carduelis flammea)*

THE KING OF THE FISHERS

This forenoon I saw a kingfisher fluttering in the brook and supposed he had a trout, which he could not swallow. On going to him I found he had driven his bill into an old rotten stick with such force as to bury it clear up to his eyes ... hard and fast. I took him with the stick to the house and called Jones and Phillips to see the curiosity. It was with difficulty that his bill was pulled out again.

—*Journal of James Swan, July 10, 1865, Neah Bay, Washington Territory*

Last week, I carried my morning tea onto the back deck to breathe in the fresh, still air and listen for bird songs. Barn swallows chattered through the air, nipping at insects to feed their near-to-fledging young. Like a broken record, a white-crowned sparrow repeated its rapid, buzzlike "see, me, pretty-little-me."

Suddenly a reverberating, metallic call—a rattle that sounded like a machine gun—fired above me. I looked up to see a strong, staccato wing beat, with white wing patches flashing a Morse-code pattern. The large-headed bird circled wide over the bluff repeating the loud ruckus, then landed on a low-hanging limb of an alder tree. There was no mistaking the showy, noisy belted kingfisher, the only kingfisher species found throughout most of the West.

Stocky and short-legged, this bird's power is in its large, strong head and sharp bill. The king of fishers hovers over water then dives headfirst to pince prey in its bill. Emerging from the water, the bird flies back to a perch. There it juggles the meal—usually a fish or aquatic invertebrate—into position and gulps it down.

The thirteen-inch kingfisher is adorned from head to tail in beautiful slate blue highlighted by a wide white collar and white belly. A conspicuous, shaggy double-pointed crest crowns this king. For years ornithologists confused the male and female. They assumed incorrectly that the more dramatically plumed bird was the male as is typical with most avian species. However, it's the female kingfisher that sports the brightest colors. She also wears a distinctive rusty bellyband, or belt, across her white breast. Mature males lack the rusty belt, though immature males have a partial one for a short time.

The belted kingfisher's scientific name, *Ceryle alcyon*, was derived from ancient Greek mythology. *Ceryle* means seabird. According to legend, Alcyone was the daughter of Aeolus, god of the wind. After Alcyone's husband unexpectedly drowned at sea, she was so distraught that she threw herself into the ocean atop her husband's floating body. As she kissed his lips, both Alcyone and her husband were transformed into kingfishers. To help Alcyone, her father ordered the winds to stay calm during the brooding period so that the floating nest of the kingfishers would not be disturbed. Calm summer days are still known as "halcyon days."

Two aspects of this briny legend are misleading. The kingfisher is not a seabird. Its toes are not webbed, thus it can't propel through water the way real seabirds can. Although the belted kingfisher does nest near sheltered watercourses, both salt- and freshwater, the nests do not float as in the myth.

However, the kingfisher's nesting behavior is intriguing. Using its strong bill and feet, the bird digs a horizontal tube or burrow into a sandy cliff or protected riverbank. The bird's feet are especially adapted for digging with two forward-pointing toes fused together for strength. As the birds excavate, telltale blasts of sand are kicked out of the hole. The burrow typically extends three to six feet into the bank, but can be as long as fifteen feet. Both the male and female help construct it. Once it's built, the couple assembles a nesting saucer of grass or leaves deep in the hole where the female lays six to seven white eggs. Kingfisher eggs require a relatively long incubation period, up to twenty-four days, before hatching.

After three weeks in the burrow, the young leave the nest and fishing lessons begin. The parents drop dead prey into the water for the fledglings to practice retrieving. After only ten days of training, the young birds are able to catch live fish and survive on their own. The parents then force the young from the home territory. The young disperse to find and claim their own feeding territory. In areas where the water remains free of ice and food is available, kingfishers stay year-round. In colder parts of the West the birds migrate south. Here in Puget Sound where winters are mild, the rattling call can pierce the morning air during any month of the year.

When I finished my tea and returned inside to my office, I looked up what one of my favorite nature writers, Henry David Thoreau, wrote about kingfishers. In April of 1854, the year he published *Walden*, he observed the same species of kingfisher that we enjoy here in the West:

> The kingfisher flies with a crack cr-r-r-ack and a limping or flitting flight from tree to tree before us, and finally, after a third of a mile, circles round to our rear. He sits rather low over the water. Now that he has come I suppose that the fishes on which he preys rise within reach.

It's nice to know that some morning enjoyments don't change with time or miles.

HERON WISDOM

When one tugs at a single thing in nature,

he finds it attached to the rest of the world.

—*John Muir*

For generations my mother's family summered at a cabin located about a mile south of where I now live on Whidbey Island. When I was a child, many weekends and a part of my father's limited two-week vacation were spent at the beach cabin. It was there that one of my earliest bird-related experiences occurred.

I remember sitting at low tide on the warm, sandy beach, looking out over the wide mudflats. I must have been about six. Near the water's edge a large heron, which I later learned was a great blue heron, stood frozen. Knee-deep in the calm water, the magnificent creature stretched its long brown-gray neck out over the water in front, then cocked its head to an odd, unbalanced angle watching for fish under the water's surface. It waited and I watched, thinking it would surely topple over. Then there was a flash and wham! The heron's sharp bill jabbed into the water and emerged with a small, wide fish, probably a sole. It shuffled the fish in its beak, then swallowed it whole, with a forward-jerking movement. I scrunched up my face, thinking about the spiny fish slithering down the heron's long throat. A few moments later, just as the heron finished its meal, a neighbor's dog exploded onto the beach and frightened the giant bird into flight. Its gangly frame lifted awkwardly, gaining both momentum and height as its pterodactyl-like call, "krohnk, krohnk, krohnk, krohnk," sounded over the water. Leaping to my feet, I scolded the dog, but my soft voice had little influence over its retriever instinct.

I looked skyward to watch the now graceful, deep-winged flight of the heron and decided this long-legged solitary aviator was a special creature. The heron radiated a mysterious intensity, both strong and quiet. Like me, it was an observer. At that young age I sensed that the heron and I, so different from each other, were connected to the same sandy beach and, therefore, were somehow related. I vowed to watch for it and protect it from the dogs.

The great blue heron, sometimes mistakenly called a crane or an egret, is one of the most often noticed birds. Its penchant for standing still on beaches and docks makes it easy to observe. Elegant yet somewhat prehistoric in appearance, the great blue is the largest heron in North America. It stands nearly four feet tall with the same six-foot wingspan as the bald eagle. Gray-blue plumage covers the heron's back and wings while its shoulders and upper legs sport patches of rusty brown. A long, snake-like neck holds a black-and-white head, with lemon yellow bill and eyes. During breeding season, filmy white plumes augment the head, neck, and back feathers.

Data from banding projects indicate that the great blue heron can survive up to twenty-three years in the wild, which makes them one of the longest-living birds. Here in the West they are permanent residents, but east of the Rockies this species generally prefers to winter in the Tropics.

What fascinates me most about the GBH—that's what birders call them—is its choice of when to be sociable and when to be alone. Most birds stake out breeding territory, keeping all intruders away while nesting. Later, during the off season, they hang out together in flocks. GBHs do the opposite. They congregate into tight colonies to breed, choosing a stand of deciduous trees usually fairly near water, where they build large, flat nests of sticks. When not breeding, GBHs spread out along fresh- and saltwater beaches, establishing and defending a feeding territory. If one heron ventures into another's feeding territory, the defender sounds its pterodactyl call and lifts into the air to chase away the intruder. Once its solitary life is reestablished, the heron settles back into a passive hunting strategy. It wades into shallow water and stands motionless waiting for prey—which are mainly fish but also frogs, snakes, crayfish, or crabs—to come into view.

The West also hosts another smaller and more secretive heron, the green heron (some books still refer to it as the green-backed heron). The green body of this chunky, short-legged bird is mixed with blue-gray and becomes chestnut around the neck. Lovely, dark-green crown feathers sometimes display a shaggy crest. The green heron prefers small bodies of fresh water with a cover of trees and shrubs for fishing. It often perches motionless in brush or on logs where its plumage provides excellent camouflage.

This pint-sized heron, one-third the size of the GBH, displays its "wisdom" in a different way. Apparently it has developed a few more brain cells, because it has an extra trick when hunting for fish, cleverly dropping a feather or twig on the surface of the water as a lure. The green heron has also been observed whittling down a twig to make it small enough to be convincing bait. The next time you see a heron, stop and take a good, long look. I'm sure you will agree that these birds are special avian treasures.

Over the years since I first noticed the GBH on the beach at my summer cabin, I've observed this widespread species many times in places as distant as Baja California, Guatemala, Oregon's Rogue River, Southern Florida, and as far north as Alaska. When I bought my new Swarovski scope last year, the first bird I observed through the lenses was a great blue heron. As it did when I was a child, this species still evokes a familiarity and I sense a tugging when I see one, reminding me of my connection to nature.

Some Native American traditions hold that herons contain the souls of wise men who have returned to the earth on mysterious pilgrimages. If true, these wise souls made a good choice: a magnificent bird with a quiet, reflective spirit capable of waiting, watching, and seeing below the surface. Perhaps the Native American tradition explains why this bird has been tugging at me all these years. In a way, these wise souls have been quietly speaking to me, encouraging me to enjoy, appreciate, and help protect nature. Perhaps the tugging of the heron has shown me that it is, as John Muir said, attached to the rest of the world.

THE BIRD-FISH CONNECTION

Oh Wilderness, have I not yet reached your center.

—Lao Tzu

As Bill and I waited to board our Seattle-to-Anchorage flight, I noticed a large percentage of the passengers carrying fishing rods, carefully protected in long, narrow cases. I too carried a case, but it was short and fat and held my spotting scope, the collapsed tripod of which Bill hauled. The man in front of us in line said he and his Florida buddies fish the Kenai River every year. By the end of our ten-day trip, I realized that in July, Alaska's Kenai Peninsula is all about fishing. Perhaps a minority of only two—Bill and myself—were looking for a bird-fish connection.

Sportfishing enthusiasts from around the world come to cast their hooks into the peninsula's rivers, all teeming with salmon traveling upstream. At the same time, Alaskan residents flock to the mouths of these rivers where they dip handheld nets into waist-high water to capture their state-allocated salmon limits. In nearby Cook Inlet, commercial fishers drape long set-nets perpendicular to the shore to snare fish as they travel toward the rivers' mouths. Offshore, skippers of commercial fishing boats drop gill nets to harvest fish traveling up the inlet. Somehow, enough salmon make it through this gauntlet to spawn and sustain the run year after year.

It was the commercial fishing that lured Bill and me to Kenai. Our Whidbey Island friends Tim and Paula Keohane have fished Cook Inlet and Prince William Sound for many years. In 1976 Paula became one of the first women to skipper her own commercial boat in the inlet. When Tim casually dropped an invitation to come north and fish with him, Bill accepted on the spot. He wanted to experience Alaskan commercial fishing firsthand. I was more interested in activity above the water, rather than the fishy depths where most everyone else's attention was focused. Except for a brief trip to Alaska years ago, I'd never been "up north" to see the northern breeding grounds of seabirds, gulls, terns, and ducks. Also, the Kenai Peninsula, the northern terminus of West Coast forests, is home to several boreal species unique to Alaska that I wanted to chase down, such as the boreal chickadee and common redpoll.

After landing in Anchorage, we rented a car for the six-hour drive down the peninsula to the town of Kenai. Our first stop, at the 564-acre Potter Marsh, offered a boardwalk over a wetland where we viewed a large duck called the canvasback, a species we commonly see back home in the winter. The mottled-brown female duck dove into the shallow marsh to lift up aquatic vegetation for her flock of young to nibble. Mallards and grebes also searched for their midday meal. The marsh was teaming with birds, but my favorite observation was a close-up look at two downy gray baby mew gulls. They called plaintively as their parents flew off to fish the nearby Cook Inlet's open waters.

Returning to the car, we drove south along Turnagain Arm, a long, narrow, winding fjord, passing huge glacier-covered mountains, snowfields that extended down to the highway, cascading waterfalls, and sparkling waters. A herd of eight scruffy Dall's sheep fed on a grassy patch next to the road. Along the way, we lingered at Tern Lake, where the road to Seward intersects the Kenai-to-Homer highway. Deeper than the Potter Marsh, this lake attracted arctic terns that wheeled through the air, then dove straight into the water for fish. This champion traveler, which depends solely on fish to survive, migrates 31,000 miles on its round-trip flight from northern breeding grounds to winter near the Antarctic ice pack. On the lake's marshy perimeter, common loon parents took turns diving for fish among clumps of bright-green grass and doting over two preteens. All these species had flown north for the fishing, as had so many humans.

That evening as we settled into our room at a bed-and-breakfast near the town of Kenai, I noticed heavily lined block-out curtains. In Alaska during July, instead of flipping a switch to turn out the lights at bedtime, one shuts the blinds to block out the midnight sun. In fact, during our ten-day visit, I don't remember seeing darkness. As someone accustomed to watching the sun rise from one horizon, arc across the sky, and set on the opposite horizon, I was fascinated by the Alaskan summer sun. Here the giant orb followed a leisurely route. After barely gaining elevation above the northern horizon, it circles wide around to the south, then continues circling before easing down to the horizon near where it launched. For a few hours in the middle of the night the sun dips below the horizon, leaving a glow lingering in the sky. Breeding birds take advantage of the twenty hours of sunlight to feed their fast-growing young, presumably one of the primary reasons why they migrated to these northern climes in the first place.

During the days when Bill fished with Tim, I hiked trails near the bed-and-breakfast to seek out forest birds. My favorite trail descended a hill through a mixed forest of familiar alder and cottonwood to the Kenai River delta, but the dominant tree was an unfamiliar tall, black pipe cleaner, which I recognized as a black spruce. On my first morning jaunt, I easily found a gray-brown backed boreal chickadee that was conspicuously perched on a tall spire of fireweed and pierced each pink blossom with its bill in its search for nectar. When its cousin, the familiar black-capped chickadee, called from a nearby spruce, I studied the differences between the two birds. Four quiet gray jays then swooped through the cottonwood trees. These jays, mountain birds of the lower forty-eight, inhabit low elevations here in the northlands. Evidently these soft-spoken cousins haven't heard that jays are supposed to be loud and raucous.

Near the river, I noticed a small brown finch-like bird and almost ignored it, thinking it must be just another boring house finch. Then remembering that house finches don't extend this far north, I looked again. As the bird preened in a willow tree, the sun glanced off its forehead showing a brilliant crimson cap. I had almost missed my first sighting of a common redpoll.

Each morning and evening from the deck off our room I gazed over the Kenai River flats through my spotting scope. Without fail I would see a sandhill crane foursome, two adults and two full-sized young, grazing and announcing their position with a trumpeting call. Caribou also fed in the marshy fields.

When Bill wasn't fishing with Tim, he and I hiked in the mountains, walked on the beach, and explored freshwater lakes. In the lakes we were delighted to encounter our scoter friends from Puget Sound. Here in these much calmer waters is where they nested. On a hike through a lowland forest we encountered a large female moose, up-close and personal. Striding along a trail, we rounded a corner and came face-to-nose with the beast. For a moment, a long, wrinkly, hairy jaw loomed above me, then the moose bolted off into the underbrush while I leapt into the air and grabbed Bill for protection. I'm still not sure which of the three of us was more surprised.

The highlight of our Alaskan adventure was a boat trip from Seward to observe marine mammals and nesting seabirds. Here was the rugged Alaska I was looking for, the raw, remote, geologically new edge where the cold forbidding North Pacific pounded against the steep cliffs of the Kenai coast. Motoring south through Resurrection Bay, Bill and I stood on the windy deck and watched sea otters roll on their backs and tumble through the waves, while Dall's porpoises surfed the bow wake. As black-legged kittiwakes and sooty shearwaters played in the gray skies, we passed some of the fastest moving rocks in the world. Two geographic plates come together in the middle of the bay, moving at half the speed that fingernails grow.

We turned west along the rugged, glacier-capped edge of Kenai Fjords National Park, and heavy rain forced us to retreat inside the cabin. The boat dipped into swells from the open ocean and sent waves of salt spray across the bow. Motoring into Aialik Bay, we stopped to watch a calving glacier—an immense wall of bluish ice, broken and cracked with chunks the size of ten-story office buildings breaking off and plunging into the bay. Next we departed the bay and headed out to the Chiswell Islands, nesting grounds for more than 50,000 seabirds. We approached an offshore island surrounded by sheer black cliffs that dropped so steeply into the water that the sixty-foot boat could maneuver close to them. Even in the protected bay, the water roiled beneath us, but Bill and I donned our foul-weather gear and staggered back on deck. For several minutes I scanned the black cliffs through a heavy, gray rain, looking for dots of white, the heads of horned and tufted puffins. The heaving boat made using binoculars impossible, but by straining my eyes and with the help of Bill, who is blessed with excellent distance vision, I could pick out the long, creamy tufts on the tufted puffins that distinguish them from the horned puffins. The latter bird was a first sighting for both of us, and we exchanged rain-soaked smiles. Then we looked down into the churning black water and noticed a cormorant diving for fish. We had been hoping to see another new species, the red-faced cormorant. It took several concentrated but quick looks as the bird surfaced between dives before we were convinced of our second new sighting. Later a parakeet auklet, a small, dark seabird with a blood-red bill, became our third life bird of the day. Still we motored past large colonies of common murres, their nests carefully positioned on the cliffs so there was a safety net of water below, rather than rocks. The first flight attempts of their offspring are often unsuccessful.

On our return to Seward the clouds remained low, obscuring

the 1,000-square-mile Harding Ice Field, the largest in the United States, which tops the coastal range that we passed. Despite this disappointment, we returned with images of seabirds, gulls, and kittiwakes crowding the ledges and swirling together in huge balls to dive for food.

On our last evening in Alaska, we stopped by the local Kenai harbor to watch the fishing fleet offload their catch. At 10:15 P.M. the sun still shone and the birdwatching was excellent. Gulls, knowing the arrival of the fishing boats signaled an opportunity for a handout, flew wide circular patterns ready to dart in for scraps. Every twenty minutes or so a parasitic jaeger, a darker, faster gull relative, blasted through the air above the harbor, chasing gulls until they coughed up their scavenged morsels.

Driving back to Anchorage, I began to think about the bird-fish connection. More than 13 percent of the bird species in North America survive by eating fish; many more consume aquatic vegetation and invertebrates. We'd seen this aquatic food chain in action, spurred by the midnight sun: loons, grebes, scoters, and terns fishing in calm freshwater marshes, seabirds and cormorants feeding in roiling saltwater coves, gulls scrounging for bits of dead fish in the harbor, and a jaeger stealing fish bits from the gulls. The Kenai Peninsula is, in fact, all about fishing, but we humans aren't the only fishers.

When we arrived at the Anchorage airport, we checked in a forty-pound box of Tim's frozen salmon. And safely tucked in Bill's suitcase were two of Paula's brine recipes for smoking the salmon. Many other returning passengers hauled in boxes and coolers of fish. As I looked around the waiting room I guessed that most of these people had only focused on the underwater half of wild Alaska. We, however, also brought home a list of sixty-three bird species, including six new bird sightings for our life lists. And with that list came a deeper understanding of an eons-old, intricate connection between what swims in the sea and what flies above it.

Brushed by Feathers

CHAPTER EIGHT

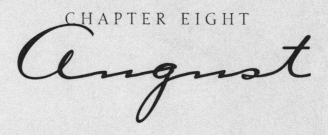

August

The early morning is a whisper cooler. A lazier sun rises over the north end of Hat Island. Alder and maple leaves have traded their spring emerald for a dry, faded olive. Without my noticing, ocean spray blossoms have metamorphosed from upright, vanilla whipped cream swirls to floppy caramel clusters. The dry, unkempt stubble of weeds we call lawn no longer satisfies the bunnies that now nibble at my heather, ferns, and ornamental grasses. I leave them alone: the August doldrums have arrived.

Snoozing western sandpiper

Adult birds, mostly retired from parenting duties, look spent, their breeding plumage faded from months of nest tending. Juvenile birds that are wearing their first, drab plumage also lack color.

Sitting on the back deck, I hear the "kuk kuk kuk" call of a large, red-crested pileated woodpecker from the direction of the Douglas fir trees that hold fast to the edge of our bluff. As I look in the direction of the call, something doesn't jibe. Beyond the firs, a woodpecker attempts to perch in the limp, gangly outer branches of a young wild cherry tree. I laugh as I watch the silly bird going after the red fruit. Its claws, so perfectly adapted to grasp the flat surface of tree trunks with both forward- and backward-facing toes, can't manage the thin, flexible branches. Plus the woodpecker's heavy body bends the branches, causing the bird to flap its large wings to maintain position. A second woodpecker, probably the parent, properly positioned on the Douglas fir trunk calls again, and the explorer returns to familiar territory.

Red-crested pileated woodpecker

August is the month when young birds attempt strange things, perhaps sorting out the ways in which their species is best adapted to behave. Some birds go exploring and end up in unusual places. I call it August Walkabout. Yesterday I received an e-mail from a woman who saw a "white heron" while golfing at a course not far from here. "It was up in a tree. Could it be an albino great blue heron?" she asked. I trolled my brain for an explanation. Then I remembered it was August. Occasionally around this time of year, great egrets wander over from the eastern side of the Cascades for a vacation at the beach. Long-tailed mourning doves are common on Whidbey Island, but don't come to our feeders, except in August. Late in the month, ravens roam away from their nesting territories and on rare occasions explore our bluff, noticeable by their low "cronk, cronk" from beyond the treetops.

Other birds have their work cut out for them in August: south-bound migration. Early migrating shorebirds start trickling south in mid-to late July. Their numbers build in August, and by September clouds of them fill the migration routes. For the first time since last spring, I heard the early morning yodeling call of a loon when I paused on my deck this dawn. Later I saw eight spotted sandpipers stopping to feed on our beach and a single horned grebe offshore as it headed south. Occasionally, high above our bluff a turkey vulture floats south on thermals after spending the summer farther north, perhaps in the San Juan Islands or on British Columbia's Vancouver Island.

A small percentage of birds diverge from their typical migration routes and land, at least for a time, off the beaten path. Last year, while watering a newly planted azalea, a yellow-rumped warbler, stopping by on its fall migration, darted in to take a bath in the hose spray. I'm guessing it was a juvenile from the far north who hadn't developed a fear of humans. That same year, a lemon yellow Wilson's warbler, which typically consumes insects, visited our seed feeder for several days.

This last full month of summer is also the time we get the most window fatalities. A couple of times a day I'm startled from my work by a thud against our family room windows. First-year birds testing their wings often hit the windows and fall to the ground dazed. Most manage to hop up and fly off again, their slower speed and flexibility seemingly saving them. (I place decals on the windows and hang brightly colored ribbons or glittery dangling ornaments to divert the birds away from the windows. Closing blinds also helps.)

During August Walka-bout we also have adult strangers to the neighborhood who crash at full speed and occasionally don't recover. One year a beautiful male Cooper's hawk died after hitting an upstairs window. I sealed the bird in a plastic bag and labeled it with the date, location, and my contact

Common raven

151

information. Later a friend dropped the bag at Seattle's Burke Museum of Natural History and Culture to add to its collection of bird skins.

Glaucous-winged gull

This month we head to the beach to do some lazy beach birding. Along with the shorebirds heading south, the first of the fall gulls have arrived on the coast and it's time to put down your summer reading and take up a challenge: gull identification. Swallows are more visible this month, gathering on electrical wires before heading south to their winter homes in the Tropics, so we'll focus on the common swallow species. Also, I tell the tale of our avian housemates during our house remodel.

Birds introduced this month:

❑ Brown Pelican *(Pelecanus occidentalis)*

❑ Heermann's Gull *(Larus heermanni)*

❑ Mew Gull *(Larus canus)*

❑ Ring-billed Gull *(Larus delawarensis)*

❑ California Gull *(Larus californicus)*

❑ Glaucous-winged Gull *(Larus glaucescens)*

❑ Western Gull *(Larus occidentalis)*

❑ Thayer's Gull *(Larus thayeri)*

❑ Herring Gull *(Larus argentatus)*

❑ Bonaparte's Gull *(Larus philadelphia)*

❑ Violet-green Swallow *(Tachycineta thalassina)*

❑ Barn Swallow *(Hirundo rustica)*

GULLS REALLY CAN BE
IDENTIFIED

Whosoever wishes to know about the world

must learn about it in its particular details.

—Heraklietos of Epbesos

My first attempt at beach birding was frustrating. It was 1967, and I was living in California's Ojai Valley near Santa Barbara. About noon I donned a bikini under my loose cotton miniskirt, tossed my binoculars and field guide into a beach bag, hopped in my lemon yellow Volkswagen bug convertible, and drove forty minutes to my favorite surfing beach. The mid-afternoon sun glared off cresting waves whipped up by a strong north wind. But I didn't see a single bird. So I flopped down on the warm sand and lathered myself with sun lotion. The binoculars worked fine for watching the surfers, but by the end of the afternoon they made a scratchy sound when I changed the focus; sand particles lubricated with sunscreen had worked their way into the moving parts. Just as I was packing to leave, a line of fifteen brown pelicans flapped and glided just above the tops of the waves, the only species for my bird list. The surf, strong wind, and human activity kept any other birds away.

My next coastal birdwatching trip, in Oregon near Lincoln City about five years later, was frustrating in a different way. The fall weather was calm, cold, and drizzly; however, I ventured out on the sandy beach to look at seagulls. I was able to approach quite close to the large birds, sat on a beach log, and took out my field guide and binoculars—I'd had them cleaned—and watched the large birds eat some soggy French fries left by picnickers. Then I searched for *seagull* in the index of my field guide. There was no listing, so I paged through to find pictures. There were pages and pages of pictures of seagulls. For the next fifteen minutes I looked at the birds, then at the pictures, and then back at the birds, but I couldn't distinguish between the different species. They all looked alike. Frustrated, I slammed the book closed and retreated back to town for a warm cup of coffee.

Fast-forward thirty-some years. The bikini is long gone, replaced by a more conservative one-piece suit. I've bought new binoculars and learned how to keep them clean. My sporty little Volkswagen bug got traded for a more practical family-style station wagon. And I've spent many beach holidays watching gulls and gleaning the fine points of their identification.

There's no doubt gulls have a bad rap with bird-watchers who are trying to identify specific species. Beginners don't even attempt to separate the nine species appearing regularly along the West Coast. Intermediate birders shrug their shoulders, and even experts can't always agree on identification of sub-adult or hybrid species. The differences between species are often quite subtle; they do pretty much look the same with a white body and gray back and wings. They also usually have a yellow bill and pink or yellow legs and feet and, just to make it more confusing, some gulls are mottled brown. But don't give up like I did back on the Oregon coast. Gulls really can be identified. Stick with me to the end of this chapter, and I'll provide the tools to identify most adult gulls seen along the West Coast.

Here's the single most important thing to know about gull identification: there is only one seagull. You find it in bookstores and its full name is Jonathan Livingston Seagull. All the rest are *gulls*. As I learned back on the Oregon coast, the word *seagull* can't be found in birding guides. That bit of knowledge already moves you from the beginner to intermediate level of *gull* identification.

Imagine the typical gray-and-white gull sitting on a piling at the wharf or flying near interior lakes; these are adult gulls. The brownish ones are young gulls—one, two, or three years old—that have not developed their adult plumage. We won't tackle the details of identifying young gulls in this book. If you need a name for them, call them "immature gull species." Even the experts get away with that on the Audubon Society's annual Christmas Bird Count.

A brief, broad-brush explanation of habitat and migration helps with gull identification. Most gull species of the western United States breed in Alaska, northwestern Canada, or the western interior states, and for the fall and winter move south and west into bays and estuaries along the Pacific Coast. Only a couple of species actually breed along the West Coast, making adult gull identification during May through early July quite simple. In the greater Puget Sound region, for example, the glaucous-winged gull is the only breeder. So during those months the typical "fish-and-chips-shack" gull will most likely be the glaucous-winged gull. South of Puget Sound along the Washington, Oregon, and California coasts, the western gull is the only common breeder. Voila! You are a gull expert for two months. Beginning in July, the arrival of migrant gulls will begin to compromise your expert status. So, either keep your mouth closed for the other ten months of the year, or read on.

Before those migrants arrive, get a good grasp on the identification of the glaucous-winged and western gulls. The word "glaucous" means gray. Granted, almost all gull species have gray wings, but this is the only gull commonly found along the West Coast with gray wings *and wing tips*. So think of this gull as the glaucous-winged (tipped) gull. (On a standing gull the wing tips appear at the very rear and might be confused with the tail.) The other gulls all sport very dark or black wing tips, many with white dots. The glaucous-winged gull is also the largest and heaviest gull in our area, twenty-six inches long and 2.2 pounds. The western gull, only slightly smaller at twenty-five inches, has a charcoal gray back and wings and black wing tips. Both these gulls have pink legs. The glaucous-winged gull (found in the Puget Sound and farther north) and western gull (found south of Puget Sound) don't migrate away and will remain the most common gulls in their areas.

Ready for the migrants? Pull out your field guide and take a close look at the California gull, mew gull, and the ring-billed gull. Okay, I know they all look superficially the same—white heads, fronts, and tails with gray backs—but there *are* differences. To keep our expert status we need to look at detail. Focus on the color of the wing tips, legs, and bill; also, begin to get a sense of relative size. Picky, picky, I know, but at least I'm not asking you to look at the color of the eye, which most field guides mention.

The twenty-one-inch, mid-sized California gull breeds in the interior of Washington and Oregon and throughout Idaho, Montana, and Alberta. It spends the nonbreeding season along the West Coast from southern British Columbia south. When it arrives in July, notice the gray back, black wing tips, and *greenish legs*. Any other gull with gray-green or greenish yellow legs? Nope.

The mew gull is one of our smallest gulls at sixteen inches, about the size of a small crow. This gull migrates a longer distance since it breeds in Alaska and northwestern Canada. This diminutive gull has yellow legs. Don't get too excited yet—there are other gulls with yellow legs—but this one also has a plain yellow bill. Remember: yellow legs and plain yellow bill. This gull also has a fairly large white spot on the wing tip, decreasing the amount of black on the wing tip.

The third mid-summer migrant is the ring-billed gull, which also arrives from the western interior. This smallish-sized gull is similar to the mew gull with yellow legs, but it has a black ring on its yellow bill. So far it's not too difficult, right?

Let's review gull populations in August. There are four common gulls, in three size ranges. About 70 percent of all the gulls will be either the big, bulky glaucous-winged (tipped) gull or the western gull. Fifteen percent will be the mid-sized California gull with dull greenish legs. Another 10 percent are divided between the cute little mew gulls, with yellow legs and a plain yellow bill, and the ring-billed gull, with the ring around its bill. Also in August we begin seeing the distinctive and much smaller Bonaparte's gull. With its swift, darting flight manner, this gull acts more like a tern than a gull. In fall it joins into large flocks. The Bonaparte's gull does not wear the typical plumage we have been discussing. Instead it sports a solid black head and bill and bright red legs and feet. During its fall molt, the bird loses the black hood but retains a black splash behind the eye.

Later in the fall, gull identification gets more complicated. Still, the most common species are our good friends the glaucous-winged (tipped) gull or the western gull; the second most common are the mew and ring-billed gulls. By now most of the California gulls have moved south into California for the winter.

We need to examine two more very similar gulls: the Thayer's gull and the herring gull. The rest of the world has no difficulty separating these two species, but here on the West Coast, the only place where they both live, it's tricky. They used to be combined into one species; they were all just herring gulls. Both species are pale gray with pinkish legs, nearly as large as the western gull. The Thayer's gull's legs can be brighter, almost bubble gum–pink, and the back is slightly darker than the herring gull's, but both gulls are variable and these identification pointers don't always work. The underside of the Thayer's wing tips is paler gray, but most bird-watchers, myself included, have trouble seeing this. I vote we put them back into the same species and call them all herring gulls like we used to.

One very different looking gull pauses along the West Coast on its fall migration and winters in California: the Heermann's gull. The size, shape, and jizz tell you it's a gull, but the gray-brown body and dark-red bill separate it from the typical fish-and-chips gulls and make it easy to distinguish.

There you have it, nine gull species that account for 98 percent of the adult gulls along the West Coast. Some good news with gull identification is that the sexes look alike. You don't have to distinguish between the gulls and the boys. If you have trouble telling the gulls from the *buoys*, I suggest you get some better binoculars.

REMODELING WITH BIRDS

It is not the strongest of the species that survive,

nor the most intelligent,

but the one most responsive to change.

—*Charles Darwin*

As Aretha Franklin blared on the boom box, Chad was up on the roof cutting skylights with a chainsaw while Jeff was down below pounding in window frames with a pneumatic hammer. Amidst all this chaos, Mamma Barn Swallow stuffed insects into her babies' insistent mouths up under the eaves. Who would have thought?

When Bill and I purchased our bluff home with white stucco walls and fake red-tile roof, it resembled a tired Taco Bell stand. I loved the view; Bill had dreams for the large storage shed that could house a woodworking and stone-carving workshop. We started planning the remodel soon after we bought it, the project finally coming to fruition a few years later.

When the construction crew arrived, I worried that the project would scare away the feathered friends that nest on or near our home. That spring I carefully watched the nesting activities of birds around the house and was amazed at the results. By the time the eight-month project ended, the scorecard for the breeding season showed one loss, one reposition, and two gains. Evidently the avian population "approved" of our design to turn the Taco Bell stand into a Spanish mission–style house.

Before the remodel, our home hosted two bird species. Each year barn swallows produced one or two batches of babies in a mud nest above our front door, while American robins established their abode in a well-protected wisteria vine under the eaves of the garage. We tried to invite more nesting bird life by setting out bird boxes. But the violet-green swallows' nest box above the garage was regularly shunned, and a hanging wren box on our eastward facing deck was royally snubbed. However, after Chad, Jeff, and Aretha arrived, the birds evidently decided that something exciting was happening and fluttered over to join the action. A chestnut-backed chickadee couple immediately asserted squatter's rights in the wren box. Unfortunately, the box hung near the site of a new sunroom we were constructing. The chickadees held their ground until a concrete pump truck arrived with a twenty-foot boom. Deciding that this metal tree branch flying around overhead was not the best environment for raising their expected brood, the chestnut-backed chickadees retreated, but didn't go far, finding lesser quarters in the violet-green swallow box over the garage. There they produced and fledged a full quota of four babies.

At about the same time, the barn swallows returned from Central and South America and discovered the front doorway piled to the eaves with batts of insulation. Despite much twittering and scolding, the swallows couldn't convince Chad and Jeff to remove the offending barrier. So, ever resourceful, the swallows moved around back, which offered unobstructed eaves and spectacular views. Those frazzled parents seemed to relax a bit when Aretha sang the blues, and they ultimately produced two batches of young.

The violet-green swallows, a different member of the swallow family, migrated back later in the spring. They hit town just about the time the chickadees finished nesting. Having paid no attention to "their" box in the past, they ensconced themselves the minute the chickadees left. A quick rearrangement of the furniture was all the swallows needed. Five weeks later, three babies fledged with a lilt of "R-E-S-P-E-C-T" in their song.

When Chad and Jeff finished and left, the only avian loss was the American robin. Their favorite wisteria bush had been removed, and they didn't attempt any other spot that year. Guess they didn't appreciate the pounding, or maybe they prefer country western music instead of Motown. The final tally for that nesting season: we kept the barn swallows, gained the chestnut-backed chickadees and violet-green swallows, and lost the robins.

The following spring the robins returned to a thick Douglas fir tree near the garage, and they've nested in a protected spot nearby each year since. The barn swallows maintain their nest under the back eaves year after year. However, most springs the chestnut-backed chickadees and the violet-green swallows ignore their (shared) nest box. No birds have shown interest in the wren box, so we are back to housing only two species (plus Rocky the pigeon) as we did before the remodel.

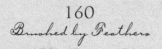

I often think back to the noisy summer and wonder about the nesting activity that accompanied our remodel project. I've considered inviting Chad and Jeff back to increase the activity level, or perhaps I'll play Aretha on full volume to advertise my home to more species. But if that doesn't work, I draw the line at climbing onto the roof with a chainsaw.

NESTING ABOVE
THE FRONT DOOR

Swallow means porch-bird, and for centuries

and centuries their nests have been placed

in the closest proximity to man.

They might be called man's birds,

so attached are they to the human race.

I think the greatest ornament a house can have

is the nest of an eave-swallow under the eaves—

far superior to the most elaborate carving, coloring,

or arrangement the architect can devise.

—Richard Jeffries,
The Open Air, *1885*

I worked out a compromise with Ma and Pa Barn Swallow this year. Each spring I welcome these V-tailed super-fliers to my house to raise their young. But this year, after they began slapping mud on the new light fixture above the front door, I decided to relocate the welcome mat. Knowing these long-distance migrants are flexible, I encouraged them to move their accommodations.

I usually don't mind stepping over their droppings just about anywhere, but I draw the line at the front door. I hung a six-inch plastic strip in their flight path to encourage them to flutter around to the back deck where, for a while, they considered nesting above the barbecue. After a couple of conveniently timed grilled dinners, they decided that the heat and activity were incompatible with their potential family needs. This coaxed them to the perfect spot for both the birds and me, under the eaves just outside my bedroom.

Barn swallows and the other five swallows that summer throughout the West—tree, northern rough-winged, violet-green, bank, and cliff—are neotropical migrants. They breed in the United States and

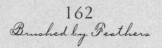

Canada and winter in Mexico, Central America, and South America. All swallows depend on insects for food, so they provide an invaluable free service for us by keeping insect populations under control. Swallows often arrive at their northern breeding ranges just as insect populations begin to hatch. The birds depart when cold weather forces insects into a dormant life cycle stage, thereby decreasing available food supply.

The most celebrated arrival of swallows are those that come, year after year, to the old Spanish mission of San Juan Capistrano in southern California. Like clockwork, a large colony of cliff swallows swoops into town on March 19, St. Joseph's Day, to build nests and raise young in the old church buildings.

Although the swallows of San Juan Capistrano continue to arrive on schedule, the migratory timing of some birds has changed. Scientists, who have studied records of arrival dates during the last thirty years, see new patterns. One study of twenty migrants, including barn swallows, found that the birds arrived up to twenty-one days earlier in 1994 than in 1965. Tree swallows, another local breeder, nest on average nine days earlier than they did thirty years ago.

Scientists have also found that in recent years many birds are breeding farther north. The band of favorable habitat for nesting and raising young is moving into cooler zones. If this trend continues, our country may experience a loss of bird species as breeding birds move north into Canada. The Baltimore oriole could disappear from Baltimore and Washington's state bird, the American goldfinch, may become difficult to find in this state. Many scientists relate these changes to global warming.

Another concern that stems from global warming is that many birds won't be able to adjust if habitats change and disappear. If sea level rises somewhere between 3.5 inches to 2.9 feet in this century, as various scientists project, coastal marshes and estuaries that now support millions of waterfowl and other birds could change dramatically. For many bird species—already stressed by loss of habitat—this could be the last straw. Like the proverbial "canary in the mine shaft," birds provide early warnings regarding changes to our environment. Their documented responses to climate change may well be signals that global warming should be a very real concern.

As I sat on my back deck and watched Ma and Pa Barn Swallow swoop out from their nest and dart after mosquitoes and gnats, I contemplated the balance we humans must continually attempt to strike between consumption of resources and stewardship of the earth for wildlife. Encouraging the barn swallows to nest on the back of our house rather than the front benefited us both. It is not always that easy to find a win-win solution. Yet, we must keep trying.

CHAPTER NINE

September

September 21 marks the autumnal equinox, midway between the early dawn of June and the late sunrises of December. The sun now emerges at 6:56 A.M. to the south of Mount Pilchuck, halfway between the boundaries of Mount Index to the south and Whitehorse to the north. The cobalt blue sky holds round, fluffy cumulus clouds with flat bottoms that look like a machete-wielding giant chopped off their bottoms. These clouds always remind me of my friend Larry who once asked if I knew why the clouds had flat bottoms. When I couldn't answer right away he responded, "So they won't tip over."

We've just enjoyed three solid weeks of sunshine, what my mother used to call an Indian summer. Looking out the window toward the maples and alders heavy with green leaves and interspersed with clear vistas stretching to the Cascades, I'd guess it still was August. But once I move outside, no illusion remains. More than the cooler temperatures—the thin, sharp air reminds me of biting into a crisp apple—it's the smells that define September.

September manifests what I call a

Wild blackberries

ripe blackberry smell, dry and lusciously fruity. Stepping off the deck, the scent draws me around the house to the meadow where wild blackberries hang in tempting bunches. The scent also brings to mind a lesson on selecting ripe blackberries offered by my father years ago. He explained, probably following my ingesting a few unripe and very sour berries, that you can tell if a berry is sweet by look and touch. First the berry must have a slightly dulled satin finish, not shiny black. Also, the berry must drop off into your fingers with just the slightest tug. His message still with me, I carefully reach between thorny vines to the deep purple fruit and select the ripest, sweetest berries to add to my morning cereal.

Along with the warm, fruity smell, a medley of grassy, dusty-harvest dryness permeates the air. Over the previous months, the weedy meadow has dried to bunnylike dappled brown, seemingly perfect camouflage for the furry creatures. Perhaps they unwisely depend on this for safety, given that last week Bill watched a Cooper's hawk catch a young rabbit just eight feet outside our sunroom window.

Finally, near the end of the month, the rains come—a soft, steady drizzle that awakens new fall smells, musty like an unheated cabin that has been closed up for the winter. On my morning walk along the county road, I step around slugs also awakened by the climate change. They come from nowhere and unknowingly travel across the road where they are smashed by the hundreds. The native, six- to eight-inch-long banana slug, more Dijon mustard than banana colored, glides around looking for detritus to consume. The smaller, nonnative black slugs swarm to my vegetable garden to munch fall lettuce, brussel sprouts, and droopy beet tops. Today a banana slug oozes up the window next to the bird feeder, leaving a slime trail. It must be enjoying the smooth sailing of the glass, or perhaps it is scheming how it will make a quick jump to the feeder.

If August is quiet of bird songs, September is dead. Breeding season has finished for the year, and with no demands from their young for feeding, the resident birds slip quietly through a lazy fall routine. During the non-breeding season, the section of a songbird's brain that controls singing actually shrinks, making it unable to sing, even if the urge arose. Many adult migrants head south as soon as parenting responsibilities end, and their offspring follow soon after. If spring migration is exciting and attention grabbing with new species arriving day by day, the fall exodus is the opposite. The nomads just quietly depart. As the month progresses, a few waves of warblers or swallows from farther north quietly pass through as they also head south. Many birds go through a fall molt in September. Old, worn-out feathers drop out to be replaced by new ones. Yesterday I watched a great blue heron fly overhead, gaps in its outstretched wings reminding me of a five-year-old's toothless grin.

Rocky seems languorous and pouty. He too is molting. None of his usual gentle cooing can be heard, and he hangs out on the lamp fixture longer in the morning. Instead of a robust burst of energy as he takes off for his morning exercise out over the bluff, he flutters softly to the deck table, perhaps stopping to check what flight feathers have dropped out during his morning preening. Like a crusty old bachelor who doesn't bother to bathe every morning, Rocky now rarely flies around to the front of the house and the three-tiered faux-Mexican fountain for his morning splash. Instead, at molting time, he just returns to the light fixture and waits patiently for his new feathers to grow in. The area under his favorite light fixture looks like someone dumped out the insides of a feather pillow. He is almost bare around the neck, causing visitors to ask, "Is your pigeon sick?"

"No," I reply, "just changing clothes."

Banana slug

Great blue heron

Birds introduced this month:

❑ Double-crested Cormorant *(Phalacrocorax auritus)*

❑ Osprey *(Pandion haliaetus)*

❑ Common Raven *(Corvus corax)*

❑ Western Bluebird *(Sialia mexicana)*

❑ Mountain Bluebird *(Sialia currucoides)*

❑ Brown Thrasher *(Toxostoma rufum)*

BIRDS AND BASEBALL

The only connection that I remember between birds and base-
ball was when Randy Johnson, pitcher for the Arizona Dia-
mondbacks, hit a dove with one of his fast balls. It was an
exhibition game with the San Francisco Giants when the Big
Unit beaned that bird. Pretty amazing pitching that was!

—Bill Graves, baseball fan

Bill realized soon after we met that I loved birdwatching, and I learned that he loved baseball. As our relationship developed, we came to understand that life together would have to include some of both. That's happened. Bill became a convert to birdwatching, though my enthusiasm for baseball has only advanced from cold to lukewarm. Still, I often join Bill at Seattle Mariners home games. We share excellent season tickets, just a few rows behind third base.

A couple of years ago, Bill thought that having a real baseball cap might make me a more avid fan. He correctly guessed that the Mariners' compass insignia wouldn't do it for me. So, after considering all the team hats, he decided on a Baltimore Orioles cap with a bright orange-and-black oriole on the front. Now when we go to an "M's" game, I wear my Orioles hat and carry my lightweight 10x25 binoculars around my neck. I'm good for a couple innings before I start looking around the stadium for something more interesting.

When the Mariners played in the enclosed Kingdome, birdwatching was limited to a flock of rock pigeons (Rocky's distant relatives) that hung out up on the top girders and an occasional house sparrow on the outside ramps pecking at peanut shells. Only if the "M's" played the Toronto Blue Jays or the Baltimore Orioles were other "birds" in sight.

The Kingdome's dearth of birdwatching opportunities allowed me plenty of time to contemplate the use of birds as sports team names. In major league baseball only three teams selected bird names. Toronto chose the blue jays, an eastern cousin to our western Steller's or scrub jays. Feisty birds, known for stealing eggs from others birds' nests and fighting off much larger birds, jays are a good choice for a team moniker. It seems the name has helped the Toronto team. Bill told me they won the World Series not too long ago. Saint Louis selected the watermelon-red cardinal as their team symbol. This eastern and southern U.S. bird is not known for being aggressive; it is really just a pretty face. Saint Louis should have known that. They have had some showy faces, such as home-run hitter Mark McGuire, but that has not translated into any recent World Series appearances. The Baltimore oriole (there really is such a species of bird) is known for making elaborately woven nests. These birds expend much time and effort building beautiful homes. Not surprisingly, the Baltimore Orioles baseball team occupies what is generally considered to be one of baseball's finest ballparks, Camden Yards.

None of these baseball teams expresses the pizzazz that some football teams have shown when selecting bird names. A sea hawk, the bird moniker for Seattle's team, is a colloquial name for the osprey, which can fly at great speed and builds large, showy nests near water on tops of trees, cliffs, or poles. The Atlanta Falcons and the Philadelphia Eagles also have strong, aggressive birds as their symbols. But look at Arizona, another team of pretty cardinals. They should have learned from the baseball team. Baltimore's football team gets my vote for choosing the most fascinating bird—the raven. Not only a strong, fearsome bird, it is considered the trickster of the avian population. And, according to many legends, it embodies mythical and supernatural powers. Perhaps this explains how the Ravens came from nowhere to win the Super Bowl in 2001.

A few college teams possess bird names, too. Three cheers for the University of Oregon Ducks. At last here's a team that can't possibly take itself too seriously as they quack, waddle, and dabble. Their symbol looks more like Donald Duck than any real species, yet in recent years they have beat up on the University of Washington Huskies more often than not and were contenders for the national championship in 2001–02. Another favorite college team name of mine is the Temple University Owls. Exceptional hunters, owls also symbolize wisdom. Some species hunt for food during the day, some at night, some both. They fly swiftly with wings that muffle any noise to allow them to sneak up on their prey.

In July of 2000, when the Mariners moved into their new home at Safeco Field, birdwatching became, shall we say, a whole new ball game. On nice afternoons or evenings with the roof retracted, the bird-watching possibilities are practically unlimited. During the second inning of the very first game in the new ballpark, an osprey flew high over the park. Later, while Edgar Martinez batted in the ninth I spotted a double-crested cormorant. Occasionally, I get so caught up in birdwatching that Bill has to nudge me to get my binoculars pointed somewhere near the baseball action.

This month, while most of the crowd is watching for foul balls, I'll be on the lookout for the fall gulls. Glaucous-winged and California gulls are common above Safeco Field, just blocks from Puget Sound. Ring-billed gulls are migrating into the area, and a mew gull or even the small Bonaparte's gull might be seen during the last weeks of the base-ball season.

Some of my best Safeco Field birdwatching occurred during a series with the Yankees last year. We had a slew of relatives in town who wanted to see the game, so we augmented our usual tickets with several extra. When I learned the extra seats were at the top of the center field bleachers, I quickly sacrificed my third-base seat to my mother-in-law. The extra seats were way out there—only with my binoculars could I see the name on the *back* of Ichiro's uniform. But the birdwatching was superb. The Mariners didn't win, but I scored with an unusual red-tailed hawk sighting. It soared directly over the ballpark, made a wide curve, and flew, flew away out over the left field wall.

Ain't birdwatching great?

WATCHING JUST ONE BIRD

One touch of nature makes the whole world kin.

—William Shakespeare

We say, "I'm going *bird* watching" not "I'm going *birds* watching." Yet the goal of most birding outings is to seek out as many bird species as possible, listing those identified and judging the success of our day by the number of species recorded. Ads for fancy birding trips to exotic locations boast the huge number of potential sightings. During May birding teams compete in the "World Series of Birding" to spot as many different species as possible within a twenty-four-hour period. In this chapter, however, I explore the joys and values of watching just one bird.

Learning to watch one bird was forced on me during an ornithology course while attending college in Illinois. Along with class lectures and early morning bird walks along the banks of the Mississippi River, Professor Doc Wanamaker required each student to monitor and report on one bird during the spring nesting season. A classmate helped me locate a male brown thrasher—obviously birding was not an innate skill of mine—as it established a nesting territory in the open deciduous woods about a mile from campus.

Each day after my last class, I'd walk or jog to the site, dripping with midwestern humidity-induced sweat by the time I reached the nesting area of the thrasher, a robin-sized bird with a reddish brown upper body, a heavily streaked breast, and a long, slightly curved beak. For nesting, the brown thrasher had chosen a grassy meadow encircled with tall trees. In the middle of the meadow, a shed-sized tangle of blackberries provided a protected nest site.

At first, my stakeout was monotonous and boring. I'd hang around for an hour or two and every thirty minutes or so "Brownie" would fly to a treetop and sing. After about a week his long, melodious song lured a female to his territory and the activity level increased. The pair chased each other from tree to tree, and once I saw one bird pick up a twig and hop toward the other while chirping and fluttering its wings. I also observed the birds carrying bits of dried grass in their beaks. I drew a map in my journal and noted the trees where Brownie perched and sang and the number of trips per hour the thrashers made into the blackberry thicket. Brown thrashers nest near the ground and choose the thickest part of the briar patch as protection from predators. If any intruder, including me, came near the thicket, Brownie loyally defended it, scolding and dive-bombing as if his life depended on it. As I continued to record my observations, I learned that every action had a purpose and the actions fell into patterns. Soon I could predict Brownie's location and what he would do next. One afternoon, after much searching and suffering scratches up and down my arms, I found the nest of dried grass and leaves deep in the thicket. Four white eggs with tiny reddish spots were nestled into the soft grassy lining.

Doc Wanamaker's mandate to pick one species and study it carefully stuck with me. Some thirty years later, I can still remember Brownie, his meadow, the trees where he perched and sang his little heart out, and the tangle of blackberries where he hid his nest. Brownie represented an individual within a species, not just a tick on my bird-watching checklist. That experience opened a window into a whole new world, which grew to include an appreciation of birds not only as beautiful objects in themselves, but also as a necessary part of an ecosystem.

Ever since Brownie opened my eyes to *bird* watching, I've observed other birds, one at a time. When I lived beside Lake Washington near Seattle, a bald eagle flew in every morning to sit in a neighbor's stand of cottonwood trees. The eagle always flew in from the south, rested for an hour or two, then departed straight east over the water. I noted in my journal what time it arrived and approximately when it left. A year or so later the property changed hands, and I heard that the new owners wanted to remove the cottonwood trees. Using my journal notes as documentation, I explained the value of the trees as an eagle perch. The new owners thinned the stand of trees but left a few for the eagles.

This September Bill and I are enjoying a family of California quail that have begun visiting our feeders. Earlier in the summer when the family first peeked out on the lawn between our house and the bluff, the eleven hatchlings couldn't have been more than a day or two old. The male quail is a dapper bird—spotted and streaked with black, white, and gray, and sporting a flashy topknot, a feather that shoots straight forward from the bird's forehead and waves around its head like a plume in a woman's hat. On that day, first the father of this family, we dubbed him Papa Quail, strutted out onto the lawn to be sure it was safe. He then stood guard, clucking softly, as the female—brownish in color with a shorter topknot—led the chicks across the exposed lawn to the north side of the house and the bird feeder. They scurried around the base of the feeder looking for spilled seed but, when Papa gave a warning call, scuttled themselves into nearby blackberry tangles.

Each day I paid careful attention to the covey. I counted to be sure all the babies were still there, and then looked closely at their soft-brown downy plumage to see if any juvenal feathers (a special molting phase between the downy hatching plumage and the adult plumage) were poking through. Gradually the downy feathers were replaced with the mottled brown-and-white juvenal plumage. And recently, the juveniles began molting into their adult plumage. Finally, the most entertaining part of this transformation was the emergence of the stubby little topknots. Like young bucks with hopelessly small stubs of antlers, the young male quails strutted around with scrawny, out-of-place feathers lifting off their foreheads. Bill and I couldn't help but be reminded of the odd teenage hairstyles of our own boys.

I'm a bit embarrassed now to admit how much pleasure Bill and I received from that quail covey. Perhaps it's because we don't have grandchildren to dote on, or perhaps it's simply because Bill is almost retired and we take more time to linger over our morning coffee and tea while watching the activity around the feeder.

One morning around the end of the month, Bill called from the kitchen, "Look, we have an interloper." A second adult male quail—we dubbed him Uncle Pete—had joined the covey. He didn't display the status or responsibility of Papa; instead he acted more like an older brother. A week later, another female and three more young allied themselves to the flock. We never figured out the relationships, if there were any, in this swelling extended family. We now had ample opportunities to enjoy watching this particular bird species. If for no other reason, we'd keep the feeder full to keep our quail family in residence.

Sometimes communities adopt one bird species. Last September Bill and I stumbled into one such community during a trip we took to my cousin Janet's log cabin, which is tucked in a valley in the Okanogan Mountains in northeastern Washington. We left Whidbey, crossed over the Cascade Mountains, followed the Columbia River north, and turned east at Tonasket, closing in on our destination. Outside the town of Tonasket, we followed the Aeneas Valley Road, which separates a flat, agricultural valley from the rolling hills, which are dotted with golden-needled western larch, deep-green Ponderosa pine, and Douglas fir. Hand-stenciled political signs marred the landscape; the race for sheriff demanded the most attention. American kestrels monitored the fields from electrical wires and black-billed magpies patrolled the farm buildings. A fence stretched along the roadside.

Shortly after we started up Aeneas Valley Road, we noticed wooden birdhouses mounted on fence poles every tenth of a mile along the road. The sixteen-inch-tall houses, each with an entry hole near the top, were carefully placed about four to six feet off the ground, facing south. Each birdhouse had a number, which we counted as we drove up the valley: 1, 2, 3 ... 10 ... 20 ... 30. Eventually we counted 115 houses. I had read about the Aeneas Valley bluebird trail, but it wasn't until we started counting the birdhouses that I realized that, quite by accident, we were smack dab in the middle of it. A bluebird trail is a series of houses—made and installed exactly to specifications for bluebirds—to encourage the birds to nest. The houses were spaced so that the birds had elbow room but also to create the advantages of living in a loose colony. Where these cavity-nesting birds have lost natural nesting habitat, populations have decreased, and the installation of birdhouses such as this bluebird trail has encouraged populations to grow.

A few mountain bluebirds, sparkling like a bright blue sky reflecting off an alpine lake, lingered around the houses. The brilliant blue males outshone the females' soft, ashy gray bodies with blue wings and tails. (The western bluebird, another common bluebird in the West, exhibits deep purple-blue on its upper parts and a chestnut belly.) Groups of twenty or so birds fluttered and swooped from fence posts to small shrubs, probably gathering into flocks for their southward migration within the next few weeks.

Bill and I needed a break from driving and something to drink, so we stopped at the Aeneas Valley General Store, an old log building with a huge rack of antlers above the door. Over a beer, I asked about the bluebird houses. The middle-aged woman with black shoulder-length hair behind the counter explained, "The birds are here—always have been—we just give them a home. We made our own houses but then the Bluebird Society came in and put up the boxes with numbers." I asked about the lingering flocks of bluebirds and she responded, "They leave before the snow—just know when to go—then come back in spring."

As we turned off Aeneas Valley Road and wound up the gentle hills toward Janet's cabin, we noticed more bluebird houses. Each of the farms had joined in the fun and nailed houses to a fence post or tree. The community was full of bluebird fans, each encouraging this charismatic species by providing homes. I bet these locals watch for the birds to return each spring and hope that a pair will select one of their own houses to nest in. There's probably conversation at the General Store when the first young begin to fledge, and there'd be a lot of disappointed folks if the birds ever stopped coming to the valley. Perhaps those bluebirds will inspire a local to start a habitat conservation project.

It only takes one bird to get the ball rolling.

I go to nature to be soothed and healed

and to have my senses put in tune once more.

—*John Burroughs*

September now brings a pair of ravens to my bluff. During the summer breeding season the birds are off in an unknown corner of Puget Sound and I never see or hear them. But for the first time since we moved here a pair has begun to spend the nonbreeding season along my bluff. In 2001 they arrived on September 11.

Early that morning I was quietly sipping tea when the phone rang. A familiar but somber voice on the other end said, "Mom, I'm okay." I couldn't imagine what my older son, Munro, who lives in Brooklyn just across the river from Manhattan, was talking about. He continued, "Mom, I just want you to really understand that I'm okay." There was a long pause. "And you probably want to turn on your TV." During that tearful conversation my son explained how he had heard an explosion, later climbed to the roof of his apartment building, and watched the second World Trade Center tower collapse.

An emotional blur consumed the rest of my morning. By noon I'd learned that my stepdaughter, Laura, who lives and works within a few blocks of the Capitol in Washington, D.C., was unharmed and calm. I'd also contacted my younger son, Alex, by e-mail. Though he lives and works in Manhattan, Alex was safely removed from the terror of the morning, attending a conference in a remote area of Croatia. If I'd awakened that morning knowing one son would be close to a disaster, I would have assumed it was Alex visiting Eastern Europe. Instead it was Munro, at home in our own country.

Shaken to the core, but with the immediate family accounted for, I longed for the refreshment of the clear blue September day. In a short time I would be leaving for a meeting, but before departing I yearned for a quiet moment with nature. I stepped outside and felt the warm sun on my head and face. The air smelled like it was on the edge between summer and fall. Lilies and sweet peas hung a ripe sweetness in the air near the door, yet a few steps away, the mowed weeds smelled as dry as an old hay bale. With no breeze to muffle it, the faint cascading sound of the nearby creek, weak from a dry summer just ending, rustled into my consciousness. The fresh air and calming sound slowly assuaged my tense body and troubled mind.

Then came the odd sense of no ambient noise of aircraft high above. I looked up, but saw no soft jet trails crossing the deep ultramarine backdrop. Instead a dark shadow above the shed caught my attention as two coal-black ravens circled quietly against the blue sky. Living here for two years, I've heard the faint, distant calling of ravens perhaps four times and had seen the birds only once or twice before, but never circling above our meadow. The ravens, which I had observed many times in other habitats where they are plentiful, carried on like their species has for hundreds of thousands of years. The pair caught the updraft, warm from the dry grass and impervious areas of metal roof and asphalt driveway, and soared high above.

The scene transported me away from surreal images of airplanes smashing into buildings and 110-story towers collapsing like sand castles. Watching the ravens allowed me to stop, disconnect from the vivid television scenes that mesmerized me all morning, and tune into a bigger picture. For at that moment, I realized there *was* order in our crazy world. I could grab hold of the natural world for stability. I could trust it. The ravens suggested that someday I would once again feel safe. I've collected myths and stories about ravens and this one came to mind:

> *The raven has a very significant place in the culture and religion of Pacific Northwest Native Americans. Several myths consider Raven to be the god who brings life and order. It was Raven who first brought light to the world and then proceeded to create water. It was Raven who, when tired of flying, created the land by dropping pebbles into the sea. Raven continued to create tides, weather, salmon, and finally, humans.*

Within thirty seconds, the pair of ravens drifted behind the treetops and out of sight. But that brief sighting offered a lifeboat for my downward-spiraling emotions. I went back indoors, picked up my keys, and left. During the afternoon meeting, there were times when tears pooled in my eyes and a choking sensation caught in my throat. What if my children had been killed? Anger began to fester. Then I remembered the coal-black ravens circling against the ultramarine sky, and I felt as if I was being calmed by a lullaby.

During the next few days I rode a roller coaster of reactions— horror, grief, confusion, and helplessness. I regularly called my children, donated money to the Red Cross of New York City, and attended services and gatherings in my community. My immediate worry for my own family shifted to concern for those directly involved in the attack, for our country, and for the stability of our global village. And I wondered whether my actions were just for my own healing or if they could be felt by those in need thousands of miles away. Then I remembered another attribute of Raven's powers.

> *A master flier, Raven often carries messages, especially to those in distress. If a ceremony is performed in a place separate from the tragedy, it is Raven who is called upon to transport the good medicine to the victims of disaster. Raven holds the courage and strength and delivers it in a way so that those in difficulty can feel the love of the distant peoples.*

Four days after the tragedy, while working quietly inside my house, I heard the distant call of a raven. I craned my neck at the window to locate the hoarse sound. Four low, throaty calls, "croak, croak, croak, croak," came from a tree overhanging the bluff far to the south. If this had been one of the common birds in my garden, I might not have paid attention. But encountering this uncommon species twice within one week made me pause. The midnight-black bird flew along the top of the bluff toward me and landed in another tree. Again, "croak, croak, croak, croak." It paused and then flew to the top of the Douglas fir tree outside my window. "Croak, croak, croak, croak." It repeated the call then followed the bluff north, stopping every hundred yards or so to sound the call.

Over many years I've learned that the source that sustains me comes through nature and that my pathway to nature usually starts with birds. For me, birds are Shamans that offer a link to the lessons of nature. Raven had offered me comfort, but I also needed healing, more secrets of the world, to help me move beyond the terror and fear.

I remembered that Raven is not just the divine cultural hero of the North Pacific coastal Indians, he is also a trickster. Years earlier I was downhill skiing at a Cascade Mountains resort. The earth seemed frozen in quietness as I rode the upper chairlift through alpine trees into a high bowl. Suddenly a raven called from the top of the hill and flew down parallel with the chairlift. With as much crowd-dazzling chutzpah as the Navy's Blue Angels, the raven did a quick 180-degree roll, flew upside down for a moment, and then reversed back to its normal flight pattern. Cheers erupted from the stunned chairlift audience. The hotdogs in the chair behind me announced that they must have had one too many drinks back at the lodge.

That carefree day in the mountains now seemed part of a different life—a life of innocence and freedom separate from the darkness that had descended on our country. I began worrying. Where would the terrorists strike next? Would our country go to war over this? Determined to conquer my fear, I went for a walk on the road along the bluff. On the way back I stopped at the mailbox. On the top of the pile of mail was *The New Yorker* magazine—the cover solid black with a barely perceptible silhouette of the Twin Towers.

The color black means many things in Native teachings, but it does not mean evil. Black can symbolize searching for answers. Raven's iridescent black feathers speak to the stirring of darkness and bring an awakening during the darkest hour.

Here on the shores of Puget Sound tides pull and push the water in and out twice daily. This regular, dependable cycle of emptying the bay then filling it up again offers a daily metaphor for my life. Life is made of cycles and when it swings too far in one direction, it will swing back again. As I read more about Raven, I was surprised to learn that, along with all his other powers, Raven created the tides.[4]

How Raven Made the Tides

A long time ago, the old people say, the tide did not come in or go out.

The ocean would stay very high up on the shore for a long time and the clams and the seaweed and the other things to eat would be hidden under the deep water. The people were often hungry.

"This is not the way it should be," said Raven. Then he put on his blanket of black feathers and flew along the coast, following the line of the tide. At last he came to the house of a very old woman who was the one who held the tide-line in her hand. As long as she held onto it the tide would stay high. Raven walked into the old woman's house. There she sat, the tide-line held firmly in her hand. Raven sat down across from her.

"Ah," he said, "Those clams were good to eat."

"What clams?" said the old woman.

But Raven did not answer her. Instead he patted his stomach and said, "Ah, it was so easy to pick them up that I have eaten as much as I can eat."

"That can't be so," said the old woman, trying to look past Raven to see out her door, but Raven blocked the entrance. So she stood up and leaned past him to look out. Then Raven pushed her so that she fell through the door, and

[4]This version of the legend is from *Native American Stories* told by Joseph Bruchac (Fulcrum Publishing, Golden, Colo., 1991).

as she fell he threw dust into her eyes so that she was blinded. She let go of the tide-line then and the tide rushed out, leaving all kinds of clams and crabs and other good things to eat exposed.

Raven went out and began to gather clams. He gathered as much as he could carry and ate until he could eat no more. All along the beach others were gathering the good food and thanking Raven for what he had done. Finally he came back to the place where the old woman still was. "Raven," she said, "I know it is you. Heal my eyes so that I can see again."

"I will heal you," Raven said, "but only if you promise to let go of the tide-line twice a day. The people cannot wait so long to gather food from the beaches."

"I will do it," said the old woman. Then Raven washed out her eyes and she could see again. So it is that the tide comes in and goes out every day because Raven made the old woman let go of the tide-line.

I reflected on this story and it helped me see that a cycle of recovery was needed. It was time to let go of the emotional tide-lines of pain and anger in my own life.

A few weeks later my son Munro and I were talking. He had visited the site where the towers had stood and watched the clean-up efforts. "Mom," he said, "come to New York. That's what people need to do. Now is not the time to freeze up with fear."

Four months later Bill and I followed his advice. The late February day when we visited Ground Zero was clear and mild, not the dark, gray day I had envisioned. We arrived at the time indicated on our tickets and stood in line for our turn to walk out onto the viewing platform. While we waited, the police officer in charge chatted with the children in our group of twelve, which helped put us all at ease. As we reached the viewing area everyone quieted. I looked out over a void, a huge empty cubic space where nothing existed anymore. Things that I held as real—hundreds of floors of concrete, metal, glass, and people—were gone. No skeletons of buildings remained; the clean-up efforts had removed those vestiges. My eyes scanned the void for something to focus on, something living and moving. Far on the opposite side of the site a line of dump trucks, like toy trucks across a schoolyard, crawled out of underground tunnels and disappeared into the city streets beyond.

The scene haunted me, stayed at the edges of my consciousness for weeks. But that sunny February day also signaled my tide was changing. It had gone way, way out and now was already moving back in. The downward spiral had reversed and, like the two coal-black ravens against the ultramarine sky, my emotions were beginning to cycle upward.

The Raven's power was not limited to the Native traditions of the Northwest Coast. Legend claims that England will not fall if ravens live in the Tower of London. Unwilling to tempt fate, the British government still keeps a flock of wing-clipped ravens on the grounds.

Messenger, comforter, creator, trickster, protector, and keeper of the tides, this bird with a blanket of black feathers takes many forms. Like a long mythical journey, the stories of Raven offer many lessons about our lives. For me, ravens also offer solace. Though I dread the pain of every September 11 anniversary, I know the ravens wintering on my bluff will give me strength, perspective, and confidence to confront my darkest fears.

CHAPTER TEN
October

Columbus Day, the middle of October. Even before opening my eyes, I know a thick fog has tucked itself into the waters around the island. The ferry, which begins its weekday run at 5:10 A.M., sounds a deep, hollow fog alarm as it exits the dock. The two-part monotone mixes into my early morning dreams and briefly brings me close to consciousness. Then I slip back to sleep, pulling myself even deeper underneath my comforter.

Later, I'm sipping tea on the deck, my thick terry cloth robe pulled tightly around me, sniffing the air and listening for birdcalls. The flat, gray, foggy backdrop obscures everything beyond the pewter silhouette of maple, alder, and fir trees, and yet occasionally a call pierces through. Today, as happens on about 10 percent of October mornings, my shivering is rewarded with the plaintive call of a loon. Hearing the clear, strong yodeling spreads a warm smile across my face.

Common loon

For Thoreau, the loon's call made "the woods ring with its wild laughter." To me the call possesses a wild, primitive quality that encapsulates the vastness and untamed nature of our world. It transports me to secluded northern lakes awash with warm summer sun and crowned with periwinkle blue skies. Laurens Van der Post, a British writer who wrote about Africa, suggested that birds sense and forecast cataclysmic changes in our world and that the birds of Africa hushed immediately prior to the fighting of World War II. Hearing the loon's call makes me feel that all is right with the world, at least for the day. Like an overture setting the tone for an opera, the loon's call announces the fall arrival of hundreds of ducks and seabirds into our bay. The species' numbers increase this month then peak in November.

Steller's jay

About noon the sun breaks through the fog's last wispy skeins and Bill and I head outdoors to tackle some fall chores. The bright-red apples on our two dwarf trees are ready for picking. As we round the house we notice a deer stretching into the branches for its own lunch. Bill lunges to chase it away. It prances off, apple between its front teeth, looking like Rudolph the Red-Nosed Reindeer.

Deer aren't our only apple thieves. One fall afternoon I observed six bird species feasting in one apple tree: a robin, Steller's jay, dark-eyed junco, white-crowned sparrow, northern flicker, and the most unlikely pirate, a pileated woodpecker. The bird's weight kept it from perching on the ends of the branches where apples hung, but it tried amazing acrobatics to reach the apples. When it did manage to get close to the prize, its long, sharp bill glanced off the wobbly fruit, like the old game of dunking for apples.

Moving away from the apple tree, we hear "tisk, tisk" and much clucking from the Nootka rose shrubs near the old maple tree. We quietly hold still so the quail family will venture across the open lawn to the feeder. In twos and threes they chance out and skitter across the exposed area like whirly wind-up toys. All the young birds are fully clothed in adult plumage, but it is still easy to pick out Papa, who stands guard during this risky maneuver. When all fourteen quail are accounted for, he scurries along behind.

Bald eagle

Unconcerned by the commotion below, an eagle soars along the bluff, banks upward with talons outstretched, and grasps a favored perch atop one of our Douglas firs. It immediately begins summoning its mate who is circling above, with three sweet chirps followed by six quickly descending notes, like a rusty gate opening. The second bird lands inches from the first. As they perch side by side we can determine their sexes, the female being about 20 percent larger than the male. These are the same eagles that nested here last spring. Each August they leave for a couple of months—perhaps to feast on the fall salmon run along the Skagit River farther north, though we don't really know.

The return of "our" eagles signals the beginning of fall and winter raptor watching along the West Coast. One hot spot for winter raptors is off the northeast end of Whidbey Island at the Skagit Flats, a wide, agricultural river estuary, which becomes the winter home for a great diversity of hawks, falcons, and eagles, as well as swans and geese. One goal for serious birders is to experience a five-falcon day, views of all five North American falcons (American kestrel, merlin, prairie falcon, peregrine falcon, and gyrfalcon), a possibility on a lucky winter day at the Flats. I've never experienced a five-falcon day, but I have counted more than sixty red-tailed hawks in five hours.

On a recent trip kayaking the middle section of the Skagit River, we counted forty-eight bald eagles perched in alder and cottonwood trees. The eagles sat digesting their morning meals of spent salmon carcasses. As we floated down the swiftly moving river I looked for "our" eagles, but the white heads and tails all looked the same to me, a mere human.

The second bird lands inches from the first

New birds this month:

❑ Rough-legged Hawk *(Buteo lagopus)*

❑ Golden Eagle *(Aquila chrysaetos)*

❑ Merlin *(Falco columbarius)*

❑ Clark's Nutcracker *(Nucifraga columbiana)*

❑ Yellow-headed Blackbird *(Xanthocephalus xanthocephalus)*

❑ Brewer's Blackbird *(Euphagus cyanocephalus)*

❑ Gray-crowned Rosy-Finch *(Leucosticte tephrocotis)*

LIGHT AS A FEATHER

From the integument of the skin originates also that beautiful

plumage which peculiarly characterizes the class of birds. ...

But it is impossible to follow up this ornamental attire

through all its wonderful features of graceful curve and irides-

cent colouring—of downy delicacy and majestic strength—

from the tiny rainbow that plays on the neck of the humming-

bird, to the bed of azure, emerald, and hyacinth, that tessellate

the wing of the parrot tribe, or the ever-shifting eyes that

dazzle in the tail of the peacock. ...

—John Mason Good,
The Book of Nature, *1839*

Feathers are a bird's defining characteristic. No bird lacks them and no other mammal possesses them. Strong, flexible, lightweight, waterproof, heat retaining, repairable, replaceable, multicolored, sometimes irides-cent, capable of producing sound—feathers are an engineering and artis-tic marvel.

A couple of years ago, while teaching a birdwatching class, I began with the question, "How many feathers does one bird have?" The students' guesses ranged from fifty to 1,000. Anyone who has plucked a chicken or game bird could attest that these estimates were low. Most students were amazed to learn that the number varies from about 5,000 feathers for small songbirds to about 25,000 for swans. I explained to the class that some of those thousands of feathers are short and fluffy to pro-vide insulation; others are long and strong for flying. There are also con-tour feathers, which cover the bird, providing protection from rain and often adding beautiful colors to their appearance. Some birds even have specialized feathers for breeding display, such as the heron's long plumes, the peacock's fancy tail feathers, and the woodpecker's flashy red crests.

Birds' feathers are almost unlimited in variety in color and pattern and play an important role in distinguishing one species from another. It's feathers that create challenges for bird-watchers by making birds so mobile, and it's feathers that allow birds to survive on every landmass in the world, even remote, cold islands. Yet without feathers, I doubt that birdwatching would be the popular hobby it has become.

Years ago, while enrolled in an ornithology class, I was assigned to monitor the amount of time birds spent preening—cleaning and arranging their feathers. Before the project I'd assumed that birds spent most of their time looking for food and just a few minutes preening, certainly no more than the twenty minutes I spend primping each morning. As I watched several birds spend more time preening than looking for food, I discovered that the exact opposite of my assumption was true. Since that early exercise, I've noticed that all birds, whether they be swallows sitting on a wire, gulls standing around on the ferry dock, or bald eagles in the Douglas fir on our bluff, spend most of the time when not feeding maintaining their 5,000–25,000 feathers.

Birds preen by running their beaks through their feathers, smoothing out the ruffled edges and realigning the zipper-type mechanism that holds the feathers' fine branches together. Preening removes dirt and parasites from the feathers and provides an opportunity for birds to waterproof their feathers by distributing oil from an oil duct near the base of the tail. Anyone with a birdbath knows birds enjoy splashing and bathing their feathers. In dry climates birds bathe in dust, which serves some of the same functions as a water bath.

Even the best-maintained bird feathers don't last more that a year; most fall out and are replaced at least yearly, a process called molting. For the majority of birds, molting occurs in late summer and fall over a period of two weeks to two months. This process is important for birdwatchers to understand since some birds replace old feathers with new ones that are of different colors. For example, brightly plumed male ducks replace their colorful breeding feathers with somber feathers similar to those of the females. Goldfinches transition from bright lemon yellow to dull green. Loons lose their green head feathers and jeweled necklaces and replace them with a plain dark-and-light pattern. Pigeon guillemots turn from shiny black to mostly white.

Other birds make less-dramatic changes and merely dull down a bit. During their fall molt, some gulls add brown speckling to their white heads, while the colorful feathers of many shorebirds are replaced by a mottled black-and-white pattern. Woodpeckers, wrens, owls, raptors, and many other birds have one style of plumage, but even then they replace worn-out feathers with new ones. The fall molt also gives birds living in cold areas a chance to put on a winter coat; these birds can grow many additional insulating feathers. Birds that change colors in the fall go through a second molt in winter or spring to restore their breeding plumage. Birds aren't trying to confuse bird-watchers with these changes. Over the eons their genetic codes have taken note that less-noticeable plumage acts as camouflage and increases chances of surviving the winter to enjoy another breeding season.

In the past, birders have used many confusing terms to label plumage at different times of year. Recently they've begun to standardize the terminology. Late fall and winter plumage (after the fall molt) is "basic" plumage. Summer or breeding plumage is "alternate" (or "breeding") plumage. Another common term is "juvenal" plumage. This defines the clothes that teenagers wear once they are out of the nest but not old enough to breed. Have you ever seen a robin with spots on the breast? Young robins sport this camouflage look until their first fall molt.

The young of some species carry their juvenal plumage through several molts. Young gulls, raptors, and other large birds take two to four years to become adults, so bird-watchers often see this immature plumage. The coffee-with-cream plumage on young gulls is an example. Juvenile red-tailed hawks lack a red tail and juvenile bald eagles wear a dark—rather than "bald"—head and tail. A bird's juvenal plumage may signal to the adults that the young birds aren't a threat during breeding season. Consequently the young are left alone. The more somber colors of juvenal plumage also help to camouflage these inexperienced birds and protect them from predators.

Observing the way birds maintain and change plumage through the seasons adds a deeper level of appreciation to birdwatching. When we watch a gull sitting on a log preening its feathers, we can admire the task of cleaning 20,000 feathers. When we observe a scraggly winged crow with a couple of feathers missing, we know the bird is molting. And when we see male mallards dressed in dandy breeding plumage, we can marvel at the amazing ability of feathers to decorate birds.

Each year during early October I rummage around the bushes below the Douglas fir where the bald eagles sit and preen. I'm full of the hope of finding a discarded wing feather. I haven't found one yet, but one day I expect I will. My conscience may not allow me to keep the feather since I know it is illegal to take eagle feathers, but that doesn't keep me from searching. If I do find a feather, it will be strong, lightweight, flexible, and a symbol of the freedom, power, and wonder of the bird that recently shed it.

COLOR

Our ability to perceive quality in nature begins, as in art,

with the pretty. It expands through successive stages of the

beautiful to values as yet uncaptured by language.

—*Aldo Leopold,*
A Sand County Almanac

October, the month of black cats, witches, and bats, got me thinking about black birds. It began one afternoon as I was sitting in a local park watching a small camaraderie of crows pecking around the tables and garbage cans for bits and pieces of picnic leftovers. Crows are thoroughly black, without a whisker of any other color. Why, I wondered, do some birds have color and others don't?

I remembered that the common raven, too, looks completely black: feathers, eyes, claws. The whole bird is black, except for the gray-based neck feathers, but those parts of the feathers are hidden and only visible up close when the feathers are parted. As I watched the crows walking and bobbing their heads, I tried to think of other completely black birds. I mentally scanned through the blackbird family. Red-winged blackbirds sport bright-red wing patches; yellow-headed black-birds have yellow heads. Even the very black Brewer's blackbird displays a yellow eye.

When I returned home, I paged through a field guide looking for completely black birds and found only two: the American crow and the common raven. The rest of the approximately 850 bird species in North America show some white or other color. The large majority of birds wear a blend of brownish, grayish, greenish, or creamy colors, and most are mottled. Many of these dull-colored birds display color accents: some owls have yellow eyes, gulls have pink or yellow legs, and wood-peckers have a splash of red. A small number of birds exhibit strong vibrant colors such as the lemon yellow warblers, iridescently jeweled hummingbirds, and bright blue jays. The Tropics, with its toucans, tro-gons, quetzals, and macaws, seem to have an even larger percentage of brilliantly colored birds.

Plumage color identifies and separates the different species, enabling birds to locate their own kind. The dramatic coloration on some male birds, especially ducks and warblers, helps females to zero in on the males of her species. Anyone who has watched a male peacock spread its large fan-shaped tail knows that birds also deploy color to communicate. The male peacock is effectively saying to a female, "Hey, babe, look at me!" The male red-winged blackbird delivers a different message when he flashes his bright-red shoulder patches. It warns other male blackbirds invading his space, "Stay away, dude, this is my territory!"

For most birds, plumage coloration is designed to camouflage and protect. Birds of the open sage and grassland tend to be lighter and grayer than birds of the deep forest. A family of killdeer feed on the beach below my bluff. They prefer the rocky area near a modest sandy point, and every time I walk past I look and look for the birds. I know exactly where they are but I can't pick them out because their feathers perfectly blend in with the pattern of rocks. I walk slowly and deliberately up to the spot but, even so, it is only when they call or fly off that I see them.

Many birds are dark on their backs with light-colored bellies, a pattern called countershading. The dark backs hide the birds from predators overhead. Light bellies allow birds to blend into a light sky, concealing them from predators lurking below.

Another camouflage tool is disruptive coloration. A striking pattern helps to break up the outline of the bird against either a light or dark background, making it hard for predators to discern where the bird begins and ends. The black-and-white stripes on the head of the white-crowned sparrow are a good example, as is the head pattern on chickadees and nuthatches.

I've often wondered why two very common birds, the spotted towhee and the dark-eyed junco, have black hoods over their head and shoulders; both birds show off flashy white on other parts of their bodies. The junco wears bright-white outer tail feathers and the towhee has white spots on the wings and the tip of the tail. This coloration may serve as a distracting mechanism. The contrasting colors misdirect a predator to the tail and outer wing feathers—areas of the bird that can be replaced—while the head and upper body remain "protected" in the black hood.

Bird feathers display color in two ways. Most colors are a result of pigment, a chemical compound in the feathers or skin—the robin's red breast, the chickadee's chestnut back, or the eagle's yellow talons. The iridescence that flashes from the feathers of hummingbirds is a result of the structure of the barbules, the zipperlike mechanism that smoothes feathers together. The barbules of iridescent feathers contain flat surfaces that rotate to reflect incoming light, such as the brilliant, strong red of a hummingbird's gorget. Our rock pigeon also sports iridescent feathers that look plain bluish until the light hits the barbules a certain way, then beautiful iridescent greens and purples shimmer from his plumage.

It is curious that with so many reasons to evolve a colorful or at least mottled plumage, the crow and raven have remained all black. The solid black coloring may be related to communication. Ravens, who remain in pairs year-round, have no need for colorful attraction display. They have few predators, so they don't need camouflage. Ravens fly great distances, and one theory suggests that the dark body against a light sky can be seen more easily so the pair can keep track of each other.

Scientists aren't sure why crows are all black. However, Native Americans have a myth to explain it.

When the world began it was just black and white. There was no color. All the animals and birds were black. Then Crow came into the world and Crow wore all the colors of the rainbow. The other animals and birds teased Crow because he was different and, in their eyes, he was ugly. Crow became very sad and wanted to look like the other animals. So he shook himself. He shook and shook his feathers until all the colors flew out. The colors landed on all the other birds and animals. The jay was covered in blue, the robin in orange, and a bit of red landed on the woodpecker. The only color left on the crow was black, and he has stayed black to this day.

HAWK WATCH

Hawks are beautiful objects when on the wing.
I have often stood to view a hawk in the sky trembling its
wings & then hanging quite still for a moment
as if it was as light as a shadow and could find like
the clouds a resting place upon the still blue air.

—Journal of John Clare, *1820s*

Bill slowly maneuvered our Jimmy van up Antoine Creek Road in central Washington State. Alternating bands of early morning sun and deep frosty shade slashed across the gravel road, producing broad stripes like a referee's uniform. As we passed from shade to sun and back to shade, the temperature display on our van's dashboard jumped from thirty-one to thirty-nine degrees and back to thirty-two degrees. Bent over the map, I calculated we were still 2,000 feet below our destination of 5,675 feet and the Chelan Ridge Hawk Watch station.

We rounded a bend and the morning sun illuminated a steep hillside, showcasing clumps of school bus–yellow willows sparkling against deep-green Ponderosa pine, checkers on a dry checkerboard. Dark-eyed juncos crossed the road in a scattered drove. A Clark's nutcracker—named in honor of William Clark, coleader with Meriwether Lewis of the 1803–05 exploration of the plains and far West—flashed its black-and-white tail feathers as it dropped down the canyon beside the road. I scanned the cobalt blue sky for soaring raptors, but nothing interrupted the vast expanse of thin air.

Clinging to the side of Cooper Mountain, we turned onto a forest service road and slowly negotiated sharp bends with sheer cliffs to our left. Below, a haze of fog and smoke from a controlled burn to the east blanketed orchard-covered valleys. Above, a series of ridges piled atop one another and faded to the horizon. Bill drove deliberately, but I couldn't help holding the passenger grab handle and pressing my right foot to the floorboards to help him break as we maneuvered the sharpest hairpin turns. Heights unnerve me.

The day before, Bill and I had caught the 4:00 P.M. ferry off our island and driven east up Steven's Pass and over the Cascade Mountains. As the daylight faded we stopped for a quick dinner in Leavenworth, an intriguing faux-Bavarian alpine village plopped in the middle of Washington. Around 9:00 P.M. we checked into the Apple Inn in the town of Chelan. After an early breakfast at the Apple Café—you can probably guess the industry that keeps Chelan going—we started the last leg of our excursion to the Hawk Watch site. For more than a month I'd been communicating with Eric Dinkel, education coordinator of the Chelan Ridge Hawk Watch project, hoping to set up a visit; however, until just a few days before, the site had been closed to visitors because of the Deer Creek forest fire. The six or so staff at this site had taken forest service fire training, which allowed them to enter the station for the ten-week fall migration season between mid-August and late October. Our visit caught the tail end of the monitoring for the year.

"Dress warmly and bring a lunch," Eric had advised in a voice mail. The site was located on a long northwest-southeast ridge where raptors tended to catch thermal updrafts to assist them on their long fall migration. This late in the year, I expected a bone-chilling rocky ridge.

Ears popping, we reached the top of the ridge and stopped at a dusty parking lot where a canvas yurt and two portable toilets comprised the field camp. Two men emerged from the yurt and introduced themselves as Bob Davies, site coordinator, and Mark Leavens, one of two hawk counters. Both had the air of field biologists: dirty boots and well-worn REI clothing in shades of gray-green. Bob's scruffy, graying beard marked him as a contemporary to Bill and me. Mark, a fresh-faced twenty-two-year-old college student from Pennsylvania, was completing fieldwork for his degree in environmental interpretation. In two sentences Bob planned our day: first we would join Mark at the observation point, later we would move to one of the banding stations. Bill and I picked up the lingo quickly: first to "ob one" and then to "North Blind." A quick radio call to the staff at the blinds launched the plan into motion.

We shouldered our daypacks and followed pink plastic trail markers tied to low, wind-shaped sagebrush for a moderate thirty-minute walk. Treeless Cooper Ridge reached its crest to our right and plunged into a bottomless valley on our left. Charred snags and downed trees, remnants of past forest fires, littered the hillside; no new growth had attempted life in the sandy patches between piles of rocks. A quarter mile ahead, we picked out a steeply pointed promontory topped with a pole and plastic owl—"ob one."

At the far horizon Bill spotted a dark object soaring toward us. We paused, lifted our binoculars, and watched until it grew into a red-tailed hawk, obviously attracted to the "owl" on the pole. First the red-tailed curiously circled the owl, then rose above it and dove down to strike. Sensing something phony, the hawk diverted and looped around once more before continuing south. Mark exclaimed, "That's an exiting way to start the day!" We hiked to the base, then scrambled up the sharp rocky pyramid toward the observation point. I forced myself to avoid looking down the dizzyingly deep canyon and repeated my silent mantra: "Keep your eyes on the horizon."

As we assembled at the observation point, Mark took weather readings and recorded our first red-tailed sighting. The wind was surprisingly forgiving, south to southwest at just one mile per hour, with gusts to two. The sun beat down and I shed my jacket. After that dramatic first act, the raptor show quieted and we satisfied ourselves by watching the gray-crowned rosy-finches cavorting among the rocks. These birds weren't passing through; high alpine ridges are their normal habitat, although they move to lower elevations in the snowy winters. Mark handed us a long panoramic diagram with the names of the surrounding mountains and ridges: Cooper Mountain, In Between Ridge, Washington Butte, Little Goat, Big Goat, Twin Peak, The Saddle, Avalanche Ridge, Raven Ridge, Gardener, and Look Out Mountain. "Knowing the landmarks will help us point out to each other where the raptors are sighted," he explained.

A sharp-shinned hawk scouted the valley to the south. We radioed to North Blind that this long-tailed robin-sized accipiter was headed their way. During the next lull, Mark filled us in on the history of this site. A local raptor enthusiast, Kent Woodruff, researched the area by plane in 1996 looking for a viable site. The next year during an exploratory season one guy sat on this point and counted 1,400 hawks and vultures pass by on their fall migration. That evidence convinced Hawk Watch International to set up the program. In 1998, 2,300 birds were counted and the banding program began two years later. Recently, the data-gathering potential of the program had increased by attaching radio transmitters to a few birds.

Mark explained that the mission of Hawk Watch International, a fifteen-year-old nonprofit organization, was to monitor and protect hawks and other birds of prey through research, education, and conservation. The organization staffs a dozen observation stations in the western United States and Mexico. The Chelan Ridge station is the most northern station. The other sites are along the Rocky Mountains in Montana, Idaho, Wyoming, Utah, and Nevada; in Oregon's Cascades; and in New Mexico, Arizona, and Texas.

A floating black dot appeared to the north toward Mount Gardner, a jagged lump on the horizon. The dot seemed to be following a typical migration pattern. Mark called it a "project bird," meaning that at present it was too far away to identify, but as it continued to circle higher in the thermals and glide toward us, clues might fall together—wing shape, size, flight pattern—so that the bird could be identified. By noting subtle differences in plumage, experienced counters like Mark could sometimes distinguish the sex of the bird and also if the bird was a juvenile or an adult.

We were experiencing a parade of sorts. Raptors in migration to southern climes gravitate toward terrain that produces an abundance of thermals, usually mountain chains. A bird finds a thermal and floats on an upward spiral with the rising air. Then the bird glides to the next thermal, which some hawk experts suggest the birds are able to hear from miles away. By coupling together thermals, long flights are possible with a minimal expenditure of energy and without having to constantly stop to hunt along the way.

The radio crackled. Bob at South Blind announced they had captured a sharp-shinned hawk and asked if we wanted to venture down and see it. Bill replied for both of us, "No thanks, we see that species lurking around our yard back home." By eleven o'clock the wind picked up to four miles per hour, with gusts to five, according to Mark's instruments, but didn't mar the warm, mild morning. Soon the "lunch factor" set in, a midday lull in hawk activity. Mark reached for his backpack, pulled out his lunch, and explained, "Around noon the stronger updrafts pull the birds higher and they become harder to see." Then added with a smile, "Or perhaps the watchers are looking down at their sandwiches and miss counting them."

As Bill and I shared an apple, a project bird appeared from the north. We watched for several minutes (a red-tailed sighting to the east interrupted us briefly) then noticed the project bird had attracted a companion. Two large black dots floated the updrafts, circled around, paired up, and flew parallel. Slowly, slowly they inched in our direction. After ten minutes Mark identified our prizes: two golden eagles, a "hatch bird" born this year and an adult. The hatch bird displayed distinctive white windows in the dark wings and white at the base of the tail. The adult remained a large dark shape, although in my imagination golden feathers shone on the head. We watched the birds crest the closest ridge and dip into the valley to the northeast. Then they separated; one majestic bird continued south, the other veered off around Cooper Mountain to the west.

"That's the closest I've ever been to a golden eagle," Bill exclaimed. He accentuated his glee by giving me an energetic high-five, then quickly grabbed my arm to be sure his six-foot one-inch, 200-pound enthusiasm didn't topple me backward off the precipice.

By one o'clock the wind picked up. Instead of donning fleece gloves and hats, Bill and I decided to descend the point and visit the banding station at North Blind. We retraced the walk to the parking lot where Theresa, another raptor counter, greeted us. She told us Bob had just radioed from South Blind that they had caught a rough-legged hawk, a large twenty-one-inch bird with a wingspan of four and a half feet. Bob wondered if we would like them to bring the hawk for us to see. We nodded enthusiastically and I commented, "We sure don't get those at our feeder."

Ten minutes later Bob arrived with a female rough-legged hawk. Creamy white and warm-brown breast markings, dark brown back, and colorless eyes identified it as a first-year bird. Hatched in the Arctic just weeks earlier, the bird had already grown to the size of an adult bird. This novice migrant had covered perhaps 80 percent of its trip south to winter in the western United States. The bird was calm; evidently raptors aren't nervous when caught. We snapped photos from all sides including a close-up of the unusual legs, one now sporting a new silver band. Unlike most raptors with smooth, bare legs, the legs of this species are wrapped in feathers to keep them warm—thus the term "rough-legged."

When we finished photographing, Bob looked at me. "Do you want to launch it back into the air?" he asked. I've held hundreds of small birds, and even large raptors in education programs, but never a large, wild raptor like this. The size and wildness of the bird intimidated me, but I heard the word "Sure!" escape my lips without due consideration. The bird seemed calmer than I was as Bob instructed how to firmly grasp first one leg and then the other. From behind the bird, I maneuvered my bare hands into the soft tarsal feathers and encircled the legs. The stiff shaft of thighbone felt scrawny with a surprisingly thin padding of muscle. It took no effort to hold this hollow-boned, lighter-than-expected bird. The hawk softly rearranged its wings and adjusted its balance, then turned to look at its new handler. Earlier Bob had encouraged us to feel the sharp keel bone with no surrounding fat reserves and the empty crop indicating the bird hadn't eaten recently. I looked into the calm, pale eye and thought of the tremendous expenditure of energy needed, even with the help of the thermals, to migrate thousands of miles each fall. I sent a blessing to this long-distance traveler for a safe journey and a full meal soon. But I knew that most hatch birds don't make it through their initial winter. Only 10 to 20 percent survive their first year.

I stepped into a clearing, faced south, and, as Bob instructed, raised my arms and let go. As if the hawk and I had practiced a thousand times, it lifted off, flapped its large wings, and flew up into the air. Maneuvering past some low pine trees, it then circled back to perch on a snag. Bob said they often do that—land to peck at the new silver band on their leg and preen flight feathers before heading down the ridge to catch the next thermal. The feeling of those firm but scrawny legs, the pale eye so close to my own, and the launch back into the wild hung at the periphery of my mind as we walked down a trail to North Blind.

There we met Luke, a bander, and Lonnie, a volunteer; both were young, energetic, and genuinely pleased to share their passion for raptors with two visitors. Although South Blind had caught several birds that day, North Blind was skunked. We sat in a closet-sized box with one thin horizontal strip cut away for viewing just at eye level when seated. Out the "window" we could see the trapping area. Luke explained, "Live pigeons, starlings, and house sparrows are the bait to attract raptors, lure them to the ground and into the nets. Then those bow nets snap over their heads for a quick, safe capture. The pigeon attracts larger raptors, the starling mid-sized hawks, and the house sparrow the smaller hawks." Lonnie showed us one of the little harnesses that tie on to the bait birds and are attached to an intricate system of wires, which run through pulleys and loop over a pole. From inside the blind, Luke could work the lines like a puppeteer "popping the pigeon"—lifting the bird into the air so it would flutter and swing attracting raptors from quite a distance. Once the raptor came close, Luke "danced" the right-sized bait bird and edged the raptor toward the spring-loaded bow net. At the precise moment Luke would release the bow net. And, as we would soon observe, the bait bird was not injured.

The blind faced down the broad valley so the banders could observe birds coming from that direction. However, birds also arrived unexpectedly from over the ridge behind the blind. When a merlin, a feisty ten-inch chocolate-colored falcon, appeared out of nowhere and dove toward the pigeon, Bill yelped with excitement, exactly what Luke had instructed us *not* to do. The merlin veered away and landed on a low stump, but remained intrigued by Luke's puppets. Knowing the pigeon was too large a prey for the merlin, Luke's well-practiced fingers settled that bird and began shuffling the starling, attracting the merlin toward the smaller bait. The starling fluttered near the ground, as if wounded. We watched the merlin watch the starling. The hawk seemed interested but cautious. Luke edged the starling closer to the bow net. The merlin pumped its tail then dove toward the starling. A nanosecond before impact, Luke jumped the starling out of the way and into the target area of the net trap. The merlin landed on the ground and hopped to the starling. Luke released the bow net and—presto!—both birds were inside the net. Luke and Lonnie darted from the blind and, before I could stand from my stool, Lonnie had snatched the merlin in her hands and Luke had checked the unharmed starling and reset the bow net.

Back in the blind, Luke took up the puppet strings while Lonnie weighed, measured, and banded the merlin and checked it for parasites. Bill recorded the statistics: band number 1593-28478, weight 250 grams. Lonnie completed the measurements and declared it a fat, healthy male. We moved outside to release the bird and again I was asked if I wanted to launch it. Bill happily took my camera to record the event. This small raptor could be held in one hand. I carefully placed my hand over Luke's and firmly enclosed my fingers around the merlin's body and folded wings. "Just like holding an ice cream cone," Luke said. This time I felt the smooth flight feathers of the wings and a strong heart pounding within. This raptor's large dark eyes radiated strength and endurance. On three, I lifted my arm and released the hawk. As with the rough-legged, it circled out and perched on a nearby snag, the lengthening afternoon rays highlighted its dark-brown body and subtly banded tail.

Bill and I looked at our watches, remembered our five-hour drive home, and offered Luke and Lonnie our good-byes and gratitude. Luke replied, "Hey, you guys brought us good luck. Come on back next year."

Back at the parking lot we copied notes from the large board with sighting and banding statistics. So far this year the site had recorded fifteen species of raptors and one species of vulture for a total of 2,451 birds. Of those, 676 birds had been banded. These figures were low compared to other banding sights farther south where hawks from all over the West funnel into well-traveled flight paths. Hawk Watch sites in Texas could record four times those numbers *in a single day.* In Veracruz, Mexico, watchers might see 500,000 migrating hawks in one very good day. That site records more than 6 million birds each fall.

Navigating the forest service road back down the ridge, Bill drove slowly but I still pressed my foot to the floorboards as he cautiously maneuvered the road's tight bends. My nervousness of heights finally subsided as we reached the upper valleys where cottonwood and aspen leaves shimmered like lemon Jell-O. To the west the sun set over the Cascade Mountains and a sun dog shone brightly, a prism of colors in the clouds predicting rain within twenty-four hours. Quietly, I wished the rough-legged hawk and merlin safe sailing and hoped they would be well south of these mountains before the October rains arrived.

CHAPTER ELEVEN

November

Today the weather forecasters predict a high of fifty-two and a low of fifty degrees. That narrow temperature band indicates the moist marine air will hang around all day. I check the tide table to see when I can sneak in a beach walk. Winter reverses the cycle of the tides, pushing the lowest tides to the night hours and the highest tides to daytime, so I must plan ahead to guarantee solid ground at the base of my bluff. About 11:00 A.M., I descend the seventy-two steep, earthen steps down the ravine to catch the lowest tide of the day, six and a half feet. There won't be a wide beach, but I'll have time to walk to the old sawdust dock and back, about three miles. Near the bottom of the stairs I spy a small sphere of gnawed apple and wonder what critter—coyote or raccoon, perhaps—snatched the fruit from below our tree and scurried down the bluff to consume it in private.

Clouds fill the panorama spread out before me, obscuring the mountains but allowing a view of Hat Island and the foothills beyond. I remember the words of my watercolor teacher at my Midwest college. Hearing I was from the Seattle area he remarked, "Oh yes, I spent a summer in Puget Sound.

Great blue heron

Bufflehead

Wanted to learn to paint clouds. Got plenty of chances." Below the clouds, a light southern breeze fractures the water's surface into thousands of dark-gray brushstrokes.

A dozen red-breasted mergansers scurry along the shoreline feeding on surface bits, a single common loon floats quietly well off shore, and a huge mix of scoters—some orange-and-white billed surf scoters and a few white-winged scoters—huddle like a raft beyond. A passel of American coots, solid black waterbirds with whitish bills and foreheads, preen on a scant patch of sand at The Point. Several camouflaged killdeer pose like statuesque rocks until I am almost upon them, and then lift with a commanding "keer, keer" that reminds me I'm intruding. A kingfisher joins the defense team, rattling in flight as it swoops to a distant, overhanging alder tree.

I strike off south along the beach, which is delightfully free of houses, bulkheads, or other human alteration. Maple trees billow out from the bluff. A few dandelion-yellow leaves the size of dinner plates cling to the branches but will drop with the next November windstorm. The leaves of the alders remain a dull green, unlikely to paint the bluff with fall color. Soon they, too, will litter the ground.

I've walked this beach ever since I learned to walk. Every time I step over the drift logs near the bluff or shed my shoes to run on the sand, I marvel that the beach has remained unchanged. Houses, such as my own, are perched unseen well back from the top of the bluff. This circumstance leaves the beach in its natural state for me, as well as for the birds and mammals that share this neighborhood.

Ahead I spot the old sawdust dock. As a child I remember watching a Foss tug pull an empty barge across the bay from Everett and snug it up to the end of the dock right under the spout of a large metal pipe. The pipe hung from tall scaffolding mounted high above the dock, then the pipe climbed the bluff to a lumber mill at the top. Sawdust was pumped down the long pipe and into the waiting barge. After several days of pumping, the barge was mounded with sawdust and the tug returned to drag its load back to Everett, where the sawdust was turned into paper products. In my young mind, my father's evening newspaper came from that same sawdust.

The sawdust dock, which hasn't seen any sawdust for decades, now functions solely as a roosting place for birds. Eagles, cormorants, kingfishers, gulls, crows, herons, and swallows all can be seen at various times perching on the aging scaffolding. One year pigeon guillemots nested high atop a support piling.

I reach the dock and notice horned grebes and Barrow's goldeneye ducks thronging near the base of the pilings: the grebes are diving for fish and the goldeneyes are nibbling at mussels and barnacles. A lone bufflehead floats just beyond. A great blue heron that has staked out this beach as its winter feeding territory flies in from the south and takes up guard on the end of the dock. A kingfisher perches on the rusting sawdust pipe.

Suddenly, I become aware of the incoming tide. I turn around and notice the narrowing beach and the water filling in my footprints. Not wanting to scale the steep bluff or perch in an overhanging alder tree for the night, I walk quickly back to my seventy-two steps and retreat up the ravine.

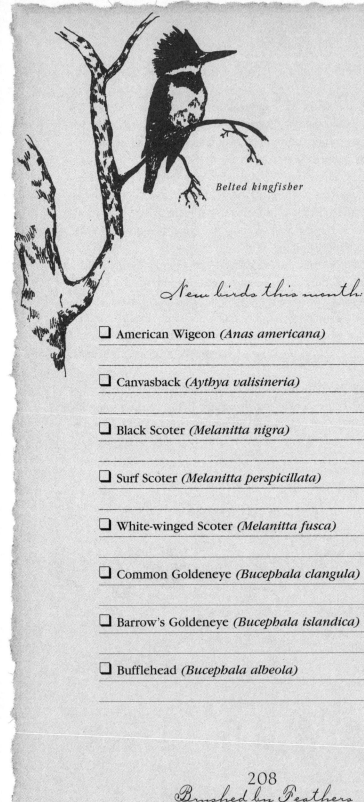

Belted kingfisher

New birds this month:

❏ American Wigeon *(Anas americana)*

❏ Canvasback *(Aythya valisineria)*

❏ Black Scoter *(Melanitta nigra)*

❏ Surf Scoter *(Melanitta perspicillata)*

❏ White-winged Scoter *(Melanitta fusca)*

❏ Common Goldeneye *(Bucephala clangula)*

❏ Barrow's Goldeneye *(Bucephala islandica)*

❏ Bufflehead *(Bucephala albeola)*

❑ Red-breasted Merganser *(Mergus serrator)*

❑ American Coot *(Fulica americana)*

❑ Cactus Wren *(Campylorhynchus brunneicapillus)*

❑ Rock Wren *(Salpinctes obsoletus)*

❑ Canyon Wren *(Catherpes mexicanus)*

❑ Bewick's Wren *(Thryomanes bewickii)*

❑ House Wren *(Troglodytes aedon)*

NOW PLAYING:
THE RETURN OF THE BUCEPHALA

The migration of birds has been, and still is, quite a
mystery. It is undoubtably a matter of instinct, and also
of example from older to younger birds. That these birds have
any idea of the exact time of an advancing season
is not to be accepted.

—*Anonymous,*
Scientific Digest, *1899*

I call the game "beat the season." The goal is to see how late into the fall I can eat my lunch outside without getting chilled or rained on. Perhaps I'm trying to prove that rainy, cloudy Puget Sound weather isn't all that bad.

Today, November 7, is a record win. The day mimics late September with calm warmth to the air. I don a down vest over my wool sweater and carry my bowl of hot, homemade vegetable soup out on my deck. A California quail calls "chi-CA-go, chi-CA-go" from deep in the Nootka roses on the bluff to the south. Then comes the "tick, tick" from a bevy of dark-eyed juncos trying to keep track of each other. A cacophony of gull calls draws my gaze out over the bluff to the calm powder blue of Possession Sound where the *Nile III*, a crab boat from Seattle, circles around its buoys, a spattering of white dollops on a field of blue. Above the commotion, Mount Pilchuck displays the first fall snow in the deeper valleys near the top. To the north, Whitehorse glimmers in sharply angled planes of white, and Mount Baker, an ice cream cone of smooth white, peeks from behind the Douglas fir trees.

Back on the water, rafts of black dots spread out across the bay. I reach for my binoculars and the dots grow into identifiable characters: ducks, grebes, goldeneyes, and scoters. Most members of these groups breed in the northern parts of the United States and Canada and, during fall, escape south and west into the protected coastal bays and lakes where mild weather and ample food supplies keep them happy all winter. Hundreds pepper the bay below my bluff.

My soup cools as I examine the bright fall plumage and watch the players mingle, lift into the air, circle around, and splash down again. One of the greatest migration shows on earth is performing right in front of me. I feel like a vaudeville barker announcing the matinee presentation. "Step right up, step right up. No need to wait in line or buy a ticket to view the exciting fall showing *The Return of the Bucephala*. With it you can also catch, again at no cost, *The Return of the Aythya and Anas*." I want to tell the world that the show will continue all this month and into winter. It runs all day long. The goldeneyes (*Bucephala*) and ducks (*Aythya* and *Anas*) and the scoters fill the starring roles. A supporting cast of thousands exhibit live action, beautiful costumes, and some spicy sex scenes—well, at least some pair interaction.

Since the show doesn't include subtitles with the names of the birds, a preview of the stars may increase your viewing pleasure. Fourteen species arrived by the middle of October; more arrive this month, and by December up to twenty-four different species of ducks or duck-like seabirds will be on the scene. This large number of species may overwhelm the novice birder so I'll focus on a few, which are common all up and down the coast. A complete listing by geographic area is available at the end of this essay for those who want to know it all. Situated approximately in the middle of the West Coast of the United States and Canada, Puget Sound hosts a representative sample of all the species of ducks wintering along the coast. Only a small handful of species pass through to spend the winter in warmer California waters.

Whether duck watching in Anchorage, Seattle, San Diego, or Boise, the first clue to learning to identify these birds is to watch the way they feed. Think of two very general categories. Does the bird stay on the surface to feed? (It may tip down like a mallard or just dabble around on the surface.) These are called dabblers, the first category. Or does the bird dive down and actually disappear under the water? These are called divers, the second category.

Since the dabblers are limited to food they can reach without diving, they prefer freshwater lakes, ponds, and shallow parts of saltwater bays. These species tend to be more familiar to bird-watchers since they are easily seen from shore. There are five common dabblers. The familiar mallard, the grayish gadwall, and the American wigeon, with a distinctive white forehead and cap, top the list of common dabblers. In addition, watch for the northern pintail and the northern shoveler. The northern pintail is a grayish bird with a deep-brown head and a long, white, statuesque neck, a body design that allows it to reach nearly two feet underwater as it tips down. Its long, pointed pintail doesn't serve any known purpose, except perhaps as sex appeal. The northern shoveler has a large spatulalike bill, well designed for filtering out nutrients near the surface of the water.

The divers comprise a much larger category. This group includes common representatives of the merganser, scoter, goldeneye, loon, and grebe families. Three species of scoters—it rhymes with "boaters"—are common on salt water. They get the Tony award for choreography as groups of thirty to seventy birds fly just above the water in tight formation or gather in rafts on the water and dive in a long roll similar to the Rockettes. Although they appear as black blobs, each species has distinctive markings on the bill or wings. The unmistakable surf scoter's broad bill looks like it was splattered with tangerine-orange and white. The white-winged scoter sports a white wing patch, as well as a white blaze below the eye. The black scoter wears a yellow-orange knob on the otherwise black bill.

Last month, four pochard family members arrived in large numbers. They model similar costumes: dark heads, pale flanks, and dark tails. Canvasbacks are the largest member of this family, dramatically plumaged with a dark reddish head and contrasting white back. I'll have to send you to your field guide to distinguish the greater and lesser scaup and ring-necked duck. I'm still trying to keep these straight.

The court jester also arrived last month for its winter performance. The harlequin duck could not be more justly named with its theatrical pattern of charcoal gray, rusty red, and white. For Bill's birthday on November 4, 1996, I "gave" him this bird as an addition to his life list. I rarely promise a bird sighting, and luckily we weren't disappointed. It was a typical cool, cloudy November day. We packed a picnic lunch and spent the day visiting several good birding sites on the west side of Whidbey Island. Near the Keystone-to–Port Townsend ferry terminal I spotted five of the jesters lounging on a log right at the water's edge. I'd like to say that the sun broke through and shown like a spotlight on the fabulous plumage and that the birds performed a series of acrobatics right in front of us. But if I did, I'd be lying. The birds just dozed and it started to rain, so we retreated to the car for our lunch.

This month three members of the elegant and star-studded *Bucephala* family also arrive. The Barrow's goldeneye wears a crescent-shaped, white face patch, while the common goldeneye is distinguished by a circular white face patch. Their smaller cousin, the black-and-white, puffy-headed bufflehead, is the darling of this family. This cutie arrives last, making an anxiously awaited entrée.

Hope this review helps you enjoy the fall water show. I give it "two thumbs up." It is rated "G," definitely safe for children. You'll have to bring your own popcorn, just don't share it with the performers.

As I pick up my bowl of cold soup and head for the microwave, I reflect on a simple law of show biz: the larger the audience the more likely the show will go on, and be preserved. That's my motive for shouting about the glories of these waterbirds, to promote greater awareness of this show and its cast of characters.

DUCKS GENERALLY WINTERING ANYWHERE ALONG THE PACIFIC COAST

❏ *Gadwall*

❏ *Northern Pintail*

❏ *American Wigeon*

❏ *Green-winged Teal*

❏ *Greater Scaup*

❏ *Ring-necked Duck*

❏ *Mallard*

❏ *Harlequin Duck*

❏ *Long-tailed Duck*

❏ *Surf Scoter*

❏ *Black Scoter*

❏ *White-winged Scoter*

❏ *Common Goldeneye*

❏ *Barrow's Goldeneye*

❏ *Common Merganser*

❏ *Hooded Merganser*

❏ *Red-breasted Merganser*

❏ *Bufflehead*

DUCKS GENERALLY WINTERING IN PUGET SOUND AND FARTHER SOUTH

❏ *Wood Duck*

❏ *Northern Shoveler*

❏ *Canvasback*

❑ *Lesser Scaup*

❑ *Ruddy Duck*

DUCKS GENERALLY WINTERING IN CALIFORNIA AND FARTHER SOUTH

❑ *Cinnamon Teal*

❑ *Blue-winged Teal*

❑ *Redhead*

DUCKS WINTERING IN THE INTERIOR

❑ *Wood Duck*

❑ *Mallard*

❑ *Gadwall*

❑ *American Wigeon*

❑ *Northern Pintail*

❑ *Northern Shoveler*

❑ *Green-winged Teal*

❑ *Canvasback*

❑ *Ring-necked Duck*

❑ *Lesser Scaup*

❑ *Common Goldeneye*

❑ *Bufflehead*

❑ *Common Merganser*

❑ *Hooded Merganser*

❑ *Ruddy Duck*

THOSE %*&# LBBs

So we shall come and look at the world with new eyes.

—Ralph Waldo Emerson

I first heard the term LBBs while birdwatching in New Jersey with my then future, now former, mother-in-law, Mary Galloway. An amateur bird-watcher but with few birding buddies—this was the mid-1960s—she handed me a pair of binoculars and drove us out into the eastern deciduous woods, a dazzling rainbow of fall color.

Within the family we called her Mighty Mary. Not because of her size, she was just four feet, eleven inches tall with her shoes on, but because she had great enthusiasm. As Mary and I ambled along a path deep in the trees the sparse birds we saw dove quickly into brush or darted for the treetops. Most remained nameless. As another unidentified flying object crossed our path, Mary firmly remarked, "That's definitely an LBB." I had no idea what she was talking about and stopped in my tracks. "Actually, on second glance it may be an LBJ," she said with a wee grin. I could feel my naivete glowing around me. I thought LBJ was the guy in the White House.

To save me further embarrassment, she explained: LBB was birding lingo for *little brown birds* and LBJ stood for *little brown jobs*. Both acronyms applied to the small brown wrens, sparrows, and other birds that scuttled themselves quickly out of sight before identification was possible. The bird either moved so quickly one couldn't get a good look, or the subtle markings lacked distinguishing characteristics. After the sighting of the small brown bird, it remained nameless. Mary then lifted her strict rule against using profanity and said, "I'm absolutely sure that it was a damn LBB."

Most birders include this or much stronger expletives when talking about LBBs or LBJs. It expresses the frustration they feel at not being able to identify the species. Conversely, I enjoy using the terms—without the expletive. It is an admission that I don't know all the birds, or that at times I can't identify the species because of poor light, or that I didn't get a long enough look. To me it is part of the game of bird-watching; I want the birds to win once in a while.

217

November

The term LBB also helps keep us bird-watchers honest. The hair on my neck rises sharply when casual birders, or experts, offer a name when they haven't really seen the bird. Bob Merrick, the closest thing to a shorebird guru in these parts, feels the same. Bob regularly monitors Crockett Lake, a migration flyway stopover here on Whidbey Island. Every spring and fall the shorebirds pour into this tidal estuary and feed. Bob carries a high-powered scope to help identify and count them. The lake lacks close access and many birds are beyond even Bob's mighty lenses, so this god of shorebird identification uses the word "peeps" (the generic word for several species of small shorebirds) all day long. Hawk-watchers employ the scientific family names *accipiters* or *buteos* when they can't identify the specific bird. Gull-watchers simply call their questionable sightings *gull species*.

All that said, most of the little brown birds can be identified, with practice. First, some review. Back in January, I introduced several common LBBs that come to your feeder. Hopefully by now the song sparrow, house sparrow, spotted towhee, chestnut-backed and black-capped chickadees, and the red finch trio—the house, purple, or Cassin's finches depending on where you live—have become old friends. Remember how they all looked the same back then? And now they are a snap to identify. Hold onto that confidence, because the time has come to tackle the smallest, brownest, and most skulking of the LBBs, the wrens. They rarely come to your feeder, they are all over the West—no area is untouched—and six similar species are trying their hardest to buffalo you.

Though small, wrens are chunky birds with slightly curved bills and sometimes uptilted tails. Their Latin name means "cave dweller," describing their propensity to dive into their nest holes, which once existed in hollow trees but now are found as often in birdhouses or an old berry-picking can hanging in the wood shed.

The western wrens divvy up by geography and habitat to make identification easier. Any wren north of Central British Columbia is the winter wren—very small, plain, and short-tailed. The interior dry areas offer two options: the rock wren (dull gray-brown with a contrasting cinnamon rump) and the canyon wren (white throat and a chestnut belly) both of which are relatively large by wren standards at about six inches long. Moist wooded areas along the coast have three options: the winter wren, the Bewick's wren (which has a long, sideways-flitting tail and white eyebrows), and the house wren (similar to the winter wren but longer tailed). The house wren is primarily a summer migrant along the coast and throughout the interior, and some live year-round in California.

Throughout the west, the wren of cattail swamps and reedy marshes is the marsh wren (which has white streaks on a dark back). I'll throw in one more member of the wren family that could never be considered an LBB, the cactus wren. More than eight inches long with heavily barred wings, a spotted breast, a propensity to inhabit arid landscapes of the Southwest, and a personality that fits more closely with the jay family, this species is definitely not a dull, skulking, forest-dwelling identification challenge.

I'll admit it takes time to learn to tell all these real little brown birds apart. Hopefully the next time you see an unidentified flying object cross your path you'll at least know whether it's an LBB or an LBW, little brown wren.

WRENS LIVING IN ALASKA AND NORTHERN BRITISH COLUMBIA

❑ *Winter Wren*

_____

_____

WRENS LIVING ALONG THE WEST COAST AND IN THE INTERIOR

❑ *House Wren (summer breeder)*

_____

❑ *Marsh Wren (prefers reedy marshes and cattail swamps)*

_____

❑ *Winter Wren*

_____

❑ *Bewick's Wren*

_____

❑ *Rock Wren*

❑ *Canyon Wren*

❑ *Cactus Wren (Southwest)*

THANKS FOR ALL THE BIRDS,
NOT JUST FOR THE TURKEY

I wish the bald eagle had not been chose as the representa-
tive of our country; he is a bird of bad moral character; like
those among men who live by sharpening and
robbing, he is generally poor, and often very lousy.
The turkey is a much more respectable bird, and withal
a true original native of America.

—Benjamin Franklin,
Letter to Sarah Bache, 1784

As we gather with families and friends to give thanks at November's end, I'm reminded of childhood Thanksgiving dinners. On those occasions my immediate family, plus aunt, uncle, cousins, and the odd distant relative whom I couldn't quite remember, assembled at my grandparents' home, a large house with a separate formal dining room, complete with white table linen and heavy silver cutlery. After we took our seats at the dining table, my grandmother carried in an antique china platter heaped with roasted turkey nestled in potatoes. She'd place it at the head of the table in front of my tall, stately grandfather.

Before he picked up the carving implements, the what-we-are-grateful-for ritual had to occur. Everyone took a turn contributing a solemn sentence or two about the blessings that had come his or her way during the past year. The adults took this tradition very seriously, while we kids kept an eye on the perfectly browned turkey with our mouths watering and our stomachs growling. When I was four or five, I learned that when my turn came, the words "I'm grateful for my mommy and daddy," given with my sweetest smile, satisfied all my relatives and quickly moved their attention past me. When my grandfather's turn finally came, he kept his remarks blessedly short and ended with the words, "And thanks for the turkey." An "amen" at the end of a long grace, he signaled the feasting could begin.

Other than my grandfather, I can't remember anyone in my family ever expressing gratitude for any bird. Quite the opposite, my father complained when the barn swallows built a nest above the front door, and my mother shooed the Canada geese off our lawn because of the mess they left. However, I also remember my father carrying me outside to listen to a hooting owl in the dark of winter and my mother pausing in her garden to watch a colorful tanager. If they felt any gratitude for these wild birds, though, it remained unspoken.

To mitigate those gratitude-barren years in the past, and in the spirit of Thanksgiving, I've created a list of wild birds for which I'm truly grateful. Some directly influence our lives; some play significant roles in the ecology of our forests, marshes, and open habitat; and some simply provide great viewing pleasure. For the record, I'm grateful for all 11,000 species because they each play a role in creating an infinitely rich and beautiful world. Narrowing the list to a handful of birds is as difficult for me as a mother admitting to favoritism among her children. As legislators in Congress speak for a whole constituency of folks back home, the birds I've selected represent thousands of unacknowledged species, each contributing in their own unique way to the balance of our natural world.

One species that affects me directly is the barn swallow. Each year a pair returns to nest under the eaves of our house, and each summer I follow their nesting routine and clean up the inevitable mess they create (which I'm *not* grateful for). While sitting on my deck eating lunch last summer, I observed the swallows launch up into the air and dart and swoop around our house, jabbing and snatching at flying insects. I couldn't estimate the number of insects they captured, but later read a conservative estimate that one swallow can consume sixty insects per hour. Multiplied by the number of hours in our long summer days, with a couple hours off to sit and preen, that's a whopping 840 insects a day, or 25,000 insects a month. Considering the hundreds of thousands of barn swallows in the United States, this results in a mind-boggling consumption of pesky mosquitoes, gnats, and termites. Not only do barn swallows consume bazillions of arthropods, the birds' migration patterns send them north into North America as the insects are hatching and time their departure to when the birds have cleaned our skies of critters each fall. This is a rather elegant solution to keeping the population of flying insects in balance. I'd hate to live in a world without barn swallows.

My next gratuitous vote goes to the gulls because they scavenge

Brushed by Feathers

and, secondarily, because I can't imagine the beach without their insistent "wak, wak, wak" cry. Yesterday I took advantage of a rare November low tide to walk along the beach below my bluff. In the slim margin between the water and the bluff, I climbed over driftwood and ducked under low branches. Ahead, two glaucous-winged gulls argued over a dead flounder, deposited by the night tide. One gull yanked a chunk of flesh and flew off, allowing the second to plunge in and jab at the carcass. Their cries alerted other gulls that soon arrived to join the feast. As I approached, the gulls departed reluctantly to the trees above. But after I passed they dropped back down to continue their devouring. Less than an hour later, I retraced my steps but found no sign of the fish. Not even the skeleton remained. The sandy beach was clean, with only a snarl of gull footprints to record the event.

Gulls and other scavengers—vultures, crows, and eagles—provide a free cleaning service. I've visited late-fall salmon spawning grounds in British Columbia and seen hundreds of bald eagles congregate to consume thousands of decaying fish. I've watched a company of vultures clean the bones of a dead cow in the rangeland of Wyoming. During a beach walk when I staffed a lighthouse poised on Dungeness Spit, I came upon a long-dead sea lion carcass. The vile smell forced me to hold the padded sleeve of my parka over my nose and mouth to keep from losing my lunch. After returning to the lighthouse, I watched bald eagles, gulls, and crows take their turn at the dead animal. A huge job lay in front of them, and each day I cheered them on.

Besides controlling insect populations and scavenging, birds contribute to the ecology of our native habitat. Take, for example, woodpeckers. Searching for wood-dwelling ants and beetles, woodpeckers drill holes in dead or dying wood. The woodpecker holes aid the decomposition process by opening passages for insects and water. Earlier this month I watched two pileated woodpeckers attack a large alder snag in the wooded ravine to the north of our house. Banging their stout bills into the tree, they chiseled away wood chips as efficiently as skilled carpenters. Large chunks of bark flew into the air to land at the tree base, as littered as the floor beneath a carpenter's bench. Each spring pileated woodpeckers carve out new nesting cavities. Their past years' holes are claimed by owls, American kestrels, and wood ducks, which cannot dig their own cavities. Smaller holes left by the woodpeckers become nesting sites for chickadees, nuthatches, and wrens.

Next, I must add hummingbirds to my list. By November most hummingbirds have left for Central and South America, but the Anna's hummingbird remains in coastal Washington, Oregon, and California year-round. In a previous chapter I've lauded the brilliant colors of these birds and their amazing maneuverability. But I'm also grateful for their ability to pollinate flowers throughout the West. As the birds caper from flower to flower, bits of pollen stick to their feathers and are distributed to other flowers of the same species. To ensure that each species is cross-pollinated, given the random wandering of the hummingbirds, flowers are designed to deposit specks of pollen on different places upon the hummingbirds' heads. Fuchsias, for example, dust pollen on the birds' throats, while carnations dab their pollen on the bills. If I weren't already grateful for the beauty and maneuverability of hummingbirds, I'd add them to the list simply for their role in assisting flowers to reproduce and bloom year after year.

Rainbow-hued and elegantly black-and-white-patterned birds radiate beauty. The next bird that claims a place on the list, simply for its dashing color, is the male wood duck. I often get a glimpse of this shy dandy when I monitor small lakes here on Whidbey Island. Recently I watched two males sitting on a log displaying their glossy colorful plumage; the crested heads alone exhibited most of the colors of the rainbow: red, orange, yellow, and green accented by bold black and white. As I approached, the ducks shuffled off the log and paddled out onto the lake to feed, unaware that their beauty captivated me.

The last item on my list isn't a specific bird, but is instead the fact that each species has unique plumage. This creates an intriguing, never-ending game for us humans to play, any hour of the day, any day of the year—the game of birdwatching. Birdwatching pulls me outdoors into fresh air where I focus on bird behavior and tune in with the changing seasons. Bird outings that include walking provide exercise, which helps maintain my health. Practicing bird identification keeps my mind active. The game reduces stress by drawing me away from my desk and workday challenges. Listening to the symphony of bird songs each spring enriches my soul. Watching baby birds hatch and fledge during the summer warms my heart. The intrigue of seeing new species takes me to foreign countries and allows me to meet and study different cultures. For all these benefits, I freely give thanks for birds.

Over the years my family traditions have evolved and dissolved. The house where my grandparents hosted Thanksgiving dinner was sold after they died. My parents are also gone. Marriage and remarriage have produced children and stepchildren who have other parents they need to visit, so our traditions seem to change with the tides. This year Bill and I celebrated Thanksgiving in New York with two of our sons, Munro and Alex. Munro roasted the turkey and made stuffing with oysters and cornbread. Bill mixed up his tantalizing garlic mashed potatoes. Alex had time to bake bread, and I contributed persimmon pudding for dessert, a fairly new innovation.

Long ago Bill and I decided there are better times than right before dinner to recite the list of things for which we are grateful. The only lingering remnant of my childhood tradition: we raise our glasses and say, "Thanks for the turkey!"

Brushed by Feathers

CHAPTER TWELVE
December

Winter wren

Winter is winning. Heavy rain, strong winds, and temperatures in the thirties blast me as I venture briefly onto the deck. I quickly retreat back inside as a gust of wind plasters wet leaves against the window. The shortest day of the year is only a couple of weeks away, and it doesn't get light until well after 8:00 A.M.

I sip my tea watching activity at the feeder where dark-eyed juncos outnumber all other species. Sporting dark hoods, pink bills, and flashy black-and-white tail feathers, they crowd on the platform feeder then, suddenly alarmed, zip away en masse. The threat is Rocky, circling around from the light fixture to claim his late breakfast. He lands on the platform feeder and munches grain, king of the roost. Slowly the juncos return, some settle for the ground underneath the feeder, others venture up alongside Rocky, six-inch midgets next to the twelve-inch giant.

Later, when I return to my computer after lunch, flapping and scrambling sounds outside of my home office window startle me. Five robins have discovered bunches of red pyracantha berries hanging from a trellis, not four feet from my desk. My movement sends the robins off to the alder trees, where they keep an eye on me, ready to return as soon as it seems safe.

Dark-eyed junco

American robin enjoying
pyracantha berries

Watching the robins, I realize the wind has calmed somewhat and the rain has stopped. This may be the best time to take my daily walk. The robins will be thrilled to dine in peace.

Walking out the driveway, I turn left at the county road into the face of the southern blow. I pull up my hood and snuggle my hands into my pockets. Leafless maples reach bare arms toward a steel-gray sky, dried pollen cones punctuate the ends of lacy alder branches, dried grasses clatter in the wind—everything says winter. Nature, a tired mother who has bedded down all her children for the night, seams to be hibernating, taking time off to rest herself. I stop and listen. Not a single birdcall cheers me onward. All the migrants are long gone; the winter visitors and residents are conserving energy in protected alcoves. I step quickly, heading for an old closed-off road that veers to the left along the bluff as the main road turns inland.

Twenty minutes later my mind is off in a land of its own when a whiff of cigar smoke alerts me that I'm not alone. Ahead I see the figure of Steve Raymond, an old codger whose family has owned thirty-four acres along this road since 1907. The first time I encountered Steve ambling along the road, I held back, wary of the gruff-looking, stooped stranger. I'd been warned that there were folks with very conservative ideas ("Stay off my land and leave me alone!") tucked into the back roads of this island. A couple of months later I ran into Steve, dressed up and jovial, at a fund-raising function for the Whidbey Camano Land Trust. It turns out that Steve and his wife, Joan, and the rest of the extended family decided to place their property, except for a few acres surrounding their house, into a conservation easement. The easement will protect their forest, pasture, wetlands, and saltwater beach from future development and keep it in a natural state for their heirs and for the wildlife that share their land.

I catch up with Steve and we walk along, stopping when we pass the bald eagle's nest, difficult to locate through layers of bare branches, perched out on the bluff in an alder tree. We lament the irresponsible and illegal actions of the neighboring landowners who cut down a huge swath of trees fifty feet from the nest during last year's nesting season. Fortunately, it appears the eagles have not abandoned the site. We continue on to Steve's house, then I turn back.

Passing near the eagle's nest again, the silence is broken by a familiar call from a tall Douglas fir, one eagle calling to the other. The call awakens a tiny winter wren, just four inches of warm-brown fluff and stubby tail. The wren calls a sharp "timp-timp" from a pile of dead leaves as if in response to its giant neighbor. I smile. Eagle and wren, largest and smallest of our winter birds, are the only voices on this December day.

As I near my driveway the rain resumes, I've luckily chosen the only dry part of this December day for my walk. The sky darkens and winter takes up the reins again. Approaching my house, I notice the pyracantha bushes are practically stripped of berries, the robins have had a good feast.

*One bald eagle
calling to another*

New birds this month:

❑ Trumpeter Swan *(Cygnus buccinator)*

❑ Tundra Swan *(Cygnus columbianus)*

❑ Gray Partridge *(Perdix perdix)*

❑ Ring-necked Pheasant *(Phasianus colchicus)*

❑ Spruce Grouse *(Dendragapus canadensis)*

❑ Ruffed Grouse *(Bonasa umbellus)*

❑ Varied Thrush *(Zoothera naevia)*

CHRISTMAS BIRD COUNTS

Never doubt that a small group of thoughtful,

committed citizens can change the world;

it's the only thing that ever has.

—Margaret Mead

It was Saturday, December 15, the date of our local Audubon Society Christmas Bird Count. As usual, the weather gods were blasting us with rain, wind, and cold. (Team leader Bob Merrick dubbed us "Les Miserables.") Bill and I drove to the north end of the island for our 8:00 A.M. rendezvous with a couple of naive newcomers to the annual count. At a coffee shop near our assigned counting area, we introduced ourselves, consulted maps still dry and smooth, and filled our thermoses before piling into our van.

Five minutes later we reached the first stop, a four-way intersection with a stand of Douglas firs on one corner, open fields on two sides, and a small house with three active bird feeders on the fourth corner. Sandra and Kevin, a bit younger than Bill and me, had recently moved to Whidbey Island. Years ago Kevin served a stint at the Whidbey Island Naval Air Station at Oak Harbor and now, retired from the Navy, they had returned to settle here. Sandra, a birder for years, convinced Kevin to join her in her hobby, at least for the day. Looking at the swaying fir trees and rain-splashed windshield, I wondered if they could handle being *miserable* for a day. At least they took to heart my earlier warning of preparedness. Both sported waterproof jackets, pants, and boots. I hoped their binoculars were also waterproof.

I explained the drill in the dry comfort of the van. Our task was to count *all* the birds, every sparrow, siskin, and robin in the air, on the ground, and in the trees. Bill, equipped with clipboard and a bird list, would tally. If we saw a large raptor flying overhead, we would mark the time and direction of flight so that later we could compare notes with counters in neighboring sections to avoid duplicate records.

We clambered from the van and directed our gazes in four directions as heavy rain fell from a dark, gray sky. Every year I hope for an unusual bird to take the honor of the first bird we tally; I don't expect a rough-legged hawk or anything rare, but a varied thrush or even a flock of bushtits would be nice. Instead Bill called out, "Three crows over in that field," then bent over his clipboard to make the tally. I lifted my binoculars to my eyes and continued, "One black-capped and four chestnut-backed chickadees at the feeder." Sandra added, "A junco just flew in." Bill shuffled through the pages adding ticks on the appropriate lines. Kevin said, "There's a huge flock of blackbirds in the field to my left." Bill asked, "What kind and how many?"

Ten minutes later, clothes dripping and having exhausted that corner, we piled back into the van. Kleenexes emerged to wipe off binoculars and running noses, Bill jammed the defrost fan to top speed, and we slowly drove down the road tallying birds from inside the van. Every mile or so we stopped, got out, and counted.

Bird by bird our tally grew. Between stops Kevin remained quiet, eyes peeled for raptors, but Sandy peppered the air with questions. I explained that the first Christmas Bird Count (CBC) was held in 1900 as a reaction to "side wars." Before then, the holiday tradition was for hunters to go out to see which side could kill the most feathered creatures. An ornithologist named Frank Chapman organized twenty-seven birders in twenty-five locations around the country to go out and *count* the birds. They logged 18,500 individual birds from ninety species. This practice spread and today, more than a century later, 1,900 CBCs with more than 55,000 participants are held throughout North and South America.

The National Audubon Society sponsors the counts, receives the data, and publishes the results in a special edition of *American Birds* magazine. Count data constitutes the largest and longest-term data bank of information on bird population trends. Each local Audubon society selects a day between December 14 and January 5 to conduct the count; local societies also select their area, a fifteen-mile diameter circle. The four of us were one of eight count teams for the Whidbey Audubon Society's count.

The rain decreased but the wind gusted as we slowly moved through our assigned back roads. At noon we retreated to the coffee shop for a quick lunch, then resumed our task. The tally increased throughout the latter half of the day. As the light faded along with our energy, I announced that we had one more stop to complete our section. Bill cracked the window and I pulled up my hood and stepped out, everyone else stayed in the van. The last several stops had been in heavy second and third growth woods, mostly fir and cedar with some alder. The birds were hard to see and most of the counting was by ear, although the wind made that more and more difficult. I picked up soft "piks" and "sees-sees" from the thick brush and evergreen trees and called to Bill in simplified jargon, "One song sparrow, a pair of towhees, five ruby-crowned, two juncos. I'll guess 100 siskins." He knew the ruby-crowned were kinglets, the juncos were dark-eyed juncos, and the siskins were pine siskins. He also realized that I was tiring since I didn't count every single siskin.

Task completed, we dropped off Sandra and a slightly bedraggled Kevin at the coffee shop. We proceeded to Coupeville High School to add our tallies to the team totals, where Bob Merrick, chair of the count, greeted us. A dozen other counters were exchanging sightings while trying to warm up and dry off. Bill wandered off to add our tally to the white boards displayed across the front of the classroom and then contributed our sheets, now wrinkled with rain and spilled coffee, to a woman working at a computer. I warmed my hands around a cup of cocoa. (A week later I got our total results from Bob. The whole Whidbey team counted 113 species and 23,085 individual birds, 3,000 bird sightings below average.)

I chided Bob for our very boring route, with no shoreline or large lakes (this exchange is a couple years old but I keep thinking a bit of whining might improve our assignment for the following year). When I moved to Whidbey Island and joined the Whidbey Audubon CBC team, I had no seniority. Consequently I was assigned a section that no one else wanted. Instead of offering sympathy, Bob asked, "How are the ducks? Others have noted the ducks' numbers are down." I recalled the three small ponds we'd monitored for two years and realized he was right. There were significantly fewer ducks this year than in the past.

After a bit more conversation Bill and I began our forty-five-minute drive home, rain splashing and wind howling. As Bill peered through the thumping windshield wipers, my mind jumped back three years to the Christmas before we moved to Whidbey. During that winter we spent six months training nature guides in Yucatán, Mexico, and celebrated the holidays in a small village named El Cuyo, near the Ria Lagartos Nature Preserve on the north coast of the Yucatán Peninsula.

Rodrigo, head biologist at the station, had asked me how Americans conducted a CBC and, after I explained the process, he asked me to organize one. Spontaneously we set in motion the first CBC at El Cuyo. We designated the station headquarters as the epicenter, mapped our fifteen-mile-diameter count circle, and checked calendars. The following day was the only day within the time period when Bill and I were free. Two problems loomed—Rodrigo and most of the staff were heading home for the New Year's holidays and we didn't have a car so we were limited to places we could walk to. Our team was lean: Bill, one biologist, and me.

Walking into the village for dinner that evening, Bill and I noticed a car slowing at the side of the road next to us. A blond head leaned out the window and asked in English if there were any good bird-watching areas nearby. I was surprised since I hadn't seen a gringo tourist in the two months we'd been in El Cuyo. Three Americans, a husband and wife in their thirties and a middle-aged women who turned out to be his mother, hopped out of the car and introduced themselves. My mind raced forward to the next day: here was our CBC team as well as our transportation. I casually answered, "There are fabulous places to bird and I'd be delighted to take you out first thing tomorrow." They agreed and then I asked, "Do you happen to know what a Christmas Bird Count is?" It turned out that the mother had participated in several CBCs in California, and the couple were excellent birders as well.

The next day was calm, hot, and sunny for the only CBC I've done or likely will do in shorts, T-shirt, and sandals. The "count vehicle" and half the team had to leave El Cuyo at noon, but before they departed we clocked thirty-five species. To celebrate, that afternoon Bill and I went swimming in the Gulf of Mexico. Later that week I showed Rodrigo how to e-mail our results to the National Audubon Society. After we returned to the States several months later, I found the Society's official results in the stack of mail. There, along with CBC results from all across North America, was our data, the first ever from El Cuyo, Yucatán, Mexico.

These thoughts of a warmer time in Mexico faded as Bill and I continued our drive home. When we arrived, our recently remodeled house seemed strangely cold, and I realized that a gust of wind had burst in the French doors from the deck. Leaves spread out on the tile floor and the wind whistled through the house. I shivered and pulled the doors closed. Exhausted from the long day, we went to bed listening to the rain pelting on the roof and the wind murmuring through the trees.

The next morning I was awakened by Bill calling from the entry window, "What the hell is that?" Standing side by side looking out into our entry courtyard with the late darkness of the winter morning just departing, we tried to comprehend why our recently installed skylight—a large four by four-foot pyramid—was lying upside down in the courtyard. I walked upstairs while Bill called the builder. A few hours later a crew of three manhandled the skylight back up onto the second-story roof. Evidently, while Bill and I were off counting birds, a fifty-mile-per-hour gust of wind pushed through the deck doors and popped off the skylight, which hadn't been properly screwed down.

Every year since then the CBC weather has been cold, wet, and windy. We've continued to be assigned to our boring section northeast of Oak Harbor with three small ponds and mainly winter resident birds. The duck populations have rebounded, and last year we saw a rough-legged hawk soaring over the fields. I've noticed that Bill and I complain less about the weather. It never seems as bad as the year the wind blew so hard it popped the skylight off the roof of our house.

THE TWELVE BIRDS
OF CHRISTMAS

On the first day of Christmas my true love gave to me,

a partridge in a pear tree ...

—Early English verse

With Thanksgiving under our belts, the holiday season floods in like a swiftly flowing Cascade river. With it come the incessant replays of holiday songs like the many-versed "Twelve Days of Christmas." Recently at a community holiday program, as the verses droned on and on, I began to wonder why the composer had such a fixation about birds. French hens, calling birds, swans a-swimming, geese a-laying, not to mention the partridge in a pear tree—most of the gifts in the song are birds.

The exact origin of the song is quite obscure, but most authorities agree it began in eighteenth-century England. Today, we generally assume that the theme of the song is romantic, the increasing numbers of gifts from the first verse's single partridge in a pear tree to the twelve drummers drumming offered to impress a loved one. But in this song's early iterations, the devotion was more religious. God, the "true love," bestowed gifts on His believers. And the gifts themselves generally symbolized spiritual blessings.

Though this original spiritual symbolism is lost to most of us, the selection of gifts sends me a message. These aren't big and expensive, but rather sentimental gifts that somehow ring sincere. I'm struck that the gifts are so nature oriented, which suggests to me an outing to enjoy nature and look for birds.

Recently I wondered, if I wanted to give my true love a gift of viewing all the song's birds, could I do it in the western United States? And, to add a seasonal challenge, could I locate them during late December?

"A partridge in a pear tree"

According to the book *The Great Song Thesaurus* by Lax and Smith, this first gift is rich in symbolism. In church lore, the partridge exemplifies abandonment of faith, since the partridge was known as a bird that deserts its young. To put a positive spin on the symbolism, I suggest that by placing the partridge in a pear tree the partridge was able to rise above temptation and stick around. Finding a partridge in a pear tree will be difficult. Actually, finding a partridge in any tree will be close to impossible, since the common partridge of England and Europe *(Perdix perdix)*—introduced to the United States in the early 1900s and named the gray partridge—rarely perches above ground level. It lives in grasslands and grain fields of the Midwest; in Idaho, Montana, and northern Nevada; as well as in eastern Washington and Oregon. The true love in the song must have had a remarkable, one-of-a-kind partridge, for it to agree to sit in a pear tree. To find a partridge in a pear tree, I'll try an overlay of both the bird's habitat and pear orchards. I'll probably have to settle for a "partridge *under* a pear tree."

"Two turtle doves"

Throughout history doves have symbolized peace and purity. Since doves are often observed sitting in pairs, they also signify conjugal fidelity. The European turtledove *(Streptopelia turtur),* the likely inspiration for the song, is not established as a species anywhere in the United States, although small pockets of escapees survive in the wild. One close North American cousin of the European turtledove is the mourning dove, a common dove throughout the West. They stay in pairs, so if I see one, I'll likely find two.

"Three French hens"

The reason for including a French hen was as a culinary treat (according to the romantic interpretation) or as a symbol of bountiful providing (from the religious interpretation). Research provides no answers on what was intended by the French hens. However, I'm willing to hazard a guess: since most English game birds—grouse, pheasants, partridges—are nonmigratory, the French hen may refer to the one European species of quail *(Coturnix coturnix)* that is migratory. These small quail fly from France to England each spring and return in the fall. Back in the 1700s, the female of this species might have been known as a French hen and, being more exotic than England's common game birds, would have made a very special gift. A close relative of the European quail is our California quail. This perky open-woodland bird is a common resident throughout the western states. These birds congregate in extended family groups during the winter, so seeing three will be a snap. Why *three* French hens? It probably takes that many of these small hens for a single dinner serving.

"Four calling birds"

At first, this phrase stumped me, since almost all birds *call*. Then I learned that the original song used the words "colly birds" from the term "collied," meaning coal black. The only common coal-black bird in England is the blackbird *(Turdus merula)*, a member of the thrush family to which our robin also belongs. Although not an eloquent songster like other members of the thrush family, the Eurasian blackbird chatters in a friendly way and is commonly seen in towns. Also, it holds a record as one of the longest-living songbirds, more than twenty years. Perhaps the significance of including this bird in the song is a wish of long life for one's true love. Here in the West we don't have black-colored members of the thrush family. The closest relatives of the Eurasian blackbird are the American robin and the varied thrush, which can be confused with the robin unless one looks closely and notices the black bands on the orange background. Both the robin and thrush can be found along the West Coast lowlands during winter. Neither are *colly* colored and probably not *calling* either, but during the holiday season I doubt anyone will mind.

"Five golden rings"

I always thought the rings meant jewelry. I assumed a true love could offer at least one ring at Christmas. Five gold rings, one for each finger, sounded especially romantic. I was wrong. The rings also refer to birds: ringed-necked pheasants. The bird sports iridescent bronze on its body, metallic green on its head, a fleshy red eye patch, a white ring around its neck, and a long, pointed tail. Understandably, this pheasant represents beauty and riches. It was introduced to the western United States and has remained a popular game bird both here and in England. Pheasants prefer drier, open areas, are now recovering from hunting season, and tend to be solitary at this time of year, so it will take a bit of searching to find five.

"Six geese a-laying"

Several species of geese could be the source of this verse. The key seems to be that the birds should be "a-laying." A laying goose in late December would have been a prize, since most wild birds lay eggs only in the spring. Perhaps a domestic goose, like our domestic chickens, could have been encouraged to lay eggs during winter. I found no particular symbolism surrounding geese, but much around eggs, which represent life. Canada geese have overpopulated many lakes and moist valleys; sighting a flock of them would be easy. The Brant goose winters along our coast in large numbers. We could solve the "a-laying" problem by changing the verse just slightly to read "six geese a-lying" (as in lying down rather than laying an egg). Check out any public park near water or even golf courses and you'll see huge numbers of Canada geese lying around.

"Seven swans a-swimming"

Greek and Roman mythology, which influenced Christian church symbolism, portray the swan as a transformation symbol. For example, Cycnus, the son of Poseidon, was turned into a swan (and his name became *cygnus,* the Latin name of the swan family). The familiar fable of the Ugly Duckling tells of another transformation into a swan. The early Church defined this transformation as surrendering to the power of God. A true love willing to travel can easily spot seven swans "a-swimming" during late December. Simply take your beloved to the Skagit Flats in Washington or other wintering grounds of the Tundra Swan and the Trumpeter Swan. The trick will be to tempt them from the fields where they feed and out onto water to paddle around.

"Eight maids a-milking"

Starting with this phrase, the song shifts from birds to people (maids, ladies, and lords) involved in certain acts—milking, dancing, and leaping. I like to interpret this phrase as eight maids giving endless mugs of creamy hot chocolate to warm one's true love after some vigorous December birdwatching.

"Nine ladies dancing"

I'm willing to stretch here and use the word "ladies" as a general term for females. I consider the prancing around of the female sandhill crane—strutting her long, droopy back feathers that form a "bustle" while lifting and fluttering her wings—to be a beautifully choreographed dance. Cranes winter in southern California, Arizona, and New Mexico where they form flocks in winter, so finding nine of these "ladies" dancing will be easy.

"Ten lords a-leaping"

The lords of December beaches are sandpipers, who can leap about on one leg as adroitly as pogo-stick experts while keeping the other leg tucked into warm belly feathers. Western sandpipers, the most common leaping lords on our beaches and estuaries, winter all along the West Coast. Thousands may gather in flocks, so seeing ten will not be a problem.

"Eleven pipers piping"

The piping plover, a pale-white shorebird named after its pipinglike call, can be found in flocks much larger than eleven. The problem: they are a species of the eastern seashore and by December have moved south to Florida and around the rim of the Caribbean into Mexico. This isn't a complete tragedy for soggy West Coast romantics. I'll simply convince my true love to take me south for a sunny holiday jaunt. We'll plan to do some serious looking for this rare species.

"Twelve drummers drumming"

Finally, the drummers. Several species of the grouse family use their inflated neck sacks or wings to produce a booming or drumming sound. The Latin name for one grouse, the prairie chicken, is *Tympanuchus,* which means "having a drum." I've flushed a couple of ruffed grouse on a late December trip to Hood's Canal near Puget Sound. Spruce grouse can be found, with a lot of searching, in higher elevations in the Cascades and northern Rockies. However, finding twelve "drummers" at this time of year could be as difficult as spotting Santa and his airborne reindeer. Drumming, like "calling" and "laying," is a breeding activity waiting for the spring.

A partridge, turtledoves, French hens, colly birds, ring-necked pheasants, geese, swans, dancing cranes, leaping "pips," piping plovers, and drumming grouse—these represent simple, outdoor-oriented gifts we can give during the holidays. They are gifts infused with both romantic and spiritual meaning. They also remind us of how blessed we are to coexist with birds on this planet. For me, the song's images of birds represent the thousands of bird species that bring joy, fascination, and variety into our lives.

The next time you're asked to sing through each and every one of the twelve verses, remember it could be worse: there are 11,000 species of birds out there to sing about. Thinking of the birds as symbols for peace, fidelity, bounty, longevity, beauty, transformation, life, and rising above abandonment will perhaps make it easier to sit through the endless verses of this holiday song.

ALL IS WELL

The ability to see the cultural value of wilderness

boils down, in the last analysis, to a question of

intellectual humility.

—*Aldo Leopold*, A Sand County Almanac

Like the hands of a huge clock converging on midnight, late December days inch toward the close of another year in the natural world. Hunkered in around Hanukkah and Christmas, the winter solstice marks the Northern Hemisphere's longest night, the point at which the earth tilts the farthest from the sun. As those huge hands complete the cycle, they seem to pause slightly at midnight and allow the earth one long exhalation before a new cycle, a new year, begins. If there is a moment approaching stillness in a bird's life, it occurs in the coldest, darkest days of winter. Some birds lower their heart rate during the long, cold nights to conserve energy.

In the West, the last migrants have long since settled into their wintering habitat. Ducks and seabirds float and feed in protected, ice-free lakes and bays along the coast, while shorebirds scamper and probe the muddy shore. Mountain species such as the varied thrush descend to lower elevations just before the snow level drops and tuck themselves into snow-free valleys. Local woodland residents eke out a living in familiar landscapes.

Here on Whidbey Island, Bill and I close the year as we started it: watching bird activity at our feeding station. As I sit by the window on the afternoon before the longest night, white tails flash as juncos dart into the blackberry hedge, fleeing the shadow of my hand, an unexplained challenge to their safety. That opens the feeder for chickadees or nuthatches to zip in, grab a seed, and retreat. The plump California quail, fully clothed in mature plumage, heft themselves onto the platform feeder; six or seven bend over to peck shoulder to shoulder, like football players set for a hike to start the play. More quail garner seeds scattered on the ground; the sidelined defensive lineup waiting for the offense to finish on the field.

In the half-light of day's end, I walk out to the edge of the bluff and look down on the narrow margin of winter beach. Great blue herons hold sentry posts on their winter feeding territory while a belted king-fisher crackles through the air above. Scoters huddle offshore while buf-fleheads and goldeneyes string out across the bay. A horned grebe dives below the surface fishing for food, and a single common loon floats motionless, head turned backward and bill tucked underneath its wing. I return to the house and greet Rocky, already snuggled in to his roost-ing spot on the deck light. I switch on the light for a few minutes to warm his feet, then turn back toward the bay to watch evening swallow up the last light of the solstice eve and gulp down any final bird sounds.

In the calm stillness of the darkening earth I can almost hear a town crier calling out, as in medieval times, "Five o'clock and all is well." It certainly seems well in my corner of the world. Tomorrow will bring a new day and a new earth-year, much like the one just past. The next day and the ones that follow will stretch and lengthen, pushing back winter's hold. Soon early bulbs will peek through and foretell a new spring. I know the days will brighten, the bulbs will blossom, and leaves will uncurl as they have for millennia.

But I also know that the April dawn song will not be as robust, the shorebird flocks that migrate through on my beach will be smaller, and the flycatchers and warblers that return from Mexico will be fewer in numbers. Some bird populations will experience steep drops, while for others, changes will be incremental. A few may undergo resurgence in numbers. We may temporarily be distracted into complacency as intro-duced species move in and replace our decreasing numbers of native species, but, year by year, spring by spring, the numbers of many native birds will drop.

Cities bloom on wetlands. Anchorage, Vancouver, Seattle, Tacoma, Portland, San Francisco, Oakland, Los Angles, and San Diego—our homes—all occupy rich former habitat for birds and other wildlife. Large stands of forests are cut and diced into smaller and smaller frag-ments. Former grassland and open prairies now sprout cultivated crops. Towns and cities gobble up real estate near water sources in the dry inte-rior. Birds and other species are pushed into inhospitable habitat that often lacks their natural food sources. Woodpeckers can't hollow out a hole in a metal lamppost; ducks can't feed in a covered culvert.

The birds that do survive become more precious. Until a short time ago I hardly bothered to notice the black-capped chickadees that stop by my feeder. Like the tall Douglas firs on the bluff, I assumed they would always be here. Practically every bird count I've done included dozens of this tiny black-and-white chickadee. But I read recently that their numbers have decreased in the Midwest to only 10 percent of their former population. Suddenly I've become more appreciative of their presence in my life. As I gaze out at the feeder I now wait for a black-capped chickadee to arrive mixed in with the many chestnut-sided chickadees. So far they keep coming.

Can the earth absorb these changes? Can birdwatching as we know it survive? I believe so. I believe the exponential increase in people watching birds will instigate heightened awareness of the need to protect birds and preserve habitats. Bird-watchers will turn their private property into wildlife sanctuaries, will stop using pesticides, will lobby for preservation of natural areas, and will vote for clean air, clean water, and renewable resources. We *can* scale back and balance our needs for shelter, food, and transportation with the requirement for natural areas that encourage wildlife to survive. We won't forget the spring dawn song or call of the loon in autumn. We won't neglect that which we cherish.

• ᴗ

One week after winter solstice a warm day boldly interrupts our chilly doldrums. The sun emerges in the south behind the alder trees, their leafless branches frame, rather than block, the persimmon- and cranberry-colored sunrise. At a respectable 8:00 A.M. the solar rays rise above the Cascade Mountains, bounce over the calm bay, and burst through the alders into our window. The wind and rain that has drenched the Washington coast for days, causing trees to fall and rivers to flood, backs off, at least for the moment. A cold front holds off the frigid, interior-spawned temperatures that usually accompany a clear winter day, giving us a brief sunshine-filled oasis.

A bald eagle flying south floats just off the bluff, and a half-hour later the majestic creature returns north with a long branch dangling from its talons. Perhaps the local nesting pair is building a new nest; perhaps a new pair is moving into our neighborhood. I make a mental note to try to discreetly locate the new nest construction.

About noon I take my daily walk, leaving my Gore-Tex jacket at home for the first time in months. Just as I pass by our mailbox, a vaguely familiar sound erupts from the alder grove across the road. Only three simple notes, but there is no mistaking the source. Something inside the tiny brain of a male song sparrow wants to try out a few bits of a song that will fill the grove later this spring. Then he is silent; but deep in the woods there seems to be a soft murmuring. Somewhere deep in the DNA of the trees and the birds a stirring begins. A promise is made. The hands of the clock move forward; the cycle begins anew.

Brushed by Feathers

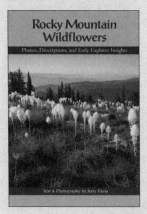